A Guide to
Patient Safety
in the Medical Practice

AMA
AMERICAN
MEDICAL
ASSOCIATION

A Guide to Patient Safety in the Medical Practice

©2008 by the American Medical Association
All rights reserved
Printed in the United States of America

Internet address: www.ama-assn.org

Additional copies of this book may be ordered by calling 800 621-8335.

Secure online orders can be taken at www.amabookstore.com.
Mention product number OP401006.

ISBN 978-1-57947-674-8

BQ13:06-P-033:10/07

Library of Congress Cataloging-in-Publication Data

Vance, James E., 1938-
  A Guide to Patient Safety in the Medical Practice / James E. Vance.
     p. ; cm.
  Includes bibliographical references and index.
  Summary: "Optimizing patient safety in the ambulatory care setting by improving and strengthening processes, information management, communications, and care coordination"—Provided by publisher.
  ISBN-13: 978-1-57947-674-8 (alk. paper)
  ISBN-10: 1-57947-674-0 (alk. paper)
  1. Medical errors—Prevention. 2. Patients—Safety measures. I. Title.
  [DNLM: 1. Patient Care—standards. 2. Ambulatory Care—standards. 3. Medical Errors—prevention & control. 4. Safety Management—standards. W 84.1 V222p 2006]
  R729.8.V36 2006
  610—dc22   2006013934

CONTENTS

ABOUT THE COKER GROUP

The Coker Group is a leading national health care consulting firm with unparalleled expertise in practice management, financial, and technology problem-solving. For more than 20 years, Coker has brought its clients the best in service, support, and results. Through careful, detailed analysis, Coker's experienced consultants are able to formulate plans and implement realistic, effective strategies.

The Coker Group offers services in the following areas:

- Practice management consulting
- Hospital consulting
- Health information technology
- Executive recruiting
- Publishing and education
- Speaking and training
- Government affairs
- Coker capital

For more information, contact:

The Coker Group
1000 Mansell Exchange West, Suite 310
Alpharetta, GA 30022
800 345-5829
www.cokergroup.com

James E. Vance, MD, MBA, is an independent health care consultant with 25 years of clinical practice and 15 years of clinical performance improvement experience. His unique background includes helping organizations improve clinical effectiveness through fostering physician engagement and clinician collaboration, improving operational efficiencies and effectiveness, enhancing patient safety, and communicating clinical and financial outcomes.

Jim has extensive group health and workers' compensation managed care and medical management experience. Previously he served as regional medical director for Humana Healthplans in south Florida, Cigna Private Practice Plan (HMO) in southern California, and The Travelers Health Network in Atlanta. He also served as chief medical officer for Conservco, a Travelers' managed care subsidiary, where he helped develop medical management programs for workers' compensation. As medical director of the Kemper Insurance Company managed care division, Jim worked with several national employers in developing integrated disability management programs. Most recently, he was vice president of clinical affairs for VHA, Inc, where he served as a resource to VHA's clinical improvement and patient safety workshop collaboratives.

Prior to joining VHA, Jim worked with a national health care consulting organization, implementing hospital clinical operational efficiency and resource management programs. While consulting with a national physician practice management firm, he worked with physician leaders and administrators in several provider organizations, helping them prepare for managed care readiness. Services included network development, managed care education, clinical resource management, data analysis, physician performance evaluation, and the development of clinical guidelines and outcome measures.

Jim served on the faculty of the Indiana University School of Medicine and followed with 15 years of private practice in south Florida prior to entering full-time health care administration. After graduation from the University of Tennessee School of Medicine, he completed his internship at the Philadelphia General Hospital, internal medicine residency training at the Mayo Clinic, endocrinology fellowship at the University of

Washington, and a physician executive MBA program at Kennesaw State University in Atlanta, Georgia. He is board certified in internal medicine, a Fellow of the American College of Physicians, and a member of the American College of Physician Executives.

INTRODUCTION

No one wants to make mistakes or, especially for clinicians, mistakes involving patient care. Yet, inevitably, errors do happen. In 1999 the Institute of Medicine (IOM), a private organization created to advise the US federal government on scientific and technical matters, published a stunning report on health care errors. The report, *To Err is Human: Building a Safer Health System*,[1] suggested that 44,000 to 98,000 Americans die each year as a result of medical errors. Although there has been criticism of the numbers provided in the IOM report, there is general agreement that extensive system changes in the health care industry are needed and that these changes will significantly reduce the number of medical errors in health care facilities and office practices. The message was clear: the medical profession must develop methods to decrease the incidence of medical mistakes.

The issues of medical errors and patient safety that were highlighted by the report immediately caught the attention of the American public and spurred action from consumer and provider organizations, health care institutions, and government. The growing momentum to improve patient safety that ensued has focused largely on hospital inpatient care. However, relatively little is known about the risks and consequences of errors and adverse events in ambulatory care, even though much of the health care in the United States is delivered in a confusing array of ambulatory settings by a variety of health care providers. The epidemiology of patient safety in ambulatory practice is impacted by increasing logistical complexity coupled with suboptimal system support for managing care. The experience encountered during a typical episode of ambulatory care often involves fragmented coordination and communication between the patient and family with multiple providers, ancillary services, and support personnel, while traversing a spectrum of handoffs and transitions between several different sites.

Passage of the Patient Safety and Quality Improvement Act of 2005, which creates a voluntary national patient safety reporting system, should change the way medical errors are addressed in the United States. Before the Act, there was no single, protected, confidential system for reporting and analyzing adverse events to help find ways to improve patient safety and quality. This legislation was one of the American Medical Association's (AMA) top legislative priorities for more than 6 years, working with a broad coalition of organizations involved in patient safety.

The AMA led passage of the Patient Safety and Quality Improvement Act, 2005, and will continue to lead physicians' efforts to measurably improve patient safety and quality of care.

Optimizing potential gains in patient safety in ambulatory care demands major infrastructure improvements in value-added decision support systems, timely point-of-care information management support, effective communication, and care coordination. Physicians, as the primary managers of most patient care, must be supported with systems for tracking and managing a number of processes in the diagnostic and therapeutic process, including clinical processes (evaluation and treatment of specific illnesses) and clinical support processes (such as ordering, performing, reporting, and interpreting diagnostic studies), as well as traditional administrative (eg, scheduling) and business (billing) processes. Nevertheless, there are many steps that can be implemented right away that will significantly impact the safety of ambulatory patient care.

The intent of this publication is to stimulate the evolution of a patient safety culture in ambulatory care, discuss practical improvements in ambulatory patient safety processes, highlight available tools for care providers, and illustrate the business case for safer ambulatory care. All ambulatory care providers, and physicians in particular, have an opportunity and an obligation to assume leadership roles in adopting and promoting a culture of safety. The future evolution to a modern-day system infrastructure and support will be made far more efficient and effective by building safe medical practice concepts into ambulatory care today.

ENDNOTE

1. Kohn LT, Corrigan JM, Donaldson MS, eds. *To Err Is Human: Building a Safer Health System.* Washington, DC: Institute of Medicine; 1999.

chapter 1

Historical Perspective

For many decades a broad spectrum of health care improvement initiatives has been under way,[1] extending from the Flexner Report in 1910 through quality assurance programs and performance improvement infrastructures in hospitals, academic medical center initiatives, and extensive health care improvement activities at individual institutions and other organizations, such as the Harvard Medical School–affiliated Partners HealthCare System. There have been efforts directed to national standardization of patient safety guidelines through the Joint Commission for the Accreditation of Healthcare Organizations, the National Committee for Quality Assurance, and others. The Institute for Healthcare Improvement has become a leader in promoting aggressive patient safety improvement reforms at all levels of the system.

The American Medical Association, along with several industry leaders, founded the National Patient Safety Foundation in 1997. The National Patient Safety Foundation promotes measurable improvement of patient safety in health care delivery, and its aim is to provide a "central voice" on patient safety and to "lead the transition from a culture of blame to a culture of safety."[2] The federal government, as a purchaser of health care services through the Medicare and Medicaid programs, established professional standards review organizations in the mid-1970s. It became evident over time that initial efforts to analyze quality assurance and patient safety issues by using aggregate statistical measures, such as hospital mortality rates, as proxy measures for patient safety were often more confusing than helpful.

Within the medical and surgical specialty societies, anesthesiology has been a leader in patient safety efforts, starting with collecting anesthetic morbidity and mortality statistics in the 1930s. They evolved into analyzing causes of anesthetic injuries in the 1970s and 1980s. In 1984 the American Society of Anesthesiologists established the Anesthesia Patient Safety program, whose mission was to "assure that no patient shall be harmed by the effects of anesthesia."[3]

Until recently, despite considerable achievements, these activities were essentially unknown to most purchasers, governing bodies, and the public. It was generally assumed that quality of care in the United States was excellent, except for a few "bad apples." Unfortunately, it often takes a major, highly publicized catastrophic event to establish the realization that medical errors can unexpectedly occur anywhere, anytime. The death of *Boston Globe* reporter Betsy Lehman from a chemotherapy overdose at the prestigious Dana Farber Cancer Institute helped bring extensive media attention to patient safety issues and the need for system solutions to prevent medical errors. The "occasional bad apple" concept for poor patient care began to dissipate.

In the past five years there has been widespread concern in the health care industry literature and the popular media and among health care professionals, purchasers, policymakers, and the general public. This is largely in response to the Institute of Medicine (IOM) report *To Err is Human: Building a Safer Health System,*[4] which declared errors in health care a major public health issue. Four recommendations were made in the report:

- Promulgate a national focus to develop leadership, research, tools, and protocols to enrich the knowledge base about safety
- Identify and learn from errors through mandatory and voluntary reporting efforts
- Raise the standards and expectations for improvements in safety through the actions of oversight organizations, group purchasers, and professional groups
- Create safety inside health care organizations through the implementation of safe practices in the delivery of care

A subsequent report from the IOM, *Crossing the Quality Chasm: A New Health System for the 21st Century,*[5] was released in 2001. It summarized current problems and health care and also urged system redesign to meet six aims, to provide health care that is:

Safe: Patients should not be harmed by the care that is intended to help them.

Effective: Care should be based on scientific knowledge and offered to all who could benefit, and not to those not likely to benefit.

Patient-centered: Care should be respectful of and responsive to individual patient preferences, needs, and values.

Timely: Waits and sometimes-harmful delays in care should be reduced both for those who receive care and those who give care.

Efficient: Care should be given without wasting equipment, supplies, ideas, and energy.

Equitable: Care should not vary in quality because of personal characteristics such as gender, ethnicity, geographic location, and socio-economic status.

The report also provided a list of rules[5] (see Appendix A) that need to be addressed by organizations in accomplishing their aims. These aims and rules are certainly applicable to patient safety initiatives in ambulatory care and will be discussed in later chapters of this book.

An update on patient safety five years after the 1999 report from the IOM[6] reminded us that the often-quoted statistic of 44,000 to 98,000 hospital inpatient deaths each year resulting from preventable medical errors was the eighth leading cause of death in the United States, exceeding the death rates from breast cancer, AIDS, and motor vehicle accidents. The report stimulated a call to take action to private and public organizations that were in a position to address the quality of US health care. Health care purchasers, industry trade organizations, accreditation agencies, and others embarked on programs of their own in the private sector.

In 2003, the Institute of Medicine came out with a new report: *Patient Safety: Achieving a New Standard for Care.*[7] Here is a brief of the report:

Every day, tens if not hundreds of thousands of errors occur in the health care system. Some can cause disastrous effects, while others — the "near misses" — slip by almost unnoticed. In recent years, patient safety reporting systems have proliferated in health care, and many hospitals now routinely capture information on "near misses" as well as disasters. However, the utility of these reporting systems is limited. The data they collect is neither complete nor standardized, and reporting is cumbersome, costly, and sporadic at best.

Improving patient safety will require much more than information systems, even if they are comprehensive and well functioning, for reporting and analyzing errors. An enhanced care delivery system must be built, one that can prevent errors from occurring in the first place. To do this, the health care industry must simultaneously set up an easy and streamlined way for health care professionals to acquire and share information related to error prevention and quality improvement.

Building on the revolutionary Institute of Medicine reports *To Err is Human* and *Crossing the Quality Chasm*, *Patient Safety: Achieving a New Standard for Care* puts forward a road map for the development and adoption of key health care data standards to support both information exchange and the reporting and analysis of patient safety data.

One of the most important messages of the report is the need for a much broader approach to patient safety that was first stated in *To Err Is Human: Building a Safer Health System.* Patient safety is defined as the prevention of harm to patients, where harm can occur through errors of commission and omission. Safety and quality cannot be separated. Achieving patient safety as a standard for care requires a commitment by all stakeholders to a culture of safety and improved information systems.

A second critical message is that access to and use of clinical data at the point of care is necessary to prevent, recognize and recover from events. The data also are essential to better understand the nature of patient safety events, how they occur, and how they can be prevented in the future. The ability to access useful data is directly dependent on a sound information infrastructure and data standards for representing the information.

To ensure that Americans receive safe care, the authoring committee addresses the need for a standards-based national health information infrastructure to support comprehensive patient safety programs for adverse event and near miss detection and analysis. The report makes detailed recommendations on the data standards needed for this new information infrastructure including standards for data interchange, health care terminologies, knowledge representation, and a common format for reporting of data related to medical errors.

This report will be of interest to individuals and organizations with an interest in patient safety, quality improvement, and the use of information technology in healthcare.

The Leapfrog Group, a coalition of large employers including many Fortune 500 companies, purchasers, and insurers, has recommended several key initiatives, "safety leaps" that may reduce adverse clinical events:

- Computer entry of physician orders
- Evidenced-based hospital referrals
- Physician staffing in intensive care units

Hospitals responding to a survey reported that 24% of intensive care units were staffed by intensivists in 2003, as compared with 12% in 2001, and use of computerized physician order entry had increased from 2% to 5%.[8]

Furthermore, in collaboration with the Agency for Healthcare Research and Quality and the Centers for Medicare and Medicaid Services, The Leapfrog Group is proposing a physician office clinical decision support system, consisting of E-prescribing, E-lab results, and E-care reminders. These initiatives will receive a lot of consumer attention and, again, represent opportunities for physician leadership and engagement.

Efforts from other organizations include the National Quality Forum endorsement of a range of patient-safety measures through its consensus process. Several state hospital associations have adopted in their improvement efforts patient-safety indicators developed by the Agency for Healthcare Research and Quality. The Joint Commission on Accreditation of Healthcare Organizations has added and continues to update patient-safety goals to the accreditation process, and the majority of eligible hospitals are reporting the quality of care data through the Centers for Medicare and Medicaid Services. The American Board of Medical Specialties has added dimensions to include demonstrated competence in providing safe, high-quality care as a requirement for maintaining board certification. System-based changes, such as reducing the work hours of medical personnel, have also been shown to be effective in reducing the rate of errors.[9] Ultimately, the result of these patient safety initiatives should be to protect the public.

The response to pleas from purchasers, consumers, and regulators, urging health care organizations to improve patient safety, initially focused on hospital inpatient care. As safety initiatives evolve into the ambulatory care arena, physician leadership and engagement in efforts to improve patient safety and quality of care are essential for ensuring success.

For its part, the AMA continues its advocacy efforts to promote a long-term approach to ensure greater patient safety in the delivery of health care in the United States. The AMA works in collaboration with the National Patient Safety Foundation, national medical specialty societies, state and local medical societies, other provider groups, and a broad range of public and private organizations to advance efforts to improve patient safety by promoting "best practices" in the delivery of health care services. The AMA and other medical groups are advancing non-punitive, evidenced-based health systems error data collection as well as strong legal protections for participants in safety programs.

The *New England Journal of Medicine* report "Improving Patient Safety—Five Years After the IOM Report"[6] cited a 2002 Gallup poll survey that noted that a majority of physicians felt that the two most effective ways to reduce errors are to require hospitals to develop systems to avoid medical errors and increase hospital nurse staffing. In 2005, the federal government enacted the Patient Safety and Quality Improvement Act (see appendix B), which establishes a nonpunitive, confidential reporting structure in which physicians, hospitals, and other health care professional and entities can voluntarily report information on errors to Patient Safety Organizations (PSOs). PSOs will analyze the data to develop patient safety improvements strategies. The legislation stipulates that patient safety information will be confidential and legally protected, and provides appropriate penalties for unlawful disclosures. It also preserves confidentiality of patient information under the Health Insurance Portability and Accountability Act of 1996.

Despite the challenges, there have been some advances in the use of technology, including computerized order entry systems, medication and patient bar coding, electronic medication pre-scribing, and support systems for information sharing. In the past few years, health systems have begun to emphasize the identification and correction of systemic issues that lead to patient safety problems. However, we will not fully accomplish our patient safety aims until there is an ingrained culture of shar-ing near misses, adverse events, and medical errors. It is hoped that enactment of the Patient Safety and Quality Improvement Act of 2005 will establish this culture of sharing and help improve patient safety.

A publication from the state of Washington noted that there are at least four types of impediments to quality and safety improvements:

- The tort system and fear of malpractice and punishment
- Lack of time
- Complexity of the health care system
- Rigid clinical boundaries

THE TORT SYSTEM AND FEAR OF MALPRACTICE AND PUNISHMENT

Discussion about patient safety issues has been traditionally cloaked in secrecy. This is largely due to fear of punishment and a culture of blame when errors occur that have permeated our liti-gious society and our legal system. Health care professionals are raising concerns about errors, and they fear that identification of an error could result in termination of employment, loss of their medical practice, and loss of their license.

The current tort system, which perpetuates a "blame and sue, don't tell" culture, is a major perpetually unresolved barrier to open reporting. The Patient Safety and Quality Improvement Act of 2005 is an effort to address this issue. The law will increase the reporting of medical errors, provide greater protections for providers who report medical errors, and facilitate the development of state patient-safety organizations to analyze patient safety data and sup-port implementation of improvements. Significant, meaningful, and lasting tort law reform will have a huge positive impact on efforts to create a culture of patient safety. There will be immediate palpable relief and it will be a highly visible sign that society believes that the "blame game" must cease in order for the health care system to con-tinue the evolution to safe care for every patient.

There must be consensus among policymaker opinions and those of the public, and in particular among the various health care professionals themselves, on the kinds of events that should be reported to the public and the systemwide support mechanisms that are essential for minimizing avoidable errors.

An open, public, national dialogue will be required in order to reach consensus.

Other important steps will be easier to accomplish, including:

- Eliminating cultures of blame in hospitals, medical practices, and other environments of patient care to allow
  - Uninhibited reporting of errors
  - Elimination of fear of punishment
- Open discussion of errors and near misses among and across all professional lines.

These are not easy goals to accomplish and will take time, patience, and commitment of all stakeholders.

LACK OF TIME

As in all competitive environments, there are financial and quality-of-service pressures on physicians, hospital staff, and other health care providers to provide timely and efficient services. Physician productivity is constantly under review, and all health care professionals are required to accomplish more in less time. Competing demands for physician time have also limited their ability to stay current with changes in evidence-based practice standards. As in other high-risk industries, such as aviation, the focus on high production rates is often associated with increased errors, largely due to the lack of essential support systems.

COMPLEXITY OF THE HEALTH CARE SYSTEM

The evolution of modern day health care over the past half-century has created a complex environment of highly sophisticated diagnostic and therapeutic technologies, physician specialization, and the concept of centers of excellence. Despite the obvious benefits of this specialization, the unparalleled complexity of the health care industry is one of the major impediments to improving patient safety. Contributing factors include the following:

- In order to go beyond basic primary care, patients often must interact with multiple health care institutions and professionals in a disconnected and confusing array of settings to obtain needed care.
- There is a major problem, obvious to patients, of ineffective transfer of clinical information and coordination of care among professionals and institutions.
- Patients and their families find it difficult to navigate this complex labyrinth of disconnected services and communication.

Therefore, patient safety improvement efforts must focus on the patient—be "patient-centered"—in coordinating care across the system and facilitating access to essential information. Who is responsible for this coordination role? An often-heard comment from patients is: "If you ever get really sick, you had better know somebody, a nurse or a doctor or somebody in the health care system who can steer you through and look out for possible mistakes. . . ."

RIGID CLINICAL BOUNDARIES

Multiple barriers to communication are entrenched in the segmented ambulatory care setting, as illustrated in Figure 1-1. In a typical primary care encounter, a patient interacts with a "vertically integrated care team" consisting of frontdesk staff, medical assistants, nurse practitioners, physician assistants, nurses, and physicians. Ideally, all are working as a team to provide the best possible service for the patient. However, the communication barriers in this vertical system are often a root cause of errors.

"Clinical silos" create horizontal fragmentation of care as the patient is referred from the primary care physician to the hospitalist, specialist, surgeon, or tertiary care center. Again, there are barriers to horizontal communication across the silos, often resulting

FIGURE   1-1

Segmented Boundaries of Clinical Care

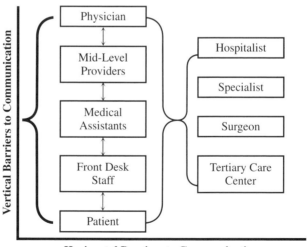

Adapted from Colley J, Heinccius L. Patient Safety and Error Reduction Initiatives in the State of Washington and Recommendations for Action: A Report From the Washington State Medical-Education and Research Foundation, July 2004. Available at: www.wsma.org/WSMERF-PatientSafetyPapers.pdf. Accessed August 18, 2005. Reprinted with permission.

in multiple efforts or services. The transfer of outcome information across the silos is often left up to the patient. These rigid clinical boundaries are solidified by system complexity and the ever-present "lack of time and resources" realized by most health care professionals. The call for creating a "patient-centered" health care system is a step forward in beginning to create permeable boundaries in our medical culture.

All of these five types of impediments to improvement interact together, often in very convoluted ways, to hamper patient safety improvements: The financial pressures causing the first two impediments (lack of time and money) often create a sense of competition among professionals and institutions that intensifies the medical silos and thwarts sharing of best practices. Efforts to create technology solutions to surmount communication barriers can divert scarce patient safety resources from other approaches, such as buying computerized pharmacy ordering, or less high-tech approaches like the slow work of changing corporate cultures.

Fortunately, despite these barriers, improving patient safety is increasingly becoming a highly visible priority for physician member organizations such as the American Medical Association and many health care institutions. Most importantly, physicians must recognize and agree that "business as usual" will not improve the safety of patient care. There is concern that many physicians have not yet embraced patient safety and quality improvement efforts.[10] Physicians must be leaders in changing culture, expanding and accelerating current efforts, and identifying and supporting new and effective patient-safety initiatives. Physicians, individually and collectively, have a key role to play in quality improvement efforts.

Without demonstrable, credible, practical, and sustainable improvements in health care safety as has been shown in other industries (the airline industry being a prime example), we will likely find surveys in the future revealing a persistent lack of confidence in the safety and quality of our country's health care system.

ENDNOTES

1. Colley J, Heinccius L. Patient Safety and Error Reduction Initiatives in the State of Washington and Recommendations for Action: A Report From the Washington State Medical-Education and Research Foundation, July 2004. Available at: www.wsma.org/WSMERF-PatientSafetyPapers.pdf. Accessed August 18, 2005.

2. National Patient Safety Foundation. About the foundation. Available at: www.npsf.org/html/about_npsf.html. Accessed August 18, 2005.

3. Siker ES. Editorial: historical perspective of APSF shows safety advocacy. Anesthesia Patient Safety Foundation. Available at: www.apsf.org/resource_center/newsletter/1996/fall/ed-histperspective.html. Accessed July 2005.

4. Kohn LT, Corrigan JM, Donaldson MS, eds. *To Err Is Human: Building a Safer Health System.* Washington, DC: Institute of Medicine; 1999.

5. Committee on Quality of Health Care in America, Institute of Medicine. *Crossing the Quality Chasm: A New Health System for the 21st Century.* Washington, DC: National Academy Press; 2001.

6. Altman DE, Clancy C, Blendon RJ. Improving patient safety—five years after the IOM report. *N Engl J Med.* 2004;351:2041-2043.

7. *Patient Safety: Achieving a New Standard for Care,* Washington, DC, National Academies Press. National Academies Press, 500 Fifth St. NW, Washington, DC 20001; (800) 624-6242, www.nap.edu.

8. *The Leapfrog Group Hospital Patient Safety Survey*, April 2003-March 2004. Washington, DC: Leapfrog Group; 2004.

9. Landrigan CP, Rothschild JM, Cronin JW, et al. Effect of eliminating extended work shifts and reducing weekly work hours on serious medical errors in intensive care units. *N Engl J Med.* 2004;351: 1838-1848.

10. Goode LD, Clancy CM, Kimball HR, et al. When is "good enough"? The role and responsibility of physicians to improve patient safety. *Acad Med.* 2002;77:947-952.

chapter 2

The Big Picture

The transition of health care improvement efforts from the relatively narrow domain of clinical experts to the nationwide broad-based focus on improving patient safety in our evolving health care system has included adapting the concepts of "safety science." With an emphasis on systematic approaches to avoid harm, the modern patient safety movement places the patient in the center, moving somewhat away from the prior primary focus of quality assurance or quality improvement movements. Safety science principles have evolved from:

- Health care research
- Systems analysis, engineering, and design
- Cognitive psychology
- Human factors/ergonomics
- Sociology and organizational behavior
- Lessons learned from other industries
- Quality improvement
- Complexity theory

The practical application of safety science concepts helps maximize the impact of current patient safety initiatives, identify the major impediments to reducing errors, and provide potential avenues to improved safety in the future. A major step forward in improving patient safety is the Patient Safety and Quality Improvement Act of 2005 (see Appendix B), whose purpose is to gather and study patient safety events, learn from them, and enhance the system to reduce adverse events.

KEY TERMS

Definition of key terms must be clearly identified at the outset. Following are frequently used terms as defined by the Agency for Healthcare Research and Quality (http://psnet.ahrq.gov/glossary.aspx):

- **Patient safety:** Freedom from accidental or preventable injuries produced by medical care.

- **Adverse event:** Any injury caused by medical care. Examples include pneumothorax from central venous catheter placement, anaphylaxis to penicillin, postoperative wound infection, and hospital-acquired delirium (or "sun downing") in elderly patients. Identifying something as an adverse event does not imply "error," "negligence," or poor quality care. It simply indicates that an undesirable clinical outcome resulted from some aspect of diagnosis or therapy, not an underlying disease process. Therefore, pneumothorax from central venous catheter placement counts as an adverse event regardless of insertion technique. Similarly, postoperative wound infections count as adverse events even if the operation proceeded with optimal adherence to sterile procedures and the patient received appropriate antibiotic prophylaxis in the peri-operative setting.

- **Error:** An act of commission (doing something wrong) or omission (failing to do the right thing) that leads to an undesirable outcome or significant potential for such an outcome. For instance, ordering a medication for a patient with a documented allergy to that medication would be an act of commission. Failing to prescribe a proven medication with major benefits for an eligible patient. For example, failing to prescribe low-dose unfractionated heparin as venous thromboembolism prophylaxis for a patient after hip replacement surgery would represent an error of omission.

    Errors of omission are more difficult to recognize than errors of commission but likely represent a larger problem. In other words, there are likely many more instances in which the provision of additional diagnostic, therapeutic, or preventive modalities would have improved care than there are instances in which the care provided quite literally should not have been provided. In many ways, this point echoes the generally agreed-upon view in the health care quality literature that underuse far exceeds overuse, even though the latter historically has received greater attention.

- **Near miss:** Also called a close call. An event or situation that did not produce patient injury, but only because of chance. This good fortune might reflect robustness of the patient (for example, a patient with penicillin allergy receives penicillin, but has no reaction) or a fortuitous, timely intervention (for example, a nurse happens to realize that a physician wrote an order in the wrong chart).

TYPES AND EXTENT OF ERRORS

Providers of care, in order to maximize patient safety efforts, must have a thorough understanding of the multiple courses of potential medical errors. Different studies over the years have used different classification approaches, but all studies agree that eliminating errors will require multidisciplinary approaches across a wide variety of service providers and settings (see Table 2-1).

SYSTEM FAILURES

The Institute of Medicine (IOM) report, *To Err is Human: Building a Safer Healthcare System,* discusses preventable adverse events/ medical errors that contribute to patient harm. These instances of patient harm/errors have been identified as largely due to system failures. That is, the complex health care system, at the macro as well as at the clinical microsystem levels, is not well designed to prevent or mitigate the potentially harmful effects of inevitable human errors. Those working or receiving services in the current system frequently focus on individuals—their competence and performance—as causes of potentially harmful events. This aspect of the existing culture, the focus on blaming individuals, is actually counterproductive to reducing patient harm because it creates incentives to hide errors rather than study and learn from them.

T A B L E   2-1

Types of Errors

- ◼ Diagnostic
    - Error or delay in diagnosis
    - Failure to use indicated tests
    - Use of outmoded tests or therapy
    - Failure to act on results of monitoring or testing
- ◼ Treatment
    - Error in the performance of an operation, procedure, or test
    - Error in administering the treatment
    - Error in the dose or method of using a drug
    - Avoidable delay in treatment or in responding to an abnormal test result
    - Inappropriate (not indicated) care
- ◼ Preventive
    - Failure to provide prophylactic treatment
    - Inadequate monitoring or follow-up treatment
- ◼ Failure of communication
- ◼ Equipment failure
- ◼ Other system failures

Source: Colley J, Heineccius L. Patient Safety and Error Reduction Initiatives in the State of Washington and Recommendations for Action: A Report From the Washington State Medical-Education and Research Foundation, July 2004. Available at: www.wsma.org/WSMERF -PatientSafetyPapers.pdf. Accessed August 18, 2005. Reprinted with permission.

GETTING PAYERS INVOLVED IN PATIENT SAFETY

Payers are beginning to recognize the value of safer patient care. Some of the insurer initiatives:

- Encouraging and actively engaging hospitals to support efforts to improve patient safety and to share information and data via initiatives such as the Leapfrog Group
- Pay for performance (PFP): PFP is a term that is being applied to incentive programs that provide financial incentives to participating entities that make progress in achieving or attaining specific quality and/or efficiency benchmarks or standards that are established by the program. PFP programs can apply to health plans, hospitals, physicians, physician groups, or other entities.
- Providing a Web site link to the Leapfrog Web site for access to a list of network hospitals that have implemented the Leapfrog initiatives
- A site survey to evaluate network provider offices and facilities
- Clinical performance and quality-of-care monitors
- Monitoring of continuity and coordination of care
- Pharmacy reviews, including systematic checks for potential drug interactions, drug utilization reviews, and polypharmacy reports
- Claims analysis to detect patient safety-related trends
- Prescription drug utilization review through access to prescription drug databases
- Online prescription drug claims adjudication systems with patient safety checks at the point of service and messages to the pharmacy, in real time, with pertinent attention to potential drug interactions, overutilization, and drug-implied disease state concerns. The dispensing pharmacist can have a discussion with the patient or, if necessary, call the prescribing physician even before the new drug is dispensed. Alerts include drug interaction, severe drug interaction, excessive daily dose, underutilization, prescribing less than the minimum daily dose, duplicate therapy, refilling too soon, drug allergy, drug during pregnancy, drug for gender, and drug for age.
- Retrospective drug utilization review to monitor formulary compliance, appropriate utilization in drug classes, and coordinated pharmaceutical care

Typical goals for insurer health management programs are to:

- Reduce unnecessary variations in care
- Increase compliance with accepted standards of care (guidelines)

- Develop interventions that result in measurable improvements in member health status
- Reduce chronic disease-associated costs for conditions such as asthma, hypertension, congestive heart failure, pneumonia, diabetes, and chronic obstructive pulmonary disease

Health management program attributes include the use of practice guidelines reflecting industry standards of care, using claims data for member risk stratification and identification of chronic diseases, disease-specific mailings to members, health management education classes, telephonic education, and wellness, smoking cessation, and prenatal programs.

The Institute of Medicine (IOM) was asked by the Centers for Medicare and Medicaid Services (CMS) to study the prevalence of adverse drug events (ADEs), or injuries due to medication, and recommend a national agenda for reducing ADEs. The IOM, in its 2006 report *Preventing Medication Errors,* has found that medication errors are surprisingly common and costly to the nation, and it outlines a comprehensive approach to decreasing the prevalence of these errors. This approach will require changes by physicians, nurses, pharmacists, and others in the health care industry; the Food and Drug Administration (FDA) and other government agencies; hospitals and other health care organizations; and patients. Here is an Institute of Medicine Report Brief, from July 2006, *Preventing Medication Errors:*

The Unacceptable Costs of Medication Errors

In hospitals, errors are common during every step of the medication process—procuring the drug, prescribing it, dispensing it, administering it, and monitoring its impact—but they occur most frequently during the prescribing and administering stages. When all types of errors are taken into account, a hospital patient can expect on average to be subjected to more than one medication error each day. However, substantial variations in error rates are found across facilities.

An ADE arising from an error is considered preventable. It is difficult to get accurate measurements of how often preventable ADEs occur. One study estimated 380,000 preventable ADEs in hospitals each year, another estimated 450,000, and the committee believes that both are likely to be underestimates. The numbers are equally disturbing in other settings. One study calculates, for example, that 800,000 preventable ADEs occur each year in long-term care facilities. Another finds that among outpatient Medicare patients there occur 530,000 preventable ADEs each year. And the evidence suggests that both of these numbers are likely to be underestimates as well. Furthermore, none of these studies includes errors of omission—failures to prescribe medication in cases where it should be. Taking all of these numbers into account, the committee concludes that there are at least 1.5 million preventable ADEs that occur in the United States each year. The true number may be much higher.

These medication errors are undoubtedly costly—to patients, their families, their employers, and to hospitals, health-care providers, and insurance companies—but there are few reliable estimates of that cost. One study found that each preventable ADE that took place in a hospital added about $8,750 (in 2006 dollars) to the cost of the hospital stay. Assuming 400,000 of these events each year—a conservative estimate—the total annual cost would be $3.5 billion in this one group. Another study looked at preventable ADEs in Medicare enrollees aged 65 and older and found an annual cost of $887 million for treating medication errors in this group. Unfortunately, these studies cover only some of the medication errors that occur each year in this country, and they look at only some of their costs—they do not take into account lost earnings, for example, or any compensation for pain and suffering.

What is most striking about these statistics is that much of this harm is preventable, since a variety of strategies and techniques exist for reducing medication errors. Many of these approaches have already been tested and shown to work in practice, while others seem promising but will require further development. Given this situation, the committee concluded that the current state of affairs is not acceptable and it recommended a series of steps that should be taken to prevent medication errors.

A Paradigm Shift in the Patient Provider Relationship

The first step is to allow and encourage patients to take a more active role in their own medical care. In the past the nation's health-care system has generally been paternalistic and provider-centric, and patients have not been expected to be involved in the process. But one of the most effective ways to reduce medication errors, the report concludes, is to move toward a model of health care where there is more of a partnership between the patients and the health-care providers. Patients should understand more about their medications and take more responsibility for monitoring those medications, while providers should take steps to educate, consult with, and listen to the patients.

To make this new model of health-care work, a number of things must be done. Doctors, nurses, pharmacists and other providers must communicate more with patients at every step of the way and make that communication a two-way street, listening to the patients as well as talking to them. They should inform their patients fully about the risks, contraindications, and possible side effects of the medications they are taking and what to do if they experience a side effect. They should also be more forthcoming when medication errors have occurred and explain what the consequences have been.

Patients or their surrogates should in turn take a more active role in the process. They should learn to keep careful records of all the medications they are taking and take greater responsibility for monitoring those medications by, for example, doublechecking prescriptions from pharmacies and reporting any unexpected changes in how they feel after starting a new medication.

Also, the health-care system needs to do a better job of educating patients and of providing ways for patients to educate themselves. Patients should be given opportunities to consult about their medications at various stages in their care—during consultation with the providers who prescribe their medications, at discharge from the hospital, at the pharmacy, and so on. And there needs to be a concerted effort to improve the quality and the accessibility of information about medications provided to consumers. The committee recommends that the FDA, the National Library of Medicine, and other government agencies work together to standardize and improve the medication information leaflets provided by pharmacies, make more and better drug information available over the Internet, and develop a 24-hour national telephone helpline that offers consumers easy access to drug information.

Using Information Technologies to Reduce Medication Errors

A second important step in reducing the number of medication errors will be to make greater use of information technologies in prescribing and dispensing medications. Doctors, nurse practitioners, and physician assistants, for example, cannot possibly keep up with all the relevant information available on all the medications they might prescribe—but with today's information technologies they don't have to. By using point-of-care reference information, typically accessed over the Internet or from personal digital assistants, prescribers can obtain detailed information about the particular drugs they prescribe and get help in deciding which medications to prescribe.

Even more promising is the use of electronic prescriptions, or e-prescriptions. By writing prescriptions electronically, doctors and other providers can avoid many of the mistakes that accompany handwritten prescriptions, as the software ensures that all the necessary information is filled out—and legible. Furthermore, by tying e-prescriptions in with the patient's medical history, it is possible to check automatically for such things as drug allergies, drug-drug interactions, and overly high doses. In addition, once an e-prescription is in the system, it will follow the patient from the hospital to the doctor's office or from the nursing home to the pharmacy, avoiding many of the "hand-off errors" common today. In light of all this, the committee recommends that by 2010 all prescribers and pharmacies be using e-prescriptions.

More generally, all health-care suppliers should seek to become high-reliability organizations preoccupied with improving medication safety. To do this, they will have to take advantage of the latest information technologies and the most up-to-date organizational and management strategies. They will also need to put effective internal monitoring programs in place, which will allow them to determine the incidence rates of ADEs more accurately and thus provide a way of measuring their progress toward improved medication safety.

Improved Labeling and Packaging of Medications

Another way to reduce medication errors is to ensure that drug information is communicated clearly and effectively to providers and patients. Some errors occur simply because two different drugs have names that look or sound very similar. With this in mind, the committee recommends that the drug industry and the appropriate federal agencies work together to improve drug nomenclature, including not just drug names but also abbreviations and acronyms. At the same time, the information sheets that accompany drugs should be redesigned, taking into account research that identifies the best methods for communicating information about medications.

Policy Recommendation

Reducing preventable ADEs will demand the attention and active involvement of everyone involved. The federal government should, for example, pay for and coordinate a broad research effort aimed at learning more about preventing medication errors. Various regulatory agencies should encourage the adoption of practices and technologies that will reduce medication errors. Accreditation agencies should require more training in medication-management practices. The committee believes that the effort will pay off in far fewer medication errors and preventable adverse drug events, far less harm done to patients by medications, and far less cost to the nation's economy.

Source: Copyright ©2006 by the National Academy of Sciences. All rights reserved. Copies of *Preventing Medication Errors* are available from the National Academies Press, 500 Fifth Street, N.W., Lockbox 285, Washington, DC 20055; (800) 624-6242 or (202) 334-3313 (in the Washington metropolitan area); Internet, http://www.nap.edu.

THE INFORMED PATIENT

Patients, as consumers, are becoming much better informed and more concerned about evidence-based medical care, health care quality, and patient safety. Communication and geographic barriers have been broken down through the use of the Internet and support groups. More and more patients are well informed on the latest medical advances and treatment and are not afraid to ask informed questions and to challenge physicians as to the reasons for their treatment plan, choice of products and drugs, and the use of patient safety measures.

The American Medical Association (AMA), through media outreach and member physician grassroots efforts, advocated successfully for passage of the comprehensive Patients' Bill of Rights Act by Congress in 1998. It guarantees access to needed health care specialists; requires continuity of care protections so that patients will not have to change doctors in the middle of their treatment; provides access to a fair, unbiased, and timely internal and independent external appeals process to address health plan grievances; assures that doctors and patients can openly discuss treatment options; and includes an enforcement mechanism that ensures these rights are real. For more about the Patients' Bill of Rights, go to http://www.consumer.gov/qualityhealth/rights.htm.

PATIENTS' BILL OF RIGHTS

I. Information Disclosure
You have the right to receive accurate and easily understood information about your health plan, health care professionals, and health care facilities. If you speak another language, have a physical or mental disability, or just don't understand something, assistance will be provided so you can make informed health care decisions.

II. Choice of Providers and Plans
You have the right to a choice of health care providers that is sufficient to provide you with access to appropriate high-quality health care.

III. Access to Emergency Services

If you have sever pain, an injury, or sudden illness that convinces you that your health is in serious jeopardy, you have the right to receive screening and stabilization emergency services whenever and wherever needed, without prior authorization or financial penalty.

IV. Participation in Treatment Decisions

You have the right to know all your treatment options and to participate in decisions about your care. Parents, guardians, family members, or other individuals that you designate can represent you if you cannot make your own decisions.

V. Respect and Nondiscrimination

You have a right to considerate, respectful and nondiscriminatory care from your doctors, health plan representatives, and other health care providers.

VI. Confidentiality of Health Information

You have the right to talk in confidence with health care providers and to have your health care information protected. You also have the right to review and copy your own medical record and request that your physician amend your record if it is not accurate, relevant, or complete.

VII. Complaints and Appeals

You have the right to a fair, fast, and objective review of any compliant you have against your health plan, doctors, hospitals, or other health care personnel. This includes complaints about waiting times, operating hours, the conduct of health care personnel, and the adequacy of health care facilities.

FIVE STEPS TO SAFER HEALTH CARE

The AMA, together with the U.S. Department of Health and Human Services (HHS) and the American Hospital Association (AHA), has developed a set of evidence-based, practical tips for patients to help improve the safety of the care they receive and avoid errors related to prescription medicines, laboratory tests, and procedures and surgery. Called the "5 Steps to Safer Health Care," these tips are designed to improve communication between patients and their health care team. Good communication between patients and health care providers can often reduce potential problems in our increasingly complex health care system. In addition, getting patients involved in their own health and health care decisions can have a huge positive impact on the success of medical outcomes. Here are the five steps to safer health care:

1. **Ask questions if you have doubts or concerns**
   Ask questions and make sure you understand the answers. Choose a doctor you feel comfortable talking to. Take a relative or friend with you to help you ask questions and understand the answers.

2. **Keep a list of ALL the medications you take and bring it to your doctor**
   Give your doctor and pharmacist a list of all the medications you take, including nonprescription medications. Tell them about any drug allergies you have. Ask about side effects and what to avoid while taking the medication. Read the label when you get your medication, including all warnings. Make sure that the medication is what the doctor ordered and you know how to use it. Ask the pharmacist about your medication if it looks different from what you expected.

3. **Get the results of any test or procedure**
   Ask when and how you will get the results of your tests or procedures. Don't assume the results are fine if you do not get them when expected, be it in person, by phone, or by mail. Call your doctor and ask for your results. Ask what the results mean for your care.

4. **Talk to your doctor about which hospital is best for your health needs**
   Ask your doctor about which hospital has the best care and results for your condition if you have more than one hospital to choose from. Be sure you understand the instructions you get about follow-up care when you leave the hospital.

5. **Make sure you understand what will happen if you need surgery**
   Make sure you, your doctor, and your surgeon all agree on exactly what will be done during the operation. Ask your doctor: Who will manage my care when I am in the hospital? Ask your surgeon: Exactly what will you be doing? About how long will it take? What will happen after the surgery? How can I expect to feel during recovery? Tell the surgeon, anesthesiologist, and nurses about any allergies, bad reaction to anesthesia, and any medications you are taking.

In 2002, the Joint Commission on Accreditation of Healthcare Organizations (JCAHO) launched a patient safety campaign called Speak Up.[1] Since that time, the JCAHO has launched four more Speak Up programs: wrong-site surgery, organ donation, infection control, and medication mistakes. The aim of these campaigns is to encourage patients to become informed and active members of the health care team. Brochures, posters, and buttons are provided, urging patients to become active, informed, and involved participants in helping to prevent health care errors. Speak Up is an acronym for important safety tips to remind patients to:

Speak up if you have questions or concerns, and if you don't understand, ask again. It's your body and you have a right to know.

Pay attention to the care you are receiving. Make sure you're getting the right treatments and medications by the right health care professionals. Don't assume anything.

Educate yourself about your diagnosis, the medical tests you are undergoing, and your treatment plan.

Ask a trusted family member or friend to be your advocate.

Know what medications you take and why you take them. Medication errors are the most common health care mistakes.

Use a hospital, clinic, surgery center, or other type of health care organization that has undergone a rigorous on-site evaluation against established, state-of-the-art quality and safety standards, such as that provided by the Joint Commission.

Participate in all decisions about your treatment. You are the center of the health care team.

Organizations interested in incorporating the Speak Up program can download preprinted brochures and posters from the JCAHO Web site (www.jcaho.org/accredited+organizations/speak+up/index.htm) and reproduce them for distribution. Speak Up information can also be reprinted for use in in-house publications.

Free information regarding hospital and physician performance parameters is available to consumers through the Internet. One source is through the Leapfrog Group. A report ranking hospital standing in a hospital quality-safety survey is posted on the Leapfrog Web site (www.leapfroggroup.org). The report includes the National Quality Forum (NQF) Safe Practices for Better Health Care, released by NQF in May 2003. These 30 NQF safe practices include Leapfrog's original three leaps (computerized physician order entry, intensive care physician staffing, and procedure volume-based hospital referrals), in addition to the remaining 27 practices. Hospitals are being asked to self-report their status on the 30 practices in the survey that is available on the Web site. The survey will rank hospitals on their use of these patient safety practices.

The Centers for Medicare and Medicaid Services (CMS) provides information to consumers related to quality of care.[2] The information is reproduced in the following excerpt:

This tool provides you with information on how well the hospitals in your area care for all their adult patients with certain medical conditions. This information will help you compare the quality of care hospitals provide. Hospital Compare was created through the efforts of the Centers for Medicare and Medicaid Services (CMS) and organizations that represent hospitals, doctors, employers, accrediting organizations, other Federal agencies, and the public.

Talk to your doctor about this information to help you, your family, and your friends make your best hospital care decisions.

This website has:	How would you like to search for a Hospital?
■ **Hospital Information** Get the address, telephone number and other important information for all Medicare-certified hospitals in the United States.	**By Geography** I want to search for all hospitals within a: **State**
■ **Quality Measures** There are treatments for certain conditions that are known to get the best results for most adult patients. Certain types of hospitals have agreed to submit data on their patients with a heart attack, heart failure, or pneumonia. This website has quality measures that show how often these hospitals provide some of the recommended care for adults with these conditions.	**County** **City** **ZIP Code**
■ **Patient Tools** Hospital Checklist Your Rights When You Are in the Hospital	**By Name** I want to search for a hospital by entering all/some of their name: **Hospital Name**

The information on the Web site has been provided primarily by hospitals participating iin a national project called the Hospital Quality Alliance: Improving Care Through Information (HQA). Participating hospitals agree to submit and report additional quality information for public reporting.

The CMS Hospital Quality Initiative (HQI) Web site[3] references efforts that are in progress to provide hospital quality information to consumers and others and improve the care provided by the nation's hospitals. These initiatives build upon previous strategies to identify illnesses and/or clinical conditions that affect Medicare beneficiaries in order to promote the best medical practices associated with the targeted clinical disorders; prevent or reduce further instances of these selected clinical disorders; and prevent related complications.

For example, the American Medical Association-convened Physician Consortium for Performance Improvement (AMA/Consortium), the Centers for Medicare and Medicaid Services (CMS), and the National Committee for Quality Assurance (NCQA) have worked jointly to identify a set of clinical ambulatory measures of quality of care for chronic diseases including diabetes, coronary artery disease, heart failure, behavioral health, hypertension, osteoarthritis, and asthma, as well as for prenatal care and several preventive services including immunizations, tobacco use cessation, and problem drinking. For more information visit http://www.ama-assn.org/ama/pub/category/17603.html

THE REGULATORS

The JCAHO has taken a strong position on patient safety and continues to expand the scope. The 2006 National Patient Safety Goals (NPSGs)[4] include:

- Ambulatory care and office-based surgery
- Assisted living
- Behavioral health care
- Critical access hospital
- Disease-specific care
- Home care
- Hospital
- Laboratory
- Long-term care
- Networks

The 2007 ambulatory care and office-based surgery goals are as follows:

Goal: Improve the accuracy of patient identification.
Use at least two patient identifiers when providing care, treatment, or services.

Goal: Improve the effectiveness of communication among caregivers.
For verbal or telephone orders or for telephonic reporting of critical test results, verify the complete order or test result by having the person receiving the information record and "read-back" the complete order or test result.

Standardize a list of abbreviations, acronyms, symbols, and dose designations that are not to be used throughout the organization.

Measure, assess and, if appropriate, take action to improve the timeliness of reporting, and the timeliness of receipt by the responsible licensed caregiver, of critical test results and values.

Implement a standardized approach to "hand off" communications, including an opportunity to ask and respond to questions.

Goal: Improve the safety of using medications.
Standardize and limit the number of drug concentrations used by the organization.

Identify and, at a minimum, annually review a list of look-alike/sound-alike drugs used by the organization, and take action to prevent errors involving the interchange of these drugs.

Label all medications, medication containers (for example, syringes, medicine cups, basins), or other solutions on and off the sterile field.

Goal: Reduce the risk of health care-associated infections.
Comply with current Centers for Disease Control and Prevention (CDC) hand hygiene guidelines.

Manage as sentinel events all identified cases of unanticipated death or major permanent loss of function associated with a health care-associated infection.

Goal: Accurately and completely reconcile medications across the continuum of care.
There is a process for comparing the patient's current medications with those ordered for the patient while under the care of the organization.

A complete list of the patient's medications is communicated to the next provider of service when a patient is referred or transferred to another setting, service, practitioner or level of care within or outside the organization. The complete list of medications is also provided to the patient on discharge from the facility.

Goal: Reduce the risk of surgical fires.
Educate staff, including operating licensed independent practitioners and anesthesia providers, on how to control heat sources and manage fuels with enough time for patient preparation, and establish guidelines to minimize oxygen concentration under drapes.

Goal: Encourage patients' active involvement in their own care as a patient safety strategy.
Define and communicate the means for patients and their families to report concerns about safety and encourage them to do so.

Following are JCAHO's 2007 Hospital/Critical Access Hospital National Patient Safety Goals:

Goal: Improve the accuracy of patient identification.
Use at least two patient identifiers when providing care, treatment or services.

Goal: Improve the effectiveness of communication among caregivers.
For verbal or telephone orders or for telephonic reporting of critical test results, verify the complete order or test result by having the person receiving the information record and "read-back" the complete order or test result.

Standardize a list of abbreviations, acronyms, symbols, and dose designations that are not to be used throughout the organization.

Measure, assess and, if appropriate, take action to improve the timeliness of reporting, and the timeliness of receipt by the responsible licensed caregiver, of critical test results and values.

Implement a standardized approach to "hand off" communications, including an opportunity to ask and respond to questions.

Goal: Improve the safety of using medications.

Standardize and limit the number of drug concentrations used by the organization.

Identify and, at a minimum, annually review a list of look-alike/sound-alike drugs used by the organization, and take action to prevent errors involving the interchange of these drugs.

Label all medications, medication containers (for example, syringes, medicine cups, basins), or other solutions on and off the sterile field.

Goal: Reduce the risk of health care-associated infections.

Comply with current Centers for Disease Control and Prevention (CDC) hand hygiene guidelines.

Manage as sentinel events all identified cases of unanticipated death or major permanent loss of function associated with a health care-associated infection.

Goal: Accurately and completely reconcile medications across the continuum of care.

There is a process for comparing the patient's current medications with those ordered for the patient while under the care of the organization.

A complete list of the patient's medications is communicated to the next provider of service when a patient is referred or transferred to another setting, service, practitioner or level of care within or outside the organization. The complete list of medications is also provided to the patient on discharge from the facility.

Goal: Reduce the risk of patient harm resulting from falls.

Implement a fall reduction program including an evaluation of the effectiveness of the program.

Goal: Encourage patients' active involvement in their own care as a patient safety strategy.

Define and communicate the means for patients and their families to report concerns about safety and encourage them to do so.

Goal: The organization identifies safety risks inherent in its patient population.

The organization identifies patients at risk for suicide. [Applicable to psychiatric hospitals and patients being treated for emotional or behavioral disorders in general hospitals.]

The CMS Web site contains detailed information pertaining to its Hospital Quality Initiative.[3] As described in their introduction, CMS has several efforts in progress to provide hospital quality information to consumers and others and improve the care provided by the nation's hospitals. These initiatives build upon previous CMS and quality improvement organization (QIO) strategies to identify illnesses and/or clinical conditions that affect Medicare beneficiaries in order to promote the best medical practices associated with the targeted clinical disorders; prevent or reduce further instances of these selected clinical disorders; and prevent related complications. This page includes links to reports and other documents that describe these efforts in more detail.

ENDNOTES

1. Speak up initiatives. Available at: www.jcaho.org/accredited +organizations/speak+up/index.htm. Accessed May 24, 2005.

2. Hospital compare. Available at: www.hospitalcompare.hhs.gov/ hospital/home2.asp. Accessed May 24, 2005.

3. Hospital Quality Initiative: overview. Available at: www.cms .hhs.gov/quality/hospital/. Accessed May 24, 2005.

4. 2006 Joint Commission National Patient Safety Goals. Available at: www.jcipatientsafety.org/show.asp?durki=10289&site=164 &return=9335. Accessed February 22, 2006.

chapter 3

The Physician Office

Although a published list of types of errors was mentioned in Chapter 2, it is helpful to also categorize errors in different ways for purposes of illustrating error concepts in ambulatory care. Two types of errors were described by the Institute of Medicine: errors of execution (failure to complete a planned action as intended) and errors of planning (use of an erroneous plan to achieve a medical outcome). Errors can be further classified as errors of either commission or omission.

Errors of commission are the results of actions that are performed incorrectly (eg, wrong-site surgery,) or when the wrong course of action is taken to achieve an objective (the wrong drug is prescribed). Other examples include:

- Wrong diagnosis
- Improper management of correct diagnosis
- Lack of patient information
- Inaccessible medical record
- Incomplete patient history and/or physical examination
- Prescription errors
- Wrong drug
- Wrong dosage or duration of therapy
- Failure to recognize drug–drug interactions
- Illegible prescriptions
- Transcribing errors by office staff or pharmacist
- Failure to refill in a timely fashion
- Failure to monitor drugs that require monitoring

Errors of omission occur when an action is not performed as it should be. Examples include:

- Failure to follow up on test results, such as a mammogram
- Failure to notify patients of test results
- Lack of necessary follow-up with physician
- Failure to make a new appointment after patient or physician cancellation

- Failure to follow up after the patient fails to show for a scheduled appointment
- Failure to coordinate care with consultants
- Lack of timely evaluation
- Delay in the referral process
- Failure to communicate findings and recommendations after consultation
- Delay in diagnosis
- Failure to perform preventive care, such as vaccinations
- Failure to provide proven disease-specific care
- Failure in information transfer
  - Among covering physicians
  - Between inpatient physician and outpatient provider
- Failure to educate patients

ERROR REPORTING IN AMBULATORY CARE

The voluntary reporting of near misses and adverse events is an important but underutilized source of information on errors in the health care industry. In particular, there is little information on errors in the ambulatory setting, and physicians have not traditionally participated actively in their reporting or analysis, for reasons previously discussed. Although enormous attention has been focused on reporting adverse events that occur in the hospital, analyzing errors in the ambulatory care setting is in its infancy and is complicated by a variety of factors:

- Multiple providers and patient visits
- Fragmented communication between patients and providers
- Error reporting dependent upon patients or physicians
- Patient compliance with treatment plans

Medical error rates were found to vary from five to 80 errors per 100,000 patient visits in a review of 11 studies on the frequency and nature of medical errors in primary care practices.[1] The two most frequent types of identified errors were (1) delayed or missed diagnosis in 26% to 78% of identified errors and (2) treatment errors in 11% to 42% of identified errors. There were often multiple underlying causes of these errors, and in up to 50% of cases the causes could not be identified. The wide diversity in these published findings may have been a reflection of the varied definitions of errors and methods of detection.

A general idea of relative frequency of types of errors was illustrated by a study in which 42 family practice physicians voluntarily provided 344 error reports.[2] Three hundred thirty were thought to be true errors. Forty-four percent of the errors resulted in adverse events, including one death. Seventy-two errors occurred in the outpatient setting. The most frequent types of errors occurred in:

- Laboratory or testing processes: 27%
- Information management or charting: 23%
- Drug treatment: 18%
- Cognitive errors on the part of the physician: 13%

A similar study of a multinational group of general practitioners had similar results.[3]

The initial one-year experience of voluntary reporting by clinicians in the ambulatory setting was reported in a study designed to determine the feasibility and effectiveness of clinician-based near miss/adverse event voluntary reporting coupled with systems analysis and redesign as a model for continuous quality improvement in the ambulatory setting.[4] There were 100 reports in the one year period, increased by five from the previous year. The events were reported by:

- Faculty physicians: 44%
- Nurses: 31%
- Residents: 22%
- Managers: 3%

The adverse event categories included:

- Near misses: 83%
- Adverse events: 17%
- Errors involving medication: 47%
- Laboratory or x-rays: 22%
- Office administration: 21%
- Communication processes: 10%

Seventy-two interventions were recommended and 75% were implemented during the study period.

The authors concluded that this model of clinician-based voluntary reporting, systems analysis, and redesign was an effective way to increase error reporting by physicians and to promote system changes for improving care and preventing medical errors. This tool process can be a powerful tool for instilling error reporting and analysis into the culture of patient care.

Although attending physicians are in an ideal position to identify medical errors and realize their consequences, the scope of error detection by attending physicians is currently unknown. A prospective identification of errors by attending physicians in patients admitted to the general medicine service of a 200-bed academic hospital was undertaken from October 2000 to April 2001.[5] The objectives were to determine the types, frequency, and consequences of errors that can be detected by attending hospitalist physicians in the care of their patients and to compare the types of errors first discovered by attending hospitalists to those discovered by other providers. Two attending hospitalists identified near misses and adverse events during the course of their routine. Clinical care errors that were initially detected by other health care workers were also recorded.

Study conclusions suggested that attending physicians engaged in routine clinical care can detect a large range of errors, although there may be differences in the types of errors detected by various health care providers. There were 528 patients admitted to the hospitalist service; 10.4% experienced at least one error, 6.2% a near miss, and 4.2% an adverse event. Drug errors were the most common type of error overall. Although differences did not achieve statistical significance, most of the errors first detected by house staff, nurses, and laboratory technicians were adverse events, and those first detected by attending hospitalists, pharmacists, and consultants were near misses.

The authors discussed the fact that efficient and reliable reporting systems for medical errors must be developed in order to enhance patient safety. These systems would track errors and enable providers to identify the scope, causes, and consequences of medical errors. Current reporting systems are underutilized and fail to provide a complete and accurate record of near-misses medical errors that are necessary to prevent errors. Much of our current understanding of medical errors is based on retrospective chart reviews, which are limited by clinician reluctance to document errors in the medical record and the inability of analysts to fully assess what actually happened during clinical encounters. Consequently, actual error rates are not known, and a full understanding of the clinical factors resulting in errors is beyond our reach. Physicians do not actively participate in most prospective error systems reporting that are critical for improving safe patient care. They are used primarily by pharmacists for tracking medication errors and by nurses for incident reporting. Attending physicians possess the experience and clinical judgment that comes with being senior physicians and are well positioned to identify errors during their involvement with day-to-day inpatient care.

The Institute of Medicine and the Joint Commission on Accreditation of Healthcare Organizations (JCAHO) are also amplifying the need for voluntary error reporting by physicians to promote patient safety. Physician error tracking efforts will go a long way to heighten awareness of current safety problems in health care delivery and energize an overall sense of awareness of the importance of patient safety.

CLINICAL SAFETY PITFALLS

An understanding of possible pitfalls that can lead to errors and adverse events in ambulatory care is paramount to error prevention. Once potentials for errors are identified and understood, then systems for error prevention can be used to help anticipate and avoid potential mistakes. The question is where to start. One approach is to look at some of the most commonly identified pitfalls for medical errors in ambulatory care.

A 2002 study reported in the *Journal of Family Practice* synthesized all the available literature on medical errors and preventable adverse events in the primary care setting to come up with a classification system of errors to help reduce errors and improve patient care.[6] The study led to a classification of three main categories of preventable adverse events: diagnostic, treatment, and preventive care incidents. Process errors were classified into four categories: clinician factors (such as judgment, decision making, or skill execution), communication factors (between clinician and patient and between health care providers), administrative factors (office and personnel issues), and blunt end factors (insurance and government regulations). This is one of the many classification systems used. The most widely accepted system is the Eindhoven Classification system.

Documentation

Illegibly documenting the severity and complexity of the patient's clinical problems, assessment, and treatment plan, including prescriptions and orders, can lead to a great potential for misinterpretation and error. For example, elimination of potentially confusing abbreviations has been a focus of the JCAHO,[7] and a similar approach could improve outpatient care documentation.

Documentation deficiencies include:

- Lack of patient information
- Inaccessible medical records
- Incomplete patient history and/or physical examination
- Illegible handwriting
- Lack of a clearly defined treatment plan
- Discrepancies between specialists' diagnostic impressions and treatment recommendations

■ Lack of documented coordination of care

■ Failure to note and track comorbid conditions and complications

■ Continued use of abbreviations on JCAHO's "Do Not Use" list

■ Failure to document quality-of-care indicators

■ Delays in completing medical records

Medical record documentation should include:

■ The specific reason for the patient encounter

■ All services that were provided

■ The assessment of the patient's condition

■ Information on the patient's progress and prior treatment

■ The plan for care

■ Information providing reasonable medical rationale for the services

■ Information supporting the care given in the case when another health care professional must assume care or perform medical review

Diagnoses should be numbered and followed by the corresponding plan for each diagnosis. The plan should include therapeutic, social, advisory, dietary, and other significant modes of treatment that have been prescribed or advised. List medications not only by name, but also by amount dispensed, number of refills, and how the medicine is to be taken. Make sure to record medication samples. Note if the patient is to be sent for special tests, including dates for follow-up.

Make sure to justify the care provided (medical necessity) in the plan part of the progress note. Alternatives provided to the patient should be noted as well as consultations and referrals. This demonstrates to other readers of the record exactly what was done and told to the patient. The legal ramifications of this part of the progress note is the area where physicians may get trapped. The physician's counseling often is not recorded in the record, and the patient may disclaim facts that the physician related.

The medical record should also:

■ Be recorded in ink and be neat, legible, factual, timely, accurate, and chronological

■ Not be subjective, sloppy, secondhand, emotional, or derogatory or contain any items of a joking or demeaning nature

■ Never show erasures, overwrites, edits, whiteouts, or obvious additions to old notes (The way to correct items is to draw a single line through them and initial and date the correction.)

- Reflect descriptive terminology when relating the history, and whenever statements should be quantified with terms such as how much, how high, how long

- State facts and avoid subjectivity, eg, physicians should state what they hear, smell, see, and feel and not write ambiguous terms or phrases such as *apparently, inadvertently,* or *appears to be*

- Not contain words that denote fault or blame, eg, *wrong, stupid, incorrect, negligent,* or *incompetent*

- Include items important to patient care that may not have been part of the office visit, such as phone calls related to clinical care and advice given by a staff member

Whenever an entry is made in the medical record, it should be done with the thought that other people will eventually see it. It will reflect that the physician is the patient's advocate.

Preventing Gaps in Care

Health care is behind other industries in the availability and use of technology for critical support functions. Reminders and alerts for results of diagnostic studies, disease prevention interventions, evidence-based treatment parameters for chronic diseases, and drug allergies and incompatibilities are only a few examples where clinical decision support systems are essential.

Practicing physicians are well aware that test follow-up is often incomplete. Tests that are ordered may never get done, and test results may not be forwarded to the ordering physician. Similarly, patients may neither make nor keep appointments with specialists, or the referring physician may not receive a report from the consultant.

In a 1996 survey of practicing primary care physicians,[8] 32% reported having a fair, poor, or no test-tracking system and 72% of physicians did not notify patients of normal results. Only 55% of physicians always notified their patients of abnormal results. Additionally, after notifying patients of abnormal results, only 23% had a reliable system of ensuring that appropriate follow-up on the abnormal test was completed by the patient. These results suggest that it can be dangerous to tell patients, "No news is good news; if you don't hear from me, everything is fine." Although patients may soon be returning for an office visit, they often skip or cancel these crucial appointments. These communication lapses are not infrequently exposed in malpractice litigation cases. Decision support, alert, and reminder systems are essential oversight requirements for safe patient care in every physician office and ambulatory care service facility. The electronic health record can help fill this need and will be discussed in detail in a subsequent chapter.

Some form of monitoring is usually required for patients taking anticoagulants, angiotensin-converting enzyme inhibitors, digoxin, insulin, oral hypoglycemics, thiazolidinediones, and antiseizure medications, among others. A monitoring calendar often facilitates this task in practice. Dates for follow-up laboratory studies are entered on a patient's monitoring calendar. If the results are not received by the due date, a staff member or the physician contacts the patient to ask whether the test was performed and arranges for testing. Any follow-up monitoring is also entered on the calendar.

It is possible to keep track of a large number of patients in this manner, but to ensure that a process is used properly, it must be standardized for each practice and the tracking system must also be kept up to date. For example, physicians prescribing new medications for patients taking warfarin should always check for drug–drug interactions; relying on memory alone can lead to serious problems.

Look-Alike and Sound-Alike Drug Names

Confusing the names of drugs is a common system failure that often results in serious and sometimes fatal errors in drug administration. Unfortunately, many drug names can look or sound like other drug names, which may lead to potentially harmful medication errors. Increasingly, pharmaceutical manufacturers and regulatory authorities are taking measures to determine whether there are unacceptable similarities between proposed names and products on the market. But factors such as poor handwriting or poorly communicated oral prescriptions can exacerbate the problem.

The United States Adopted Names (USAN) Council—which is jointly sponsored by the American Medical Association (AMA), the United States Pharmacopeial Convention (USP), and the American Pharmacists Association (APhA)—aims for global standardization and unification of drug nomenclature and related rules to ensure that drug information is communicated accurately and unambiguously. USAN works closely with the International Nonproprietary Name (INN) Programme of the World Health Organization (WHO), and various national nomenclature groups. USAN's purpose is to select simple, informative, and unique nonproprietary names for drugs by establishing logical nomenclature classifications based on pharmacological and/or chemical relationships. By definition, nonproprietary names are not subject to proprietary trademark rights but are entirely in the public domain. This distinguishes them from the trademarked names that have been registered for private use. A USAN is a nonproprietary name selected by the USAN Council according to principles developed to ensure safety, consistency, and logic in the choice of names.

These principles take into account practical considerations, such as the existence of trademarks, international harmonization of drug nomenclature, the development of new classes of drugs, and the fact that the intended uses of substances for which names are being selected may change. However, these rules apply only to nonproprietary drug names, not brand or proprietary names. Drug brand names are not regulated in any way by the federal government.

USAN General Rules

1. A nonproprietary name should be useful primarily to health practitioners, especially physicians, pharmacists, nurses, educators, dentists, and veterinarians.
2. Attributes that contribute to usefulness are simplicity (brevity and ease of pronunciation), euphony, and ready recognition and recall.
3. A name should reflect characteristics and relationships that will be of practical value to the users.
4. A name should be free from conflict with other nonproprietary names and with established trademarks; it should be neither confusing nor chemically misleading.
5. Preference should be given to names of established usage provided they conform to these guiding principles and are determined to be free from conflict with existing nonproprietary names and trademarks.
6. Identical negotiations submitted by more than one manufacturer will be conducted in accordance with the Council's practice of maintaining confidentiality. The applicants involved will not be notified of the multiple sources of the submission. However, the name selected by the USAN Council will need to be accepted by each manufacturer involved in the negotiation process.
7. A request for a USAN should be made after the drug manufacturer or sponsor has submitted an Investigational New Drug (IND) application to the Food and Drug Administration (FDA) to obtain permission to initiate studies on humans.
8. The USAN Council honors requests to defer active negotiations for a set time upon receipt of written request from the manufacturer.

Source: http://www.ama-assn.org/ama/pub/category/17603.html. Accessed June 8, 2007.

In 2001, the JCAHO published a Sentinel Event Alert on look-alike and sound-alike drug names. This alert urged health care practitioners and organizations to be aware of the role drug names play in medication safety as well as system changes that should be made to prevent such errors. A safety strategy to help manage all sound-alike and look-alike drug names should be established for every medical practice. Lists of look-alike and sound-alike drugs are provided in Appendices D through G.

Continuity of Care

Flawed communication in the fragmented ambulatory care environment was previously identified as one of the root causes of medical errors. Many of the benefits of continuity of care were discussed in a study of the impact of provider continuity on the management of patients with diabetes mellitus.[9] Although the study found no association between provider continuity and completion of diabetes monitoring tests in a national privately insured population, it was felt that continuity might benefit other aspects of health care, especially the management of chronic diseases.

Continuity of care is a hallmark of primary care and can be defined as ongoing care from the same health care provider over a period of time. Studies were cited that high provider continuity may have a positive impact on quality of care because of the knowledge and personal relationship that develops between the patient and the provider.

Continuity can be associated with:

- Improved preventive care and immunizations for children
- Improved compliance with medication prescriptions
- Improved physician recognition of medical problems
- Reduced rates of hospital admissions and emergency department visits

Patients who maintain physician continuity:

- Are more satisfied with their care
- Are more likely to keep follow-up appointments
- Communicate better with their physician
- Rank continuity as a high priority in their medical care

Improved quality of care for patients with chronic diseases may be another potential benefit of continuity. Diabetes requires considerable medical management, and the review cited published studies suggesting that higher provider continuity might lead to better glucose control. When a patient is cared for by the same provider, it is easier to know when tests are required and treatment changes are indicated.

Physicians face another coordination of care pitfall during their training years as well as when on night and weekend call for their practice: handoffs and transition of care. A published discussion of this problem[10] summarized the findings of a study that followed 3146 patients admitted to a medical service and recorded the preventable errors that occurred.[11] An analysis of the risk factors for errors discovered that coverage by a second team of physicians was one of the strongest predictors—almost three times as likely as coverage by a single team—to correlate with an adverse event. These results are even more prevalent today. Residency programs have begun to have more physicians rotating through shifts, thereby creating more cross-coverage, more sign-outs, and more opportunities for error. Unfortunately, the work regulations that are supposed to improve patient safety by decreasing the number of overworked, fatigued physicians may inadvertently expose patients to errors made in the process of a greater number of handoffs. It appears that the errors result from a breakdown in the chain of communication during these transitions. In another study,[12] when a team used a computerized list to help with sign-outs, the errors in sign-outs were dramatically reduced. It appeared that physicians needed tools to communicate effectively, but even sophisticated tools can fail. Even with computerized lists, we can stumble on the confusion and slipperiness of language, including human nature in the form of resistance to asking for clarification.

Communication

Communication failures are frequently implicated as contributors to adverse events. They can be divided into three categories:

- Failure in information transfer
  - Among covering physicians
  - Between inpatient physician and outpatient provider
- Failure to communicate findings and recommendations after consultation
- Failure to educate patients

Deficiencies in communication cover the spectrum of:

- Listening to the patient
- Capturing pertinent clinical information and data regarding current and past medical problems
- Reporting and confirming patient responses to diagnostic study results

- Information sharing among providers
- Appropriate disclosure of errors when they occur

A 2004 publication from the Department of Veterans Affairs summarized studies that illustrated the magnitude of communications deficiencies in health care.[13] The study was designed to analyze the complexities of medical errors and emphasized the need for detailed models to illustrate how communication breakdowns contribute to adverse drug events so that interventions can be developed to improve communication processes. Flawed communication was the most frequently cited cause (> 60%) of medication errors reported to the JCAHO between 1995 and 2003.

It is unclear what, if any, interventions could reduce the rate of adverse events by improving communication processes. Detailed process tracing analyses of single incidents were conducted to gain understanding of how communication breakdowns contribute to adverse events. The Veterans Affairs study[13] described a complex sequence of events leading to a medication error on an oncology care ward and discussed how these events related to communication patterns and possible interventions described in the human factors literature. (A report of the tracer case is reproduced as Case Study I in Chapter 6.)

The events leading to medical error and possible interventions included:

- Local actors (such as residents) do not tailor their actions to meet the intent of distant supervisors (such as attending physicians) when events occur; the literature suggests that local actors need to know the intent of distant supervisors in order to respond to new events.
- Unwarranted shifts in planning may occur after handoffs.
- A handoff transfer of responsibility for a patient ideally occurs without an interruption in patient care. Successful handoffs avoid unwarranted changes in goals, decisions, priorities, or plans, including dropping or reworking tasks that the previous person in the role had told others would be completed.
- Unclear roles lead to confusion about responsibilities for tasks.
- Clarification of roles and responsibilities is essential for team members to know exactly what is expected of them in carrying out specific assigned duties using their own skills and knowledge. Also, to effectively coordinate activities, team members need a mutual understanding of:
  - Roles and functions of each participant
  - Routines that the team is capable of executing
  - Skills and competencies of each participant

- Goals of participants, including commitment to team success
- Difficult-to-access specialized expertise

Research by NASA space shuttle mission control indicated that it is difficult to access specialized expertise in nonroutine situations, and particularly in escalating emergency situations. This process was corrected by mission control by explicitly assigning "on-call" responsibility to controllers, who are also expected to possess a full understanding of mission status on a daily basis in preparation for the unexpected.

Reluctance to Question Authority

It has been well documented that "authority gradients" in civilian and military aviation result in people lower in a hierarchy questioning others less frequently than those who are higher in the hierarchy. This phenomenon is also present in the health care industry, often exemplified by nurse–physician friction.

The study concluded that poor communication is frequently implicated as a "root cause" of sentinel events, with many communication-related issues contributing to the medication errors. Communication proved to be important in the detection and mitigation of consequences from faulty medication administration. The patterns of communication and potential interventions identified were derived from a deep understanding of the complex interconnected nature of communication processes, providing "traction" for targeted ideas for improving patient safety.

Work Hours

Extensive studies have confirmed that fatigue associated with long work hours increases human error rates. The airline industry has imposed strict rules to for maximum flight hours for pilot and flight attendants to prevent fatigue-related errors. Attempts to impose similar work hour limits for house staff and other health care professionals have not been strictly enforced and therefore are lagging in implementation. Consequently, it was disturbing to see the results of recent studies published in the *New England Journal of Medicine* reconfirming the link between work hours and mistakes.

In the first of these studies,[14] 17 of 20 interns worked more than 80 hours per week during the traditional schedule, and all interns worked less than 80 hours per week during the intervention schedule. On average, interns on the intervention schedule worked 19.5 hours per week less, slept 5.8 hours per week more, slept more in the 24 hours preceding each working hour, and had less than half the rate of attentional failures while working during on-call nights in comparison with the traditional schedule. The study concluded that eliminating interns' extended work shifts in an intensive care unit significantly increased sleep and decreased attentional failures during night work hours. In addition, due to the obligation of interns to ensure the continued care of their patients beyond their shift, reported work hours usually exceeded both the scheduled weekly hours and the number of consecutive work hours scheduled during both the traditional and the intervention schedules. The actual work hours data revealed that the maximum number of scheduled work hours must be lowered to allow for this inevitability.

The findings of this study may apply not only to house staff working in critical care units but also to those on other rotations and specialties and to more senior residents, attending physicians, nurses, and others. It goes without saying that the physician in private practice must also be aware of and respond appropriately to the effects of current working practices on their performance and to look for future studies that will objectively measure the effect of interventions designed to improve physicians' health and patients' safety.

Although sleep deprivation has been shown to impair neurobehavioral performance, few studies have measured its effects on medical errors. A study designed to analyze this problem was published in the same issue of the *New England Journal of Medicine*.[15] The prospective, randomized study was conducted to compare the rates of serious medical errors made by interns while on a traditional schedule with extended (24 hours or more) work shifts every other shift (an "every third night" call schedule) and while working on an intervention schedule that eliminated extended work shifts and reduced the number of hours per week.

In this study, a multidisciplinary, four-pronged approach that included direct, continuous observation was used to identify incidents. Each incident was independently rated by two physicians who were unaware of the interns' schedule assignments. During a total of 2203 patient-days involving 634 admissions, interns made 35.9% more serious medical errors during the traditional schedule than during the intervention schedule, including 56.6% more non-intercepted serious errors, 22.0% more serious errors on the critical care units during the traditional schedule than during the intervention schedule, 20.8% more serious medication errors during the traditional schedule than during the intervention schedule, and 5.6 times as many serious diagnostic errors during the traditional schedule as during the intervention schedule.

In conclusion, considerably more serious medical errors were made when interns worked frequent shifts of 24 hours or more than when working shorter shifts. The elimination of extended work shifts and reduction in the hours worked per week can reduce serious medical errors by interns working in the intensive care unit. Again, the same conclusions should apply to the hectic schedules of many ambulatory care providers.

Workplace Intimidation

Intimidation in the workplace can be a problem in any industry. A survey by the Institute for Safe Medical Practices (ISMP) revealed that intimidating behavior by health care providers may contribute to medication errors[16]:

- Seven percent of 2000 health care professional respondents, including nurses, pharmacists, and other providers, indicated that they had been involved in a medication error during the previous year in which intimidation played a key role.
- Past experiences with intimidation had often altered the way they handled order clarification or questions about medication orders.
- More than one third indicated that at least once in the past year, they had had concerns about the safety of a medication order but assumed that it was correct rather than facing an interaction with an intimidating prescriber.
- Almost half of the respondents felt they had been pressured into dispensing a product or administering a medication despite their concerns regarding its safety.
- Intimidation ranged from subtle questioning of judgment to more explicit threatening behavior.
- Intimidating behavior was not limited to physicians/prescribers, but physicians/prescribers used condescending language or were impatient with questions twice as often as other health care providers.
- Sixty-nine percent said a prescriber had at least once in the last year responded, "Just give what I/the attending ordered," when faced with a question.
- Twenty-eight percent of respondents often encountered condescending language or tone of voice, and 25% indicated impatience with questions from the physician/prescriber.
- Approximately half of respondents reported having been the recipients of strong verbal abuse (56%) or threatening body language (49%) at least once during the past year.

The ISMP recommends that health care organizations create a code of conduct and values that promote behaviors that safeguard team cohesion and staff morale, a sense of self-worth, and safety. Organizations should also establish a conflict resolution process that ensures effective communication, protects patients, and strictly enforces a zero tolerance policy for intimidation, regardless of the offender's standing in the organization.

In 2001, the American Medical Association (AMA) House of Delegates adopted a set of principles of medical ethics for physicians. According to the AMA, these standards of conduct define the essentials of honorable behavior for physicians:

- A physician shall be dedicated to providing competent medical care, with compassion and respect for human dignity and rights.

- A physician shall uphold the standards of professionalism, be honest in all professional interactions, and strive to report physicians deficient in character or competence, or engaging in fraud or deception, to appropriate entities.

- A physician shall respect the law and also recognize a responsibility to seek changes in those requirements which are contrary to the best interests of the patient.

- A physician shall respect the rights of patients, colleagues, and other health professionals, and shall safeguard patient confidences and privacy within the constraints of the law.

- A physician shall continue to study, apply, and advance scientific knowledge, maintain a commitment to medical education, make relevant information available to patients, colleagues, and the public, obtain consultation, and use the talents of other health professionals when indicated.

- A physician shall, in the provision of appropriate patient care, except in emergencies, be free to choose whom to serve, with whom to associate, and the environment in which to provide medical care.

- A physician shall recognize a responsibility to participate in activities contributing to the improvement of the community and the betterment of public health.

- A physician shall, while caring for a patient, regard responsibility to the patient as paramount.

- A physician shall support access to medical care for all people. Available at http://www.ama-assn.org/ama/pub/category/8600.html. Acessed June 12, 2007.

Ambulatory Surgery

Pressures on the medical profession for cost containment have, in part, led to a proliferation of ambulatory surgical centers. The overhead costs of operating hospital outpatient surgery programs are much higher than the costs of office surgical facilities. Along with the tremendous growth of office-based surgery, questions have been raised regarding patient safety, a concern escalated by media reports of tragedies that may have been precipitated by a lack of the same resources (personnel, equipment, drugs, administrative policies, and facilities) that are present in ambulatory surgical centers or hospital inpatient and outpatient surgical facilities.

To examine patient safety in office surgical facilities, a survey was conducted by the American Association for Accreditation of Ambulatory Surgery Facilities through an anonymous questionnaire sent to its 418 accredited facilities.[17] There was a high (57.7%) response rate, with the following findings:

- During a five-year period, 400,675 operative procedures were reported.
- Significant complications (hematoma, hypertensive episode, wound infection, sepsis, hypotension) were infrequent (one in every 213 cases).
- Return to the operating room within 24 hours and postprocedure hospitalization occurred less frequently.

The overall risk was comparable in an accredited plastic surgery office facility and in a free-standing or hospital ambulatory surgical facility. The study was thought to reflect an excellent safety record for plastic surgery procedures performed in accredited office surgical facilities by board-certified plastic surgeons.

The American Society of Anesthesiologists (ASA) Closed Claims Project database was examined in a study to compare closed malpractice claims against anesthesiologists for adverse events after office-based anesthesia compared to anesthesia and surgery in other ambulatory surgical settings.[18] The Closed Claims Project database contains standardized summary data on anesthesia malpractice claims collected from 35 professional liability carriers that insure approximately half of the practicing anesthesiologists in the United States. At the time of the study there were 5480 claims in the database, including 753 claims for surgical anesthesia in the outpatient setting and 14 claims for surgical anesthesia in physician's offices (office-based claims).

Despite the small number of office-based claims, due to the three- to five-year delay for claims resolution, some interesting trends were discovered:

- Patients filing claims for adverse anesthesia events in the office-based setting had demographic characteristics similar to those of patients filing claims in other ambulatory settings.
- Most patients were middle-aged women undergoing elective surgery under general anesthesia, with ASA physical status 1 or 2.

- Dental and plastic surgery were the most common procedures performed in the office-based group.
- Patients in both ambulatory groups were generally younger and healthier than inpatients in the Closed Claims Project database.

Severity of injury for office-based claims was greater than for other ambulatory anesthesia claims. Sixty-two percent of ambulatory anesthesia claims vs 21% of office-based claims were for a temporary and nondisabling injury. Sixty-four percent of office-based claims were for death vs 21% of ambulatory anesthesia claims.

Even though these observations may reflect higher patient safety risks in the office-based setting, the lack of denominator data (eg, the number of cases performed in each setting) prevents an accurate estimation of risk or safety. Overall, the most common damaging events (the particular aspect of anesthesia management that led to patient injury) in the Closed Claims Project database were 22% respiratory system, 11% cardiovascular system, and 10% equipment-related events.

Damaging events in office-based claims involved the respiratory system in 50% (airway obstruction, bronchospasm, inadequate oxygenation-ventilation, and esophageal intubation) and drug-related events in 25% (wrong dose or drug, malignant hyperthermia, and allergic drug reaction). The apparent trend toward an increase in respiratory system events in the office-based claims compared to other ambulatory anesthesia claims was not statistically significant.

The timing of injuries in claims against anesthesiologists was similar in office-based and ambulatory anesthesia claims: 64% during anesthesia, 14% in the recovery phase, and 21% after discharge (with a trend for fewer in ambulatory claims). Forty-six percent of office-based injuries were judged as preventable through better monitoring. Thirteen percent of ambulatory anesthesia claims were preventable. All preventable office-based injuries were the result of adverse respiratory events in the recovery or postoperative periods and were considered to be preventable by use of pulse oximetry. The preliminary data from this study suggested that safety efforts involving office-based anesthesia should focus on improving care in the recovery and postoperative phases.

In response to a noticeable increase in the number of invasive surgical procedures being performed in the office setting over the past few years, the American College of Surgeons (ACS) and the American Medical Association (AMA) coordinated the development of a list of core principles for office-based surgery.[19] This report is reproduced in Appendix I. Recognizing in 2003 that many states had not issued patient safety guidelines in this area, the ACS and the AMA convened a meeting of interested specialty societies and state medical societies to discuss the surgical community's perspective on this issue. Representatives from the ASA were invited to provide information and guidance regarding ASA's anesthesia guidelines. In the end, a majority of the medical groups reached consensus on a set of 10 core principles that states should examine when moving to regulate office-based surgical procedures. This effort is an excellent example of physician leadership, through the ACS and the AMA, in developing and promoting patient safety guidelines that can have a far-reaching impact.

Following are the AMA's Core Principles on Office-Based Surgery:

Core Principle 1 Guidelines or regulations for office-based surgery should be developed by states according to levels of anesthesia defined by the ASA, excluding local anesthesia or minimal sedation (available at http://www.asahq.org/publications).

Core Principle 2 Physicians should select patients for office-based surgery using moderate sedation/analgesia, deep sedation/analgesia or general anesthesia by criteria including the ASA Physical Status Classification System and so document (available at: http://www.asahq.org/clinical/physical status.htm).

Core Principle 3 Physicians who perform office-based surgery with moderate sedation/analgesia, deep sedation/analgesia, or general anesthesia should have their facilities accredited by the Joint Commission on Accreditation of Healthcare Organizations (JCAHO), Accreditation Association for Ambulatory Health Care (AAAHC), American Association for Accreditation of Ambulatory Surgical Facilities (AAAASF), American Osteopathic Association (AOA), or by a state recognized entity, such as the Institute for Medical Quality (IMQ), or be state licensed and/or Medicare certified.

Core Principle 4 Physicians performing office-based surgery with moderate sedation/analgesia, deep sedation/analgesia, or general anesthesia must have admitting privileges at a nearby hospital, or a transfer agreement with another physician who has admitting privileges at a nearby hospital, or maintain an emergency transfer agreement with a nearby hospital.

Core Principle 5 States should follow the guidelines outlined by the Federation of State Medical Boards (FSMB) regarding informed consent.

Core Principle 6 For office surgery with moderate sedation/analgesia, deep sedation/analgesia, or general anesthesia, states should consider legally privileged adverse incident reporting requirements as recommended by the FSMB and accompanied by periodic peer review and a program of Continuous Quality Improvement.

Core Principle 7 Physicians performing office-based surgery using moderate sedation/analgesia, deep sedation/analgesia or general anesthesia must obtain and maintain board certification by one of the boards recognized by the American Board of Medical Specialties, American Osteopathic Association, or a board with equivalent standards approved by the state medical board within five years of completing an approved residency training program. The procedure must be one that is generally recognized by that certifying board as falling within the scope of training and practice of the physician providing the care.

Core Principle 8 Physicians performing office-based surgery with moderate sedation/analgesia, deep sedation/analgesia, or general anesthesia may show competency by maintaining core privileges at an accredited or licensed hospital or ambulatory surgical center, for the procedures they perform in the office setting. Alternatively, the governing body of the office facility is responsible for a peer review process for privileging physicians based on nationally recognized credentialing standards.

Core Principle 9 For office-based surgery with moderate sedation/analgesia, deep sedation/analgesia, or general anesthesia, at least one physician who is credentialed or currently recognized as having successfully completed a course in advanced resuscitative techniques (e.g., ATLS, ACLS, or PALS), must be present or immediately available with age- and size-appropriate resuscitative equipment until the patient has met the criteria for discharge from the facility. In addition, other medical personnel with direct patient contact should at a minimum be trained in Basic Life Support (BLS).

Core Principle 10 Physicians administering or supervising moderate sedation/analgesia, deep sedation/analgesia, or general anesthesia should have appropriate education and training.

Source: American Medical Association. AMA policy H-475.984, Office-Based Surgery Regulation. http://www.ama-assn.org/apps/pf_new/pf_online?f_n=browse&doc=policyfiles/HnE/H-475.984.HTM Accessed June 11, 2007.

Wrong-Site Surgery

The American Academy of Orthopaedic Surgeons (AAOS), a vocal advocate of efforts to eliminate wrong-site surgery has noted that wrong-site surgery is a system problem affecting all surgical specialties. In its Advisory Statement on Wrong Site Surgery, AAOS stated that ". . . a unified effort among surgeons, hospitals and other health care providers to initiate preoperative and other institutional regulations can effectively eliminate wrong site surgery in the United States" and urged "other surgical and health care providers to join the effort in implementing effective controls to eliminate this system problem."

The Department of Defense provided an excellent summary of efforts under way to prevent wrong-site surgery errors, a continuing problem within the field of surgery.[20] In August 1998, JCAHO issued a Sentinel Event Alert entitled "Lessons Learned: Wrong Site Surgery," based on 15 cases received in the first two years of its sentinel event policy. Risk factors identified as contributing to wrong-site surgery included involvement of more than one surgeon, multiple procedures on the same patient during a single trip to the operating room, unusual time pressures, and unusual patient characteristics, such as physical deformity or extreme obesity. Root causes noted by reporting hospitals included failures of communication, incomplete preoperative assessments, and flawed procedures to verify the correct operative site. On the basis of this information, JCAHO recommended three strategies for reducing the risk of wrong-site surgery: (1) the operative site should be clearly marked, with the patient involved in the marking process; (2) each member of the surgical team should orally verify the correct site in the operating room; and (3) a verification checklist that includes all documents referencing the operative procedure and site should be followed.

Three years later, in 2001, wrong-site surgery remained a significant concern nationwide. The JCAHO reiterated the importance of implementing the risk reduction strategies first suggested in 1998 and devoted Sentinel Event Alert issue 24 (December 5, 2001)[21] to a follow-up review of wrong-site surgery. The majority of *contributing factors* for wrong-site surgery involved:

- Breakdown in communication between surgical team members and patient or patient's family
- Absence of a policy requiring the marking of the surgical site
- Lack of a checklist procedure in the operating room to verify the surgical site
- Incomplete assessment of the patient, including preoperative assessment

The JCAHO also found root causes of wrong-site surgery to be:

- Lapses in communication
- Orientation or training shortcomings
- Patient assessment deficiencies
- Lack of timely and accurate information
- Noncompliance with procedural guidelines
- Hierarchy and distraction

The Military Health System Patient Safety Registry received several root cause analyses outlining action plans that provided the impetus to develop the following list of some of the specific actions to take to eliminate the occurrence of wrong-site, wrong-person, or wrong-procedure surgery[22]:

- At check in, identify patient by first/last name and [social security number]
- Discuss consent with patient prior to procedure
- [Operating room (OR)] circulating nurse writes each surgical case on dry marker board, specifying type and location, and receives verbal consensus from OR team
- Surgeon states on consent form the correct location/site of procedure
- Surgeon reviews H&P and consent form to confirm accuracy of documents
- Correct site policy requires surgeon to meet with patient the day of surgery *prior* to sedation to confirm procedure and surgical site.
- Utilize the preoperative checklist to verify correct operative site.
- Ensure *[sic]* three independent verifications of surgical site by OR nurse, anesthesia provider and patient in holding area and document verification in medical record
- All staff initial checklist agreeing on correct site prior to procedure
- Surgeon, anesthesia, and operating room staff verify correct patient, marking, site and procedure prior to start of case
- Circulating nurse completes documentation of surgical site verification on surgical flow sheet prior to patient sedation
- Time out prior to incision—all operating room staff pause while circulating nurse verbally verifies information from the patient's record, consent form, patient [identification], specific surgical procedure and surgical site.
- Utilize intra-operative checklist to verify correct operative site
- Revise surgical flow sheet to include: Procedure verification, site initialing and verification by surgeon with patient, site consistent with documents, interview and site verification by APU and OR staff

[Military treatment facilities], in addressing wrong site surgery, have also implemented these actions related to education, procedure and information systems:

- Hospital wide training of site verification policy
- In-service for OR staff and physicians on site verification policy

■ Development and implementation of Standard Operating Procedure to include specific procedure, surgical site, equipment needed, room crew assignments, and special patient considerations

■ Scheduling program that includes specific information about the surgical site.

It is hoped that with JCAHO's implementation of its "Universal Protocol for Preventing Wrong Site, Wrong Procedure, Wrong Person Surgery," in 2004, there will be a concerted effort within the health care industry to enforce clearly proven processes to end the risk to patients of undergoing a wrong-site, wrong-procedure, or wrong-person surgical procedure. Leadership among physicians will be essential in this effort. The JCAHO Universal Protocol is reproduced in Appendix J.

EVIDENCE-BASED PRACTICES TO PROMOTE PATIENT SAFETY

Today's health care environment poses significant challenges for physicians in addressing public concern about the quality of health care in America. Reports in the medical literature and news media indicating significant gaps between clinical performance and knowledge have led to increased demands for accountability in the health care system. However, efforts to measure quality are frequently disjointed, duplicative, incomplete, inaccurate, and of limited utility for physicians.

In 2002, the American Medical Association (AMA) convened the Physician Consortium for Performance Improvement in recognition of physicians' professional responsibility to provide quality health care, and in response to the multiplicity and variability of performance evaluation mechanisms in contrast to the paucity of measurement systems. The Consortium currently includes methodological experts, clinical experts representing more than 50 national medical specialty societies, the Agency for Healthcare Research and Quality (AHRQ), and the Centers for Medicare and Medicaid Services (CMS). All medical specialty societies represented in the AMA House of Delegates are invited to become members of the Consortium.

Physician Consortium for Performance Improvement: Vision and Mission

The vision of the Physician Consortium for Performance Improvement is to fulfill the responsibility of physicians to patient care and public health and safety by:

■ becoming the leading source organization for evidence-based clinical performance measures and outcomes reporting tools for physicians; and

- ensuring that all components of the medical profession have a leadership role in all national forums seeking to evaluate the quality of patient care.

The mission of the Consortium is to improve patient health and safety by:

- identifying and developing evidence-based clinical performance measures that enhance quality of patient care and that foster accountability;
- promoting the implementation of effective and relevant clinical performance improvement activities; and
- advancing the science of clinical performance measurement and improvement. [endnote: Sackett DL, Straus SE, Richardson WS, et al. Evidence-Based Medicine: How to Practice & Teach EBM. 2nd edition. London: Churchill Livingstone; 2000.

The Consortium aims to provide performance measurement resources for practicing physicians to facilitate implementation of clinical quality improvement programs. Physician use of Consortium measures is voluntary. Consortium members collectively seek to unify the medical profession's efforts to develop and identify effective performance measures and to promote the appropriate use of measures and measurement systems to address health care quality and patient safety issues. By providing a forum for national medical specialty societies and other organizations committed to quality improvement, The Consortium seeks to remove barriers and promote incentives for physician participation in continuous quality improvement.

Consortium activities are carried out through cross-specialty work groups established to develop performance measures for physicians from evidence-based clinical guidelines for select clinical conditions. The Consortium selects topics for performance measures development that are actionable, for which established clinical recommendations are available, and for which feasible data sources exist. Work groups review the levels of evidence provided in clinical practice guidelines that demonstrate potential positive impact on health outcomes and propose feasible measures for inclusion in a physician performance measurement set.

Following an iterative process of review and approval of the draft measures by the Consortium, a public comment period is initiated, resulting in further refinement until the final measurement set is adopted. Subsequently, The Consortium solicits partners among its member organizations and other stakeholders to test the measurement sets through demonstration projects. Projects may focus on a) testing the reliability and validity of measures; b) demonstrating the feasibility of data collection from physician offices and other practice sites; c) evaluating the use of computer-based and Web-based applications; d) increasing physician participation in practice-based research; or e) testing the feasibility of single data collection for physician-, hospital-, and health plan-level analyses. After Consortium review, results from the demonstration projects will be used to refine the measurement sets. Test results and revised measurement sets subsequently will be submitted for publication.

It is important to note that Consortium performance measures are not clinical guidelines; rather, they are resources to provide physicians with information they can use to identify opportunities to improve patient care. These measures, derived from evidence-based clinical guidelines, focus on processes and outcomes of care. One or more measures that focus on a condition or service are collectively known as a performance measurement set.

The Consortium has developed several physician performance measurement sets and related documents to guide their implementation. Measurement sets typically include definitions for the measures; specific references to the clinical guidelines from which the measures were derived; sample flowsheets for prospective data collection; specifications and tools for medical record abstraction if retrospective data collection is preferred; and sample feedback reports. Measurement sets have been developed for: Type 1 Diabetes, Chronic Stable Coronary Artery Disease, Prenatal Testing, Asthma, and Preventive Care and Screening.

The Consortium's performance measures enable physicians to identify aspects of care that may need modification to improve patient care and maintain clinical excellence. For patients, The Consortium's measures represent the consensus of experts in clinical and research fields and include those measurable activities in which physicians can participate to continuously improve quality of care and outcomes.

While measurement alone does not automatically result in improvement, measurement and feedback enable physicians to focus attention on the processes of care that are most important for achieving good outcomes and to assess the effects of changes they make to improve care. Consortium-developed performance measurement sets represent a unified, physician-driven effort to encourage improved patient care by defining standardized, evidence-based measures and providing comprehensive feedback reports that physicians and others will find useful in their management of patients.

A current list of Consortium members, work products, and additional information on Consortium goals and activities may be obtained from www.ama-assn.org/go/quality.

DO MEDICARE BENEFICIARIES EXPERIENCE VARIATIONS IN CARE?

A publication from the Center for the Evaluative Clinical Sciences at Dartmouth Medical School analyzed the finding that quality of care received by Medicare beneficiaries varies across the states and that states with higher Medicare spending have been shown to receive a lower quality of care.[23] Several research studies[24-26] have found large and persistent differences in the quality of care that Medicare beneficiaries receive across states. These variations in care can be measured through differences in the use of effective, evidence-based care, such as the administration of β-blockers after heart attacks, mammograms for older women, influenza vaccines, or eye examinations for diabetics. These procedures are rarely contraindicated, are affordable, and are known to improve medical outcomes. It is therefore of concern that the documentation of the use of these procedures varies so widely between states. As an example, in 2000 the use of β-blockers within 24 hours of admission for patients with heart attacks and without contraindications varied from 50% in Alabama to 86% in New Hampshire.

The study focused on three areas:

- Answers to the question, "Are states where there is more spending per Medicare beneficiary also more likely to provide effective care?"
- Whether high-spending states provide more care along other dimensions, such as multiple specialist consultations, hospitalizations, and use of intensive care units (ICUs) in the last six months of life. Prior research results have shown that end-of-life care is extraordinarily costly but is not correlated with the underlying sickness of the population, patient outcomes, or patient satisfaction.
- Potential mechanisms through which intensive care might crowd out high-quality care—the effect of the underlying physician workforce (generalists vs specialists) on both spending and quality differences across states

A subset of four quality measures that were available for both 1995 and 1999 from Medicare claims data from the Dartmouth Atlas project was used to assess whether the findings of the study were driven by unmeasured differences in the underlying sickness of state populations. The quality measures included β-blockers administered at discharge, mammography every two years for women aged 65 to 69, hemoglobin A1c monitoring, and annual eye examinations for diabetics.

The following parameters were analyzed:

- The relationship between changes in the use of these quality measures and changes in spending within each state
- Whether higher Medicare spending is a marker for a different pattern of spending
- The relationship between spending and end-of-life care, such as the fraction of patients admitted to the ICU and the number of days spent in the hospital
- The effect of spending on patient satisfaction

The composition of the medical workforce (one of the factors that may be responsible for the trade-off between high-quality health care and costly end-of-life care) was studied by regressing spending per Medicare beneficiary and overall quality rank on the number of specialists, general practitioners, and registered nurses per capita, controlling for the total number of physicians per capita.

The study used the 24 quality measures developed by the Medicare Quality Improvement Organization and computed at the state level by Jencks et al for 2000–2001. The measures use samples of hospital patient discharge records for the treatment of six common medical conditions: acute myocardial infarction, breast cancer, diabetes mellitus, heart failure, pneumonia, and stroke. Interventions and evaluations "for which there is strong scientific evidence and professional consensus that the process of care either directly improves outcomes or is a necessary step in a chain of care that does so" were also captured, such as prescription of warfarin for atrial fibrillation and biennial eye examination for diabetics.[25]

Medicare claims data from the Dartmouth Atlas projects were used to calculate Medicare state-level reimbursement per beneficiary.[27] Several other measures were computed from the Medicare claims data, including the number of days Medicare beneficiaries in their last six months of life spent in a hospital and the fraction of these beneficiaries admitted to the ICU. Other studies have established that, even though provision of such care does not improve patient outcomes or satisfaction, it is prevalent in areas with a lot of hospital beds and specialists. Some specifications were controlled for the number of acute myocardial infarction (AMI) discharges and AMI mortality in each state, adjusted for the age, sex, and race composition of the population, also computed from the claims data.

Study results demonstrated that higher spending is associated with a lower quality of care, and spending is not merely uncorrelated with the quality of care provided. There was a statistically significant negative effect of increased spending on 15 of the 24 quality measures and there was no statistical effect on the remaining nine. A state spending $1000 more per beneficiary dropped almost 10 positions in overall quality. Similarly, states spending $1000 more per Medicare beneficiary had β-blocker usage rates at discharge that were 3.5 percentage points lower and mammography rates that were 2.1 percentage points lower than the average usage in 2000.

What happened to the money in high-spending states, if it did not go to more effective care? It may have been spent on expensive health care with no proven positive effect on patient satisfaction or health outcomes. There was a positive relationship between Medicare spending on Medicare patients during their last six months of life in terms of the percentage of Medicare beneficiaries who were admitted to the ICU and the number of days beneficiaries spent in the hospital. Medicare patients in states that spent $1000 more per beneficiary spent an average of 1.3 more days in the hospital and were 3.9% more likely to be admitted to an ICU. These increases did not seem to be associated with higher levels of patient satisfaction.

Another question: Why are some states high spenders and provide *lower*-quality care, while others are low spenders and provide *higher*-quality care? One possible answer may lie in the composition of the medical workforce and the relationship between the medical workforce, spending, and quality. Fisher and Skinner[27] looked at the effect of changing the composition of the medical workforce in a state (physicians [specialists, general practitioners], nurses) while holding the overall size of the physician workforce constant. Together, these workforce measures explained 42% of state-level variation in Medicare spending per beneficiary. States where more physicians are general practitioners show greater use of high-quality care and lower cost per beneficiary.

Increasing the number of general practitioners in a state by one per 10,000 population (while decreasing the number of specialists to hold constant the total number of physicians) is associated with a rise in that state's quality rank of more than 10 places and a reduction in overall spending of $684 per beneficiary (statistically significant at $P < .0005$). Conversely, in states with a higher number of specialists, there is a demonstrated lower quality of care and higher cost per beneficiary. The estimated effect of increasing the ratio of specialists by one per 10,000 is a drop in overall quality rank of almost nine places and an increase in spending of $526 per beneficiary. The supply of nurses did not appear to affect either rate of high-quality care or total spending.

Study results demonstrated that, although areas with more specialists do not provide higher-quality care along these dimensions, they may be better at the treatment of more acute conditions.[28,29] It is also possible that areas "specialize" in different types of care. Some areas specialize in primary care, while others may specialize in the delivery of technologically aggressive care for heart attacks. There was no evidence of this in the study; states with more specialists have neither lower mortality rates from all causes nor reduced post-AMI mortality.

In summary, this eye-opening study provided valuable insight and recommendations. States that spend more per Medicare beneficiary are not states that provide higher-quality care. In fact, additional spending is positively correlated with end-of-life care but negatively correlated with the use of effective care. While higher spending per se is unlikely to cause a drop in the use of high-quality care, it seems to be a marker for a particular pattern of care. Analysis suggested that the mix of the physician workforce plays a critical role in the use of highly effective care. States with relatively more general practitioners have both higher rates of use of effective care and lower spending. There was no relationship between nurses and the provision of high-quality care.

A second concern might be that specialists locate in areas where patients are sicker and that sicker patients are more likely to be hospitalized for longer stays or admitted to the ICU. If this were true, then the positive relationship between specialists and end-of-life spending could be spurious. Furthermore, other researchers have found that underlying population risk does not seem to drive the presence of specialists and that outcomes are not improved by increased access to these specialists. In particular, in the area of neonatology, specialists are associated with neither higher risk nor lower mortality. The results on the ineffectiveness of specialists for the provision of high-quality care are thus consistent with the findings of a broader literature.

What, then, are the policy implications of the negative relationship between spending and quality? It clearly does not suggest that we mandate lower spending, because it is probably not spending per se that reduces quality. Spending captures many aspects of local health care delivery systems, such as physician practice styles, composition of the medical workforce, and capacity constraints. Therefore, policies that simply target spending could have the undesirable effect of reducing the quality of care in high-spending states even further. Also, the quality measures we use do not capture the totality of health care provision. Although specialists may not drive the provision of effective care, they often provide better care in their area of specialty. This suggests that specialists are clustered in areas where costly intensive care crowds out high-quality care and that one mechanism for this is a lesser presence of general practitioners. Encouraging greater

access to general practitioners, or involving specialists in the provision of effective care, could improve the overall quality of care
received by elderly Americans.

With Medicare's mounting fiscal crisis, understanding the relationship between the variation in Medicare spending and beneficiaries' quality of care is critical. The negative relationship found
between spending and quality and the factors that drive it are of
immediate concern. Policies that improve quality of care (such as
establishing national practice benchmarks for basic quality measures) need not be costly and could even improve Medicare's
financial solvency.

LOWERING THE FLAPS: A PLEA TO PHYSICIAN LEADERS

The 30-year-old Dartmouth study followed by the current
Medicare experience confirms that there has been a fundamental
failure to resolve unexplained variations in medical care across
the country. Physicians are clearly in the crosshairs of the focus on
this issue. Lack of time, productivity pressures, the complexities
of medical care, and other factors are not good reasons to not stay
current with changes in evidence-based standards of care. What if
the evidence in any given state showed that 80% of commercial
airline pilots agree to lower the flaps on landing? Would that be
any different than showing that adults received 55% of recommended care based on 439 process-of-care measures? Would the
effect on airline safety (with the best record of all industries
worldwide) be as devastating as the effect on patient care? To
answer the recalcitrant resistors, of course flying an airplane is
different than caring for a patient, but failure to adhere to accepted standards can have the same devastating effect on both.

Physician leadership is essential for reducing variation in
patient care.

SAFETY ISSUES WITH THE ELDERLY

Inappropriate drug therapy can have greater consequences for
elderly patients than for young adults, owing to generally poorer
health status and a greater likelihood of receiving multiple prescriptions. Adverse drug reactions in the elderly are a growing
concern because of the rapidly increasing elderly population and
the increasing numbers of medications prescribed to this group.
Physiological changes of aging result in altered drug pharmacokinetics and pharmacodynamics, increasing the risk of adverse
drug reactions. Polypharmacy and the presence of comorbid

diseases are frequent. As a result, the risk–benefit ratio for many drugs is unfavorable in the elderly.

Adverse drug events, especially those that may be preventable, are among the most serious concerns about medication use in older persons cared for in the ambulatory clinical setting. A study to assess the incidence and preventability of adverse drug events among older persons in the ambulatory clinical setting analyzed the experience of all Medicare enrollees cared for by a multispecialty group practice during a 12-month study period, July 1, 1999, to June 30, 2000.[30] Possible drug-related incidents occurring in the ambulatory clinical setting were detected by multiple methods, including reports from health care providers; review of hospital discharge summaries; review of emergency department notes; computer-generated signals; automated free-text review of electronic clinic notes; and review of administrative incident reports concerning medication errors.

There were 1523 identified adverse drug events, of which 27.6% (421) were considered preventable. The overall rate of adverse drug events was 50.1 per 1000 person-years, with a rate of 13.8 preventable adverse drug events per 1000 person-years. Of the adverse drug events, 578 (38.0%) were categorized as serious, life threatening, or fatal. Two hundred forty-four (42.2%) of these more severe events were deemed preventable, compared with 177 (18.7%) of the 945 significant adverse drug events. Errors associated with preventable adverse drug events occurred most often at the stages of prescribing (246, 58.4%) and monitoring (256, 60.8%). Errors involving patient adherence (89, 21.1%) also were common. The most common medication categories associated with preventable adverse drug events included:

- Cardiovascular medications: 24.5%
- Diuretics: 22.1%
- Nonopioid analgesics: 15.4%
- Hypoglycemics: 10.9%
- Anticoagulants: 10.2%

The most common types of preventable adverse drug events included:

- Electrolyte/renal: 26.6%
- Gastrointestinal tract: 21.1%
- Hemorrhagic: 15.9%
- Metabolic/endocrine: 13.8%
- Neuropsychiatric: 8.6%

The more serious adverse drug events are most likely to be preventable. Prevention strategies should include the prescribing and monitoring stages of pharmaceutical care, improving patient adherence to prescribed regimens, and monitoring of prescribed medications.

ENDNOTES

1. Sandars J, Esmail A. The frequency and nature of medical error in primary care: understanding the diversity across studies. *Fam Pract.* 2003;20:231-236.

2. Dovey SM, Meyers DS, Phillips RL, et al. A preliminary taxonomy of errors in family practice. *Qual Saf Health Care.* 2002;11:233-238.

3. Makeham MA, Dovey SM, County M, et al. An international taxonomy for errors in general practice: a pilot study. *Med J Aust.* 2002;177:68-72.

4. Plews-Ogan ML, Nadkarni, MM, Forren, S, et al. Patient safety in the ambulatory setting: a clinician-based approach. *J Gen Intern Med.* 2004;19:719-725.

5. Chaudhry SI, Olofinboba KA, Krumholz HM. Detection of errors by attending physicians on a general medicine service. *J Gen Intern Med.* 2003;18:595-600.

6. Nancy C. Elder, MD, *Journal of Family Practice,* Nov. 2002, 51:927-932

7. www.jcaho.org/

8. Boohaker EA, Ward RE, Uman JE, et al. Patient notification and follow-up of abnormal test results: a physician survey. *Arch Intern Med.* 1996;156:327-331.

9. Gill JM, Mainous AG III, Diamond JJ, et al. Impact of provider continuity on quality of care for persons with diabetes mellitus. *Ann Fam Med.* 2003;1:162-170.

10. Mukherjee SA. A precarious exchange. *N Engl J Med.* 2004;351:1822-1824.

11. Petersen LA, Brennan TA, O'Neil AC, Cook EF, Lee TH. Does housestaff discontinuity of care increase the risk for preventable adverse events? *Ann Intern Med.* 1994;121:866-872.

12. Petersen LA, Orav EJ, Teich JM, O'Neil AC, Brennan TA. Using a computerized sign-out program to improve continuity of inpatient care and prevent adverse events. *Jt Comm J Qual Improv.* 1998;24:77-87.

13. Patterson ES, Cook RI, Woods DD, Render ML. Examining the complexity behind a medication error: generic patterns in communication. *IEEE Trans Syst Man Cybernet.* 2004;34:749-756.

14. Lockley SW, Cronin JW, Evans EE, et al. Effect of reducing interns' weekly work hours on sleep and attentional failures. *N Engl J Med.* 2004;351:1829-1837.

15. Landrigan CP, Rothschild JM, Cronin JW, et al. Effect of reducing interns' work hours on serious medical errors among interns in intensive care units. *N Engl J Med.* 2004;351:1838-1848.

16. Intimidation: practitioners speak up about this unresolved problem (Part I). Available at: www.ismp.org/Newsletters/acutecare/articles/20040311_2.asp. Accessed February 22, 2006.

17. Morello DC, Colon GA, Fredricks S, et al. Patient safety in accredited office surgical facilities. *Plast Reconstr Surg.* 1997;99:1496-1500.

18. Domino KB. Office-based anesthesia: lessons learned from the Closed Claims Project. *ASA Newslett.* 2001;65(6):9-11, 15. Available at: http://depts.washington.edu/asaccp/ASA/Newsletters/asa65_6_9_11.shtml. Accessed February 22, 2006.

19. ACS Views: Patient safety principles for office-based surgery utilizing moderate sedation/analgesia, deep sedation/analgesia, or general anesthesia. Available at: www.facs.org/patientsafety/patientsafety.html. Accessed Febrary 22, 2006.

20. Special Focus: Wrong Site Surgery. Available at: www.afip.org/PSC/newsletter/summer03.pdf. Accessed February 22, 2006.

21. A follow-up review of wrong site surgery. Sentinel Event Alert, Issue 24, December 5, 2001. Available at: www.jcaho.org/about+us/news+letters/sentinel+event+alert/sea_24.htm. Accessed February 22, 2006.

22. Actions to eliminate wrong site surgery. *Patient Safety.* Summer 2002:3. Available at: www.afip.org/PSC/newsletter/summer03.pdf. Accessed February 22, 2006. Reprinted with permission.

23. Baicker K, Chandra A. Medicare spending, the physician workforce, and beneficiaries' quality of care. *Health Aff.* April 7, 2004. Available at: http://content.healthaffairs.org/cgi/content/full/hlthaff.w4.184v1/DC1. Accessed February 22, 2006.

24. Jencks SF, Cuerdon T, Burwen DR, et al. Quality of medical care delivered to Medicare beneficiaries: a profile at state and national levels. *JAMA.* 2000;284:1670-1676.

25. Jencks SF, Huff ED, Cuerdon T. Change in the quality of care delivered to Medicare beneficiaries, 1998-1999 to 2000-2001. *JAMA.* 2003;289:305-312.

26. Fisher ES, Wennberg DE, Stukel TA, Gottlieb DJ, Lucas FL, Pinder EL. The implications of regional variations in Medicare spending, part 2: health outcomes and satisfaction with care. *Ann Intern Med.* 2003;138:288-298.

27. Fisher ES, Skinner JS. Comparing the health care of states. *Providence Journal-Bull.* March 17, 2001. Available at: www .dartmouth.edu/~news/releases/2001/apr01/medicare.html. Accessed February 22, 2006.

28. Ayanian JZ, Landrum MB, Guadagnoli B, Gaccione P. Specialty of ambulatory care physicians and mortality among elderly patients after myocardial infarction. *N Engl J Med.* 2002;347:1678-1686.

29. Jollis JG, DeLong ER, Peterson ED, et al. Outcome of acute myocardial infarction according to the specialty of the admitting physician. *N Engl J Med.* 1996;335:1880-1887.

30. Gurwitz JH, Field TS, Harrold LR. Incidence and preventability of adverse drug events among older persons in the ambulatory setting. *JAMA.* 2003;289:1107-1116.

System Support

Errors may enter the picture at the point physicians directly interface with patients. It has been repeatedly shown that poorly designed processes of care, and not individual practitioner mistakes, are the primary causes of error. In one review study[1] it was found that 86% of errors could be attributed to system flaws and 14% resulted from physicians' lack of knowledge or skills. The information that follows will provide practical suggestions and tools for system support in mitigating errors in ambulatory care settings and will be aligned to address the major types of errors that have been previously identified.

A VHA Inc research series report[2] explored the adoption of information technology (IT) by physicians across the continuum of clinical settings. They looked at the broad spectrum of technology used to create, store, exchange, and use information in its various forms (clinical and financial data, voice technology, imaging, multimedia, and others).

Developing, selecting, and adopting the right IT can help health care providers and their patients navigate the system with minimal errors and maximal satisfaction. Facilitating physician adoption of IT not only can enhance patient care, revenues, and staff satisfaction, it can also strengthen the long-term competitive position of a health care organization. The study concluded the following:

- Physicians recognize the potential impact of IT on quality of care.
- Physicians are becoming aware that technology is used by their patients in seeking improved delivery of care and by hospitals for enhancing operational performance.
- Many physicians are lagging in the adoption of technology.
- Physicians may see IT as disruptive to clinical processes. Deal breakers are failures to address their concerns on:
  - Workflow
  - Payment for services
  - Liability
  - Productivity

Barriers to IT adoption fell into the following three general categories:

Technical: Issues about the technology features and functions
Social: Issues of culture, comfort with the status quo, and the environment in which technology is placed
Operational: Issues of organizational process and structure

Physician acceptance and use of IT will increase through active attention to several key enablers that include knowledge, value, communication, involvement, infrastructure and support, and leadership. Also at stake is the cost of implementation of technology support in the ambulatory care setting and the absence of enhanced revenue through such effort. However, increased operational efficiencies should lead to at least some reduction in overhead costs. An expanded discussion of technology support will follow in future chapters.

INFORMATION TECHNOLOGIES IN THE MEDICAL PRACTICE

Annually, health care expenditures in the United States exceed a trillion dollars, and yet there is a perceived lack of resources in almost every segment of the delivery system. The demand from purchasers for significant investments in support systems and changes in infrastructure requires investments of huge sums of money and creates budgetary conflicts with multiple competing priorities. Economic realities include staggering increases in malpractice premiums and declining third-party payments.

The investment and maintenance costs for patient safety programs in physician offices must usually come from practice income. In a large group practice, multiple physicians can share the costs, but for smaller groups and solo practices, the cost of investing in patient safety systems is currently prohibitive.

Fortunately, there are efforts under way to provide outside financial support for the massive investments facing the health care industry. However, the American health care industry is bogged down with inefficient, antiquated processes, outdated technology systems, dependence on paper rather than electronic records, lack of standardization of processes and procedures, and a virtual absence of decision support systems. There is a need for strong leadership, including physician, administrative, and organizational governance (board of directors) to deal with and resolve tough issues, such as widespread unexplained deviations from evidence-based care, failure to document compliance with quality standards, incomplete and illegible medical record documentation, and lack of compliance with mandated patient safety initiatives (such as use of unacceptable abbreviations that are known to lead to errors).

Innovations like electronic health records (EHRs), computerized drug order entry systems, and clinical decision support systems can improve the quality of care that patients receive and also help to increase efficiencies in medical practice. In a discussion of the use of IT tools in health care, a new Commonwealth Fund survey found that, despite the undeniable benefits, health care organizations and physicians have been slow to embrace such technologies.[3] The 2003 survey was completed by 1837 randomly selected US physicians. Overall, the survey results showed only modest adoption of IT applications, with a few exceptions:

- Seventy-nine percent reported using electronic billing either routinely or occasionally.
- Fifty-nine percent used electronic access to patients' test results either routinely or occasionally.
- Twenty-seven percent used EHRs and electronic ordering of tests, procedures, or drugs routinely or occasionally.
- Fifty-four percent sent reminders to their patients regarding routine preventive care, but only 21% had automated the process.
- Twenty-five percent used electronic clinical decision support systems, but only 6% used them routinely.

Standard office technology is also underutilized. Only 7% routinely used e-mail to communicate with other physicians. Only 3% routinely communicated with patients this way.

The predominant factor affecting use of IT was practice size. Eighty-seven percent of physicians in large group practices have access to electronic test results. Thirty-six percent of solo-practice physicians have access. Other technologies followed a similar pattern. Physicians in large group practices were more likely than solo practitioners to use EHRs, receive electronic drug alerts, communicate by e-mail with colleagues and patients, and practice in a "high-tech" office (ie, one where physicians routinely or occasionally use at least four of the tools referenced in the survey).

How physicians were compensated also significantly affected the use of IT: 34% of salaried physicians worked in a high-tech office and 17% of nonsalaried ones enjoyed that environment.

After billing, the most widely adopted clinical IT tool was electronic access to patient test results. Fifty-nine percent of respondents have computer access to such results, and 14% plan to have it within the next year.

The future of EHRs also appears to be poised for greater use. Twenty percent said they plan to begin using EHRs within the next year, which would bring the total to nearly 50%, with computerized test ordering and prescribing following a similar pattern. Use of electronic clinical decision support, patient reminders, and alert systems, however, were predicted to grow more slowly. The top three reported barriers to IT adoption were costs of system start-up and maintenance; lack of local, regional, and national standards; and lack of time to consider acquiring, implementing, and using a new system. Again, practice size plays a role, with physicians in solo and smaller practices more likely to cite barriers as causes for concern.

The authors concluded that the use of IT in medical practices was growing slowly. Not surprisingly, there appeared to be a deep technological divide between physicians in large group practices and physicians in smaller settings, as well as between salaried and nonsalaried physicians. This gap is further widened by the fact that the barriers to use, including financial barriers, were greatest for solo and small group practices.

Stimulating widespread IT adoption will require federal leadership, potentially in the form of:

- Federal grants
- Expansion of the Medicare diagnosis-related group physician reimbursement
- Revolving loans
- Additional standardization to allow for interoperability and the exchange of relevant information within the health care system

Federal leadership became more visible in 2004, when President Bush, in his State of the Union Address, called for computerizing health records as a way to avoid dangerous medical mistakes, reduce costs, and improve care. He outlined a plan to ensure that most Americans have EHRs by 2014. Called the Health Information Technology Plan,[4] it addresses the problems of preventable errors, uneven quality, and rising costs in the nation's health care system. However, the 2014 goal of having EHRs for most Americans may be optimistic. In October, 2006, researchers from Massachusetts General Hospital and George Washington University released results of the most comprehensive study to date that reliably measures the state of EHR use by doctors and hospitals, showing that an estimated one in four doctors (24.9 percent) use EHRs to improve how they deliver care to patients. However, the study found that fewer than one in 10 are using a "fully operational" system that collects patient information, displays test results, allows providers to enter medical orders and prescriptions, and helps doctors make treatment decisions.

Health Information Technology in the United States: The Information Base for Progress is a joint project of the Robert Wood Johnson Foundation and the federal government's National Coordinator for Health Information Technology. (Copies of the report are available on the Robert Wood Johnson Foundation Web site, www.rwjf.org.) The report provides a look at how doctors and hospitals are using information systems to drive improvements in quality. It shows that EHR adoption rates remain very low due to multiple financial, technical, and legal barriers. The report authors say these barriers will need to be lifted if the health sector is to meet President Bush's desired goal of ensuring that most Americans have their medical information collected, stored, and organized in an EHR by 2014.

The report was commissioned to set a benchmark for where the US stands on EHR adoption. It reflects one year of examination of dozens of studies and surveys by some of the nation's leading experts on health IT and illustrates the EHR adoption environment among physicians and hospitals, what predicts whether or not a provider will adopt an EHR, where the gaps in adoption are, how much adoption depends on location, practice size, specialty, or kinds of patients treated; and how the US can collect more precise and timely data on adoption to better enlighten policymakers.

Some key highlights of the report:

- Hospital adoption trends are unknown. Assertions to the contrary, there are not enough high-quality, reliable surveys of hospital use of EHRs. The research team reliably estimates, however, that about 5 percent of America's 6,000 hospitals have adopted computerized physician order entry (CPOE) systems, a component of EHRs, to help reduce medical errors and ease care delivery.
- There is no evidence yet of a digital divide. There remains "considerable uncertainty" about the existence and size of gaps in use of EHRs among physicians who care for vulnerable populations. Tracking the adoption and use of EHRs among these providers, understanding unique barriers to adoption, and identifying policies to close this gap are important steps. The study did find that patient characteristics matter, however. Physicians who treat fewer Medicaid patients are more likely to report using EHRs than those with a larger share of practice revenue from the insurance program.
- A better definition of EHRs is essential. There is no standard definition of what an EHR is and what adoption means.

Consequently, a lot is left to interpretation when surveys are conducted. The report says that the US could more adequately measure EHR adoption trends over time if there were a consistency in terminology and survey methods related to adoption practices.

■ Adoption depends on many factors. The report points to four key things that drive adoption: financial incentives and barriers, laws and regulations, the state of the technology and organizational influences such as the size of a practice or hospital or payer mix; and how integrated a health care system is.

As barriers to implementation decrease and pressures to improve efficiency and quality increase, it is predicted that more and more physicians will incorporate IT into their practices. Providing reliable, efficient, individualized care requires a degree of mastery of data and coordination that will be achievable only with the increased use of IT. Information technology can substantially improve the safety of medical care by structuring actions, catching errors, and bringing evidence-based, patient-centered decision support to the point of care to allow necessary customization. New approaches that improve customization and gather and sift through reams of data to identify key changes in status and then notify key persons should prove to be especially important.

CUSTOMIZED CARE

In other industries, IT has made "mass customization" possible: the efficient and reliable production of goods and services to meet the personalized needs of individual customers, by building and selling products with features broken out and offered to the consumer as choices. Examples include ordering a customized computer with your exact specifications, or designing your own tennis shoe by choosing from a handful of "uppers" and a handful of "soles" to create your own personal combination. Clinical care is, of course, extremely more complex than selling personal computers or tennis shoes, and clinicians have always strived to provide carefully individualized care. However, safe care now requires a degree of individualization that is becoming virtually unimaginable without computerized decision support. For example, tasks that are poorly performed by human prescribers without assistance can be completed by computer systems that are capable of instantaneously identifying a patient's medication intereactions and accurately calculating dose adjustments for the more than 600 drugs that now require adjustment for multiple levels of renal dysfunction.

The growing sophistication of computer-based decision support systems can play a vital role in the improvement of physician performance and patient outcomes and in reducing risks of medical errors by:

- Streamlining care
- Catching and correcting errors
- Assisting with decisions
- Providing feedback on performance

Information technology systems can reduce the rate of errors by:

- Preventing errors and adverse events
- Facilitating more rapid responses after an adverse event has occurred
- Tracking and reporting feedback about adverse events
- Decreasing the frequency of different types of errors and the probability of associated adverse events

SUMMARY OF APPROACHES TO ERROR PREVENTION

To date, studies have generally been conducted in individual health care facilities and rarely in the outpatient setting. Furthermore, only a few technologies have been well tested. However, it has been found that improving the fundamental aspects of patient care leads to large benefits, an indication that IT can be an important tool for improving safety in many clinical settings. Substantial benefits can be derived from making use of tools that are available today to improve communication, make knowledge more accessible, require key information, and assist with calculations and clinical decision.

- More research is needed to answer many questions, such as:
- How can checks be performed best?
- What is the best way to assist in monitoring?
- How can decision support be provided most effectively in complex situations?
- Why, in today's systems, are many important warnings ignored?

And there are too many unimportant warnings. Approaches have been developed to highlight more serious warnings, for instance, by displaying a skull and crossbones when a clinician tries to order a drug that has previously caused an anaphylactic reaction in the patient. However, many efforts directed at complex targets such as the management of hypertension or congestive heart failure have failed. Overcoming these difficulties will require bringing cognitive engineers and techniques for assessing and accommodating human factors, such as usability testing, into the design of medical processes.

The main strategies for preventing errors and adverse events include tools that can:

- Improve communication
- Make essential point-of-service and other knowledge more readily accessible
- Require key information components (such as the dose of a drug)
- Assist with complex calculations
- Perform real-time checks and alerts
- Assist with monitoring tasks
- Provide decision support

COMMUNICATION

Failures of communication, particularly those that result from inadequate "handoffs" between clinicians, remain among the most common factors contributing to the occurrence of adverse events. New technologies, including computerized coverage systems for signing out, hand-held personal digital assistants, and wireless access to electronic medical records, may improve the exchange of information (once links between various applications and a common clinical database are in place), as many errors result from inadequate and delayed access to essential clinical data. These are a few examples:

- The increased risk resulting from cross-coverage can be virtually eliminated by the implementation of a "coverage list" application, which standardizes information exchanged among clinicians.
- Notification of dangerous laboratory abnormalities requiring immediate notification and urgent action often does not occur and such results can be buried amid less critical data, especially when a clinician is not at hand (eg, hypokalemia, falling hematocrit, a critically low serum sodium level, or high calcium level).

Information systems can identify and rapidly communicate these problems to clinicians automatically (unlike traditional systems in which such results may be communicated to a unit clerk or left on a voice mail in a physician's office).

Another key to enhancing safety will be improving access to reference information. Medical textbooks, drugs references, and tools for managing infectious disease, as well as access to the MEDLINE database, are currently available for desktop as well as handheld computers.

Requiring Information and Assisting With Calculations

It is possible to implement "forcing functions," features that restrict the way in which tasks may be performed. This is one of the main benefits of using computers for clinical tasks. The following examples illustrate some of the uses and the impact of forcing functions:

- Applications can require constraints on clinicians' choices regarding the dose or route of administration of a potentially dangerous medication.
- Prescriptions written on a computer can be forced to be legible and complete, thereby eliminating, for example, the possibility of administering the wrong dose of a medication.
- Forcing functions built into computerized order entry systems are one of the primary ways by which physicians reduce the rate of errors.
- Barcoded patient-identification bracelets can prevent accidents, such as performing on one patient a procedure intended for another patient.

Dependent actions that imply that another action should be taken have been termed *corollary orders.* For example, prescribing bed rest for a patient would trigger the suggestion that the physician consider initiating prophylaxis against deep-vein thrombosis.[5] This approach, which essentially targets errors of omission, resulted in a change in behavior in 46% of cases in the intervention group and 22% of cases in the control group, with regard to a broad range of actions.

Similar results were found in a more recent controlled study[6] that used a computer program linked to the patient database to identify consecutive hospitalized patients at risk for deep-vein thrombosis in the absence of prophylaxis. The program used a robust, rule-based alerting system that could be triggered in a variety of ways to respond to eight common risk factors that determined each hospitalized patient's risk profile for venous thromboembolism. Each responsible physician had to acknowledge the computer alert and could then withhold prophylaxis or, on the same computer screen, order prophylaxis with multiple prompted options.

The program more than doubled the rate of orders for prophylaxis in the intervention group compared to the control group (from 14.5% to 33.5%), and reduced the overall rate of venous thromboembolism at 90 days by 41%, without an increase in bleeding or mortality rates. The reduction in clinically diagnosed and objectively confirmed venous thromboembolism was due mainly to a decreased frequency of pulmonary embolism and proximal-leg deep-vein thrombosis.

The frequency of a common human failing, errors of calculation, can also be reduced through the use of computers. Such tools can be used on demand, for example, by a nurse in the calculation of an infusion rate or by a pediatrician in calculating medication dosing adjustments by body weight for infants.

Monitoring

Not only is monitoring a task that is usually not performed well by humans, it is extremely difficult to detect problems by sifting through the large volumes of data that are often collected. However, with computerization of information monitoring, applications can perform this task, searching for and highlighting relationships and trends, thus permitting clinicians to intervene before an adverse outcome occurs. This type of monitoring can look for and highlight signals that suggest possible decompensation in a patient, signals that a human observer would often fail to detect.

A similar approach involving this technology enabled remote monitoring of intensive care patients, an approach that can reduce mortality and length of stay. With the national shortage of intensivists, such monitoring can be especially beneficial in the intensive care unit.

Decision Support

Information systems can assist in the flow of care in many important ways through implementation of monitoring decision support systems. Examples include providing key information on patients, such as laboratory values; calculating medication dosages in patients with impaired renal function; and red-flagging patients for whom an order for aspirin after an acute myocardial infarction may be inappropriate.

Rapid Response to and Tracking of Adverse Events

Decision support tools can also be integrated into EHRs to provide early identification and intervention as well as to track the frequency of adverse events. This functionality is currently missing in the patient safety-related armamentarium because, while improving processes, it is also important to be able to measure outcomes. A method for searching clinical databases to detect clues of a possible adverse drug event (ADE) in hospitalized patients, such as the administration of vitamin K in a patient receiving heparin, was pioneered by Classen et al.[7] Using this approach, 81% more ADEs were identified than using the customary adverse event reporting that is currently under development in hospitals today. Similar applications for the detection of inpatient nosocomial infections and the occurrence of ADEs in outpatient settings have been reported in other studies.

Future tools might be included for computerized prescribing in physician offices. A computerized monitor for ADEs could search the EHR for signals (such as elevated serum drug levels) that would suggest that an ADE may have occurred. Large numbers of ADEs that are not routinely detected could be identified (rather inexpensively) through this type of technology. The rates of events could subsequently be used for assessing the effect of electronic prescribing.

MEDICATION SAFETY AND THE PREVENTION OF ERRORS

Efforts to reduce medication error rates have received an enormous amount of attention in hospital patient safety improvement initiatives, using all of the previously discussed methods. Frequent causes of medication errors include:

- Physician lack of sufficient information regarding the patient and the medication(s)
- Lack of sufficient order specificity
- Illegible handwriting of orders
- Calculation errors
- Transcription errors

The benefits of implementing computerized order entry and other decision support systems have been shown[8,9,10] to not only reduce serious medication-related errors but also to provide:

- Improvements in communication and knowledge accessibility
- Clinically appropriate constraints, drug choices, routes of administration, and frequencies
- Help with calculations
- Real-time checks
- Assistance with monitoring
- Reduction in the rate of antibiotic complications
- Decreases in the number (and cost) of nosocomial infections

The addition of higher levels of clinical decision support (eg, more comprehensive checking for drug allergies and drug–drug interactions) led to an 83% overall rate of medication errors. Looking to the future, other technological tools may include bar coding medications and the use of automated medication delivery devices.

A review of reducing errors in primary care by Keenan and associates[11] provided a pertinent literature summary and some practical suggestions for avoiding errors. A meta-analysis in 1998 estimated that more than one million Americans were hospitalized because of ADEs related to prescription drug use.[12] A recent study of more than 30,000 Medicare enrollees in a large multispecialty practice determined that 1523 ADEs occurred during a one-year period in the ambulatory setting; 28% of these were deemed preventable, and preventable ADEs were more likely to be life-threatening or fatal.[13] If these data were extrapolated to the entire population of 38 million Medicare enrollees, an estimated 475,000 preventable ADEs, of which 90,000 are life-threatening or fatal, occur in this elderly population each year. In this study, the drugs most often implicated in preventable ADEs were cardiovascular agents, diuretics, anticoagulants, hypoglycemics, and nonopioid analgesics. Preventable ADEs were attributed to errors in prescribing (58%), monitoring (61%), and patient adherence (21%).

A 2003 prospective cohort study of four Boston-area, adult primary care practices found that 25% of patients had had an ADE.[14] Of these, 11% were preventable, that is, caused by an error. The overall error rate was 27 ADEs per 100 patients in these practices. In this study, the most common medications involved in preventable ADEs were nonsteroidal anti-inflammatory drugs, calcium-channel blockers, β-blockers, and angiotensin-converting enzyme (ACE) inhibitors. The bottom line is that ADEs are common, are frequently preventable, and can lead to significant morbidity.

Computerized drug order entry systems are a logical and often the first electronic decision support system to be installed in health care organizations. For the physician office, electronic prescribing software is readily available and also a logical starting point for an electronic health record.

The incidence of and risk factors for ADEs in the long-term care setting were assessed by a cohort study of all long-stay residents of two academic long-term care facilities over a period of up to nine months during 2000 to 2001.[15] The study looked at the number of ADEs, the severity of events (classified as less serious, serious, life threatening, or fatal), and whether the events were preventable. A case-control study was nested within the prospective study to identify resident-level risk factors for the occurrence of ADEs. The results showed:

■ There were 815 ADEs, of which 42% were judged preventable.

■ The overall rate of ADEs was 9.8 per 100 resident-months, with a rate of 4.1 preventable ADEs per 100 resident-months.

■ Errors associated with preventable events occurred most often at the stages of ordering and monitoring.

■ Residents taking medications in several drug categories were at increased risk of a preventable adverse event.

■ In multivariate analyses, the adjusted odds ratio was 3.4 for those taking antipsychotic agents, 2.8 for those taking anticoagulants, 2.2 for those taking diuretics, and 2.0 for those taking antiepileptics.

The findings emphasized the need for a special focus on the ordering and monitoring stages of pharmaceutical care for preventing ADEs in the long-term care setting. Patients receiving antipsychotic agents, anticoagulants, diuretics, and antiepileptics are particularly at increased risk.

It has been well established that ineffective systems of care are the root cause of most medical errors. Keenan and associates[11] summarized the work of Lucian L. Leape, MD, a well-recognized leader in medical error prevention, who drew on examples from other high-risk industries to summarize five basic principles of systems redesign in medicine[16]:

■ **Reduce reliance on memory.** Physicians have traditionally been trained to rely on memory in the day-to-day care of patients. On a daily basis, primary care physicians depend on their memory for diagnostic options and criteria; treatment choices and dosing specifics; procedure techniques; medication monitoring; preventive care parameters; and follow-up on diagnostic studies. The availability of support systems, including checklists, alerts and reminders, guidelines and protocols, are essential requirements to minimize mistakes and errors in today's complex health care environment. Manual tracking and monitoring systems can be quickly and easily put in place and then moved to computerized decision support systems that are available in electronic medical record systems.

■ **Improve information access.** Critical information for timely, effective, and safe patient care should be readily available and easily accessed at the point of care. Again, computerized medical records, pharmaceutical information, and treatment algorithms are just a few examples of essential support systems.

■ **Strive for error-proof systems.** Critical tasks and procedures should have system alerts and stopgaps that prevent errors from occurring. Examples include computerized infusion pump controls to stop incorrect flow rates, drug administration logic that prevents giving lethal doses, measures that prevent known drug allergy administration, and procedures to calculate renal disease doses.

- **Standardize processes of care.** Inappropriate or unproven variation in practice procedures that can result in errors can be minimized through the use of standardized procedures, evidence-based care plans, and protocols. The use of computerized checklists in commercial and military aviation is a prime example of the effectiveness of standardization in avoiding errors.

- **Emphasize error avoidance when training medical personnel.** Patient safety education should not only be a fundamental component in the training of health care professionals, it should be a key part of the orientation of new physicians and other professionals and staff joining a health care organization. Error recognition, prevention, and appropriate error response strategies should be emphasized.

Electronic Prescribing

Electronic prescribing, or e-prescribing, systems are receiving a good amount of attention. These programs clearly have applicability in physician offices and are available today. Simple electronic prescription programs can:

- Eliminate errors caused by handwriting and transcription errors
- Assist with dosing
- Provide quick access to drug information

More sophisticated programs can be integrated with laboratory test results or complete EHRs, and these programs have the potential to prevent drug–drug interactions, drug–disease interactions, and allergic reactions to medications. They can also assist with patient-specific dosing.

The effect of electronic prescribing in outpatients has not yet been specifically studied, but studies from the inpatient arena show impressive results. One study found an 88% reduction in serious medication errors and an 81% reduction in all medication errors following the implementation of an advanced computerized order-entry system.[17]

Computerized order entry and electronic prescribing systems are expensive at the present time. As previously noted, they lead to significant changes in physician workflow, and their impact on error reduction and the cost of ambulatory care has not been clearly defined. Nevertheless, based on cost-effectiveness analyses, electronic prescribing systems may well be a good investment for some physician practices, in particular larger group practices.

Writing Prescriptions Safely

It has been clearly established that handwritten prescriptions are prone to medication errors. Fortunately, there are several simple steps that can result in the reduction of prescribing errors

TABLE 4-1

Safe Prescription Writing

- Written prescriptions must be legible; printing is usually best.
- Include a brief note on purpose of the medication.
- Include allergies and age and weight of patient on prescriptions when possible.
- Include drug name, exact metric weight (ie, grams, milligrams, micrograms, and milliliters), concentration, and dosage form.
- Use generic names when possible; beware of sound-alike brand names.
- Write out "Units" not U; U often is misinterpreted and read as the number 0, leading to massive overdoses.
- Beware of decimal points, which can lead to excessive dosing if misinterpreted.
- A zero should always precede a decimal point if the amount is less than 1 (eg, 0.5 mg and not .5 mg).
- A trailing zero should never be used after a decimal (eg, 1 mg not 1.0 mg).
- Do not use abbreviations of drug names-not everyone uses the same abbreviations.
- Avoid Latin directions for use. Write it out (eg, "every day" instead of qd). Often the Latin abbreviations are misread.
- Give specific instructions. "Use as directed" is not appropriate.
- Specify the number of refills; do not write "refill prn."

Source: Keenan CR, Adubofour K, Daftary AV. Reducing medical errors in primary care. *Patient Care.* 2003;37:28-36. Reprinted with permission from *Patient Care. Patient Care* is a copyrighted publication of Advanstar Communications Inc. All rights reserved.

(see Table 4-1). If verbal orders (which are especially susceptible to error) must be given, use the following process:

- Spell the drug name and state each numeral of the dosage (eg, "six zero milligrams," not "sixty milligrams"; intravenous bolus of "twenty five milliliters of five zero percent glucose").
- The pharmacist or nurse should read the entire prescription back for verification.
- This is similar to a proven communication safety procedure used in aviation:

  Air Traffic Controller: "Delta two five four, descend and maintain two zero thousand."

  Delta Pilot: "Descend and maintain two zero thousand, Delta two five four."

A detailed and practical dissertation called "Safely Prescribing Take-Home Medications for Ambulatory Care Patients" appeared on the Virtual Hospital Web site (a digital health sciences library created in 1992 at the University of Iowa but discontinued in 2006).[18] Several key strategies to prevent errors during the prescribing of take-home supplies of medications for ambulatory care patients were illustrated. The information in this review was considered to be important for both new and experienced pre-scribers, since medication therapy is an essential component of treatment for ambulatory care patients.

Written prescriptions are a critical communication link between the physician who prescribes the medication, the pharmacist, and the patient. Therefore, it is critical for patient safety to ensure complete, accurate, and legible (or, ideally, electronic) prescription writing.

■ Completing of all of the "essential elements" of a prescription order will ensure that it is interpreted accurately.

■ Attention to detail will avoid callbacks from the pharmacist to clarify information and will also minimize patient delays.

The Illegible Handwriting Problem

There have been multiple warnings to health care providers from the medical literature, patient safety organizations, regulatory and accrediting agencies, the American Medical Association (AMA), the Institute of Medicine, the Institute for Safe Medication Practices, and the Joint Commission on Accreditation of Health-care Organizations (JCAHO) regarding the relationship between poor handwriting and medical errors. But the problem persists. Physicians must lead the effort to eliminate the problem through bold and effective action.

The following suggestions to avoid errors caused by illegibly written orders are reproduced from the publication by Keenan et al[11]:

■ All aspects of handwritten prescription orders must be clearly written using a ball-point pen. (For multiple copy prescription pads, felt tips and fountain pens do not generate sufficient pressure to transmit the order to the duplicate copies of the prescription blank.)

■ Care should be taken when prescribing drugs with look-alike names, especially when handwritten, eg, Inderal vs Isordil, Lantus vs Lente, Humulin vs Humalog.

■ Drug names should be legibly printed.

■ The use of drug name abbreviations should be avoided.

■ The use of medical abbreviations should be minimized because these may be misread or misinterpreted, eg, "qod" may be misinterpreted as "qid," resulting in a significant drug overdose.

■ Instructions should be written in complete English.

■ Prescriber signatures should be clearly legible, not simply recognizable (by the pharmacist, ward clerk, etc).

Additional information about safely writing medication orders may be reviewed at the Institute for Safe Medication Practices Web site (www.ismp.org).

Reducing Errors Caused by Drug Abbreviations

Hospital policies and JCAHO standards permit the use of drug name abbreviations in medication orders only if the abbreviation has been specifically approved by the hospital and it appears on a published list. Table 4-2 is the JCAHO-issued list of common abbreviations, acronyms, and symbols.

Medication orders that contain unapproved drug name abbreviations or dangerous medical abbreviations should not be considered valid, and pharmacists should be authorized to withhold dispensing of medications ordered via unapproved abbreviations. Similarly, abbreviations for chemotherapy drug names should never be permitted. Practitioners should be notified to clarify any orders using these dangerous abbreviations. Obviously, doing it right the first time will avoid the notification and the unnecessary hassle of back-and-forth phone calls.

Attention to detail when writing prescription orders obviates the need for the filling pharmacist to contact the prescriber to clarify orders, and also enhances safety and reduces patient

T A B L E   4-2

Abbreviations, Acronyms, and Symbols to Avoid as Provided by JCAHO

Do Not Use	Potential Problem	Use Instead
U (unit)	Mistaken for "0" (zero), the number "4" (four) or "cc"	Write "unit"
IU (International Unit)	Mistaken as IV (intravenous) or 10 (ten)	Write "International Unit"
Q.D., QD, q.d., qd (daily)	Mistaken for each other	Write "daily"
Q.O.D., QOD, q.o.d., qod (every other day)	Period after the Q mistaken for "I" and the "O" for "I"	Write "every other day"
Trailing zero (X.0 mg)*	Decimal point is missed	Write X mg
Lack of leading zero (.X mg)		Write 0.X mg
MS	Can mean morphine sulfate or magnesium sulfate	Write "morphine sulfate"
MSO$_4$ and MgSO$_4$	Confused with one another	Write "magnesium sulfate"

©Joint Commission on Accreditation of Healthcare Organizations, 2006. Reprinted with permission. Available at: www.jcaho.org/accredited+organizations/patient+safety/06_dnu_list.pdf. Accessed March 23, 2006.

Note: Applies to all orders and all medication-related documentation that is handwritten (including free-text computer entry) or on preprinted forms.

*Exception: A "trailing zero" may be used only where required to demonstrate the level of precision of the value being reported, such as for laboratory results, imaging studies that report size of lesions, or catheter/tube sizes. It may not be used in medication orders or other medication-related documentation.

inconvenience. The following information regarding elements that should be provided by the physician on each prescription blank or computer order entry was also reproduced from the publication by Keenan et al[11]:

- A separate prescription blank or screen must be used for each drug prescribed; multiple prescriptions on a single blank are unsafe and greatly increase the potential for medication errors.

- Patient demographics (patient name; address; hospital, clinic, or practice number; birth date) and the date the prescription is written should be written or entered on the face of the prescription or order entry screen. Templated prescription order forms or electronic medical record input screens should facilitate information input.

- Name and strength of drug. Medications should be ordered by the generic name, not by the proprietary or trade names. The dosage form (such as tablet, capsule, suspension) and the strength or concentration of the dosage form must be specified. The prescriber should also specify when the delayed-release dosage form for a medication is desired.

- Quantity to be dispensed. Quantity of ingredients should be expressed in the metric system. A zero should always be placed before a decimal expression less than one (ie, 0.1 mg) to prevent misinterpretation of the prescription. When prescribing drugs with varying dosage (eg, "1 to 2 tablets") or prescribing "as needed" dosing, an exact numerical quantity should be specified rather than writing "30-day supply" on the quantity line.

- Directions to the patient. Writing clear and concise directions on the prescription will assist the patient in appropriate use of the medication. "Take as directed" should be avoided. The patient may forget or confuse verbal directions or lose a separate note. The "PRN" designation should include the medication's purpose (eg, PRN sleep, PRN pain). An "Indication for Use" should be designated.

- Signature, printed name. In addition to signing the prescription, the prescriber should print his/her name legibly below the signature.

- Drug Enforcement Agency number

- Refill designation

- Always write or circle "no refills" or specify the number of times and/or the last date the prescription may be refilled. "PRN" is not a valid refill designation.

- Drug allergies. The patient's medication allergies should be specified in a space on one of the prescriptions for each set of prescriptions. If there are no known allergies, note or check an "NKA" box.

Effective Drug-Monitoring Systems

Some form of monitoring is usually required for patients taking, among others[11]:

- Anticoagulants
- ACE inhibitors

- Digoxin
- Insulin
- Oral hypoglycemics
- Thiazolidinediones
- Antiseizure medications

In the absence of an EHR, a calendar can be used to monitor dates for diagnostic study results, with follow-up if the results are not received by the due date. Any follow-up monitoring is also entered on the calendar. If the process is used properly, it is possible to keep track of a large number of patients. Patients receiving anticoagulant medication should ideally be followed in anticoagulation clinics. Reminders to check for drug–drug interactions when new medications are prescribed for patients taking warfarin anticoagulation prevents relying on memory for such an important task. Other approaches to tracking pertinent patient information will be discussed later in the chapter.

Geriatric Pharmacology

The primary clinical concerns in geriatric pharmacotherapy are:

- Efficacy
- Safety
- Appropriate drug and dose
- Complexity of the treatment regimen
- Cost
- Patient compliance

Because of the variables in determination of dose and in compliance, there are no simple rules for prescribing drugs for the elderly. The American Medical Association Council on Scientific Affairs published the results of an exhaustive literature search on the subject of improving the quality of geriatric pharmacology.[19] Important findings and recommendations from this study are summarized in this section. The report shared valuable information and lessons for improving the safety of drug prescribing in the geriatric population.

Concerns about medication use in the elderly are not new. As life expectancy increases, there will be efforts to discover new treatment and prevention modalities, improve health behavior habits, and continue effective pharmaceutical research.

Medicare eligible individuals currently consume nearly one third of all medications. Furthermore, elderly patients constitute a unique dimension of virtually all aspects of medication use, including basic pharmacology, drug testing, prescribing, utilization, reimbursement, and postmarketing surveillance. It has been known for some time that age is a risk factor for the development of adverse drug reactions. Studies have shown that the rate of ADRs among persons aged 65 years or older is nearly double that of younger individuals. The 1987 Omnibus Budget Reconciliation Act (OBRA) developed regulations for the use of sedatives, hypnotics, and antipsychotic medications in Medicare- and Medicaid-certified nursing homes. A Workshop on Health Promotion and Aging held by the Surgeon General in 1988 led to several recommendations in the areas of education and training, service, research, and policy to begin addressing problems related to geriatric pharmacotherapy in a comprehensive way. Many of these recommendations are still relevant today and are provided in the following extract.[19]

Recommendations of the Surgeon General's Medication Working Group (1988)

Education and Training

1. More training and continuing medical education courses should be provided that emphasize:

    a. Resources available to the prescriber

    b. Understanding of age-related physiologic changes affecting drug disposition

    c. Nonjudgmental patient-counseling skills

    d. Interdisciplinary communication skills

2. Social service providers, home caregivers, family members, and older adults should be:

    a. Trained in medication management

    b. Educated about the potential for adverse drug reactions

3. The role of pharmacists in management of and education about geriatric medication should be expanded.

4. Sites for geriatric-specific prescribing information in all practice settings should be identified.

Service

1. Access to medicine and pharmaceutical services should be included as a basic part of health care programs for the elderly, including those who are geographically isolated and mobility-impaired.

2. Community-based programs should strengthen efforts to ensure older Americans have the information necessary to participate with their physicians in medication management.

3. Reimbursement patterns should encourage better access to medical care for persons needing complex medication regimens and for isolated patients.

4. Reimbursement for pharmacy services for the elderly should be independent of dispensation or cost of the product.

Research

1. Cross-sectional and longitudinal studies and other pharmacoepidemiological research should emphasize nonlethal side effects, efficacy, risks, compliance, and cost-effectiveness.

2. National data sets should be studied further to assess medication-use patterns among older adults.

3. Studies should focus on cost-effective means of educating the consumer and the home caregiver on proper use of meditations and monitoring of side effects, and on the standardization of medication profile and drug interaction information.

Policy

1. Regulatory agencies should explore fraud and quackery by reviewing the marketing of certain drugs, vitamins, foods, and other dietary supplements used as medications.

2. The FDA should complete its guidance for drugs used in the elderly.

3. Drug labeling should be enforced and should emphasize patient education by including specific instructions for the elderly

---

Thus, going back almost two decades, there were clear-cut guidelines and suggestions urging special attention to drug use in seniors. Fast-forward through other actions that subsequently took place:

- In 1989, the Food and Drug Administration (FDA) issued a voluntary guideline intended to encourage routine and thorough evaluation in elderly populations of the effects of new drugs being proposed for federal approval.

- OBRA 1990 required all states to conduct ongoing retrospective drug utilization reviews of Medicaid prescription drug claims and prospective reviews before each prescription is filled.

- A 1995 report by the General Accounting Office, "Prescription Drugs and the Elderly," concluded that inappropriate use of prescription drugs remained a significant health problem for the elderly.

- In 1997, the FDA issued a final rule on establishing specific requirements to add a "geriatric use" subsection in product labeling.

- In 2001, the FDA released a guidance statement for industry clarifying who should submit revised labeling and explaining the implementation schedule for drugs already on the market.

Therefore, the point is not that problems with drug administration in our aging population suddenly appeared, but rather what has been done about it during the past 20 years. Fortunately, there has been progress in many areas.

FORMAL GRADUATE MEDICAL EDUCATION IN GERIATRIC MEDICINE

Formal graduate medical education in geriatric medicine has been established in several ways. Except for the obvious exceptions (eg, pediatrics), all graduate medical education programs and residencies accredited by the Accreditation Council for Graduate Medical Education (ACGME) provide specialty-specific education, training, and experience in the care of geriatric patients as a normal part of their programs of instruction. This is particularly true for the specialties of internal medicine and family practice. In a joint venture, the American Board of Internal Medicine and the American Board of Family Practice have offered a subspecialty certificate in geriatric medicine since 1988. The added certificate is designed to recognize excellence among those diplomates of the primary board who provide care to the elderly. A candidate for certification in geriatric medicine must be certified by one of the sponsoring boards, have undertaken one year of fellowship training in a program of geriatric medicine accredited by the ACGME, and have passed a cognitive examination.

The 2001 Annual Report of the American Board of Medical Specialties (ABMS) indicates that in the 10-year period from 1991 to 2000, 1779 certificates in geriatric medicine were awarded by the American Board of Family Practice and 3853 by the American Board of Internal Medicine. The small number of physicians undertaking additional training in geriatric medicine from the specialties of internal medicine and family practice likely reflects the adequacy of preparation to care for geriatric patients after completing the primary specialty program.

The American Board of Psychiatry and Neurology offers a subspecialty certificate in geriatric psychiatry. In addition to certification in psychiatry, an additional year of residency training in geriatric psychiatry at an ACGME-accredited program is required. There are 61 accredited programs in existence, with a total of 86 physicians in training. Twenty-seven percent are graduates of US medical schools. The ABMS indicates that the American Board of Psychiatry and Neurology has awarded 2508 subspecialty certificates in the referenced 10-year period.

The pharmacoepidemiology of drug use in geriatric patients has been extensively studied. Although the AMA report[19] discussed certain pharmacokinetic changes with aging that are beyond the scope of discussion in this book (the pharmacokinetic processes of absorption, distribution, metabolism, and excretion), there were other observations that are important to understand.

PATTERNS OF MEDICATION USE

Over time, it has been recognized that patients older than 65 years take more drugs than younger adults and that the number of drugs taken tends to increase with age. Nearly 75% of office visits by geriatric patients are associated with continuation or initiation of a drug prescription. Large numbers of US adults take large quantities of medications in the ambulatory as well as institutionalized population. Rates of use increase with age and are greater in women than in men for most measures.

Among individuals aged 65 years and older, 66% of men and 81% of women use at least one prescription drug weekly. One in eight men and nearly 25% of women use five or more prescription drugs weekly. When over-the-counter (OTC) drugs and dietary supplements are included, 89% of men and 94% of women use at least one product weekly; 43% of men and 57% of women use five or more; and 11% to 12% of men and women use 10 or more of these products weekly.

The most frequently used OTC entities were analgesics (acetaminophen, ibuprofen, aspirin), pseudoephedrine, diphenhydramine, dextromethorphan, nonsteroidal anti-inflammatory drugs, antihistamines, and H_2-blockers. The most frequently used prescription drugs in this study were conjugated estrogens, thyroid supplements, diuretics, statins, ACE inhibitors, progestins, nonsedating antihistamines, β-blockers, calcium-channel blockers, omeprazole, and warfarin. Overall, 16% of prescription drug users also used one or more dietary supplements.

Other survey data suggest that community-dwelling older Americans take an average of 2.7 to 4.2 prescription and nonprescription medications. Historically, at discharge from the hospital, older patients take a higher number of drugs (mean, five); nursing home residents take an even larger number.

ADVERSE DRUG REACTIONS IN THE ELDERLY

Avoidable adverse drug reactions (ADRs) are a serious consequence of inappropriate drug prescribing and use in the elderly. The World Health Organization defines an ADR as "any noxious, unintended, and undesired effect of a drug, which occurs at doses used in humans for prophylaxis, diagnosis, or therapy." This definition excludes therapeutic failures, intentional and accidental overdoses, and drug abuse. It also does not include "adverse events" attributable to errors in drug administration or noncompliance. A meta-analysis of 34 studies spanning the 1960s to 1990s estimated that in 1994 (more than a decade ago)[20]:

- Greater than 100,000 patients experienced a fatal ADR
- More than two million hospitalized patients experienced a serious ADR
- Roughly 4.7% of hospital admissions are drug-related

Once in the hospital, ADRs occur in 6.5% of patients, and approximately 28% may be preventable. Patients who are sicker and have longer hospital stays experience more ADRs. Many, but not all, studies have revealed an association between old age (older than 65 years in most studies) and a greater risk of adverse events in hospital, community, and nursing home settings. Analysis of hospital admissions suggests that 10% to 17% of acute geriatric admissions are related to ADRs. An additional complement is related to noncompliance, which also contributes to increased emergency department visits. The most recent outpatient survey estimated that 18% of elderly outpatients suffer ADRs. Correlates were:

- Number of medical problems
- Number of medications
- Lower compliance
- Presence of renal disease

Predictable ADRs are even more common (35%) in high-risk elderly outpatients (ie, those taking more than five drugs daily). It has been consistently shown that the number of ADRs increases with the number of drugs taken. This increase is exponential rather than linear; thus, an increase in the rate of ADRs with advancing age may be a simple consequence of increased exposure to multiple medications rather than an effect of aging on susceptibility per se. The increasing number of ADRs with age tends to disappear when adjustments are made for the number of drugs taken. Thus, use of greater numbers of drugs, rather than age alone, is associated with an increased risk of ADRs.

Most ADRs are dose-related and related to the number of concurrent medications. The study of ADRs in the elderly becomes more complex when one attempts to determine an age-appropriate dose for a particular medication. Many patients demonstrate an age-related decline in drug elimination. If lower doses are not routinely considered in such patients, blood concentrations of the drug will be too high for the clinical situation. In such cases, the increased rate of ADRs is a consequence of inappropriate prescribing.

DRUG LISTS

Lists of inappropriate drugs for patients older than 65 years have been developed (using consensus approaches with explicit criteria): inappropriate drug–disease combinations and/or inappropriate drug–drug interactions. The most familiar is the "Beers criteria," first published in 1991,[21] which listed 19 medications or drug categories to be avoided and 11 criteria that described doses, frequencies, or duration of medication prescriptions that generally should not be exceeded in frail nursing home residents. The list was updated in 1997[22] to apply to older people in all care settings. A severity rating reflecting the likelihood of an adverse reaction was added. Clinical information on diagnoses was incorporated when available. The updated list was expanded to include 28 medications that should generally be avoided in the ambulatory elderly, doses or frequencies of administration that should generally not be exceeded, and 35 medications that should be avoided in older persons known to have any of several common conditions (drug-disease criteria). A published update in 2003[23] identified 48 individual medications or classes of medications to avoid in older adults and their potential concerns and 20 diseases or conditions and medications to be avoided in older adults with these conditions. Sixty-six of these potentially inappropriate drugs were considered to have high-severity adverse outcomes.

OVERUSE AND POLYPHARMACY

While polypharmacy, the administration of multiple medications, has multiple connotations, in many cases the use of multiple medications is justified because of concurrent comorbid conditions and/or severe illness. When multiple medication is not justified or medically necessary, the pattern represents overuse. Physicians can contribute to overuse by prescribing a drug without a proper indication or acquiescing to patient demands for a prescription. Furthermore, prescribing additional drugs to treat drug-induced symptoms that are misinterpreted as a new sign, symptom, or disease can lead to prescribing cascades.

Patients contribute to the problem by not acknowledging or being aware of all medications (including OTC medications and dietary supplements) they have or are taking. Patients also may receive medications prescribed by more than one physician. Polypharmacy, in older patients, is the greatest risk factor for ADRs, drug interactions, reduced compliance, increased emergency department visits, hospitalizations, and nursing home admissions. It may also contribute to the development of several "geriatric syndromes" such as:

- Cognitive impairment
- Delirium
- Falls and hip fractures
- Urinary incontinence
- Diminished functional status

Polypharmacy increases health care costs, but, most importantly, studies have confirmed that the more prescriptions a patient has, the greater the risk of an ADE. Minimizing the number of medications a patient (particularly an elderly one) takes is another means of avoiding medication errors.[24]

Many medications can be removed safely from elderly patients' drug lists without incurring adverse events by paying careful attention to medical status changes.[25] Maintaining a complete and accurate patient medication list is essential for safe prescribing. It is crucial to review patients' medications, including OTC medications and supplements, during every office visit. Patients should carry a complete and up-to-date list of their medications. If they cannot maintain a list, before each visit they should bring all of their medications, including OTCs and herbals, to the visit. Routine drug reviews help the physician eliminate duplicate drugs, reduce polypharmacy, and avoid drug–drug interactions.

Research has shown that multiple errors may occur after patients are discharged from the hospital, and it is therefore important to pay attention to medication lists.[26] Patients are often confused by their medication changes and may duplicate medications by taking their "new" ones along with identical ones that they already have at home. Patients should be given a complete medication list at the time of discharge and it should be confirmed that they understand any changes from their preadmission outpatient medication regimen.

INAPPROPRIATE MEDICATION USE

Inappropriate drug use is prescribing a medication that has more potential risk than potential benefit or prescribing that does not agree with accepted medical standards. Such practices contribute to increased hospital admissions in the elderly. Categories of inappropriate use include:

- Improper drug selection
- Use of a drug without indication (including continuing use of a drug after the indication is no longer present)
- Choosing an appropriate drug but the wrong dose (too low or too high), or any of several other elements of the drug treatment plan

UNDERUTILIZATION

Underutilization is the omission of drug therapy that is indicated for the treatment or prevention of a disease or condition and raises consequences of underprescribing of potentially beneficial therapies to patients older than 65 years. Application of explicit criteria has revealed underutilization in the use of:

- Secondary prevention (β-blocker, aspirin, lipid-lowering agents) after myocardial infarction
- Treatment of hypertension

- ACE inhibitors in patients with congestive heart failure
- Treatment of cancer pain
- Warfarin in older patients with atrial fibrillation with contraindications to treatment

DETERMINATION OF DOSAGES

A useful rule for prescribing for geriatric patients is "start low and go slow and sometimes say no." With respect to medication dosage, low body weight and advanced age are major risk factors for overmedication. Physicians must recognize the need to reduce drug doses for low-weight elderly patients. Patients (mean age, 72 years) weighing 50 kg or less received milligram-per-kilogram doses 31% to 45% higher than the group mean and 70% to 88% higher than patients weighing more than 90 kg.

Reduced homogeneity is responsible for the wide interindividual variation that exists in the rate of age-related changes in physiological parameters that affect drug disposition. Chronological age and biological age are not synonymous. Thus, precise predictions for individual elderly persons are difficult to make. The clinical status of each patient (such as nutrition and hydration status, cardiac output, and renal and hepatic function) must be considered in addition to the effects of aging.

However, certain factors such as changes in renal function are readily quantifiable by use of the Cockcroft-Gault equation, and this approach should be employed routinely in clinical practice. FDA-approved product labeling for geriatric patients usually lacks specific dosage recommendations, particularly among older subsets. The elderly population represents a continuum from "fit" to "frail." However, most studies in aged individuals include only the "fit." These subjects are probably more similar physiologically and pharmacokinetically to younger people than to their chronological peers. The current pharmacokinetic database comprises mostly studies of healthy individuals aged 60 to 75 years. Few data are available to support (or refute) extrapolation of the current pharmacokinetic database to the (sick) patient population in whom the drug will be used. Similarly, the most straightforward study, single-dose exposure, may provide an incomplete understanding of pharmacokinetics during multiple-dose drug administration.

Although it is appropriate for physicians to feel hesitant about using lower drug doses without proof or product labeling stating their effectiveness, a large number of studies involving lower doses of several commonly used drugs have been conducted. A list comparing the initial doses recommended in the FDA-approved product labeling and lower effective doses reported in the medical literature is reproduced in Appendix K.

COMPLIANCE CONCERNS

Compliance is viewed as the extent to which a person's behaviors coincide with medical advice. Because most older persons handle the responsibility for taking their own medications, there are multiple variables that affect compliance with medication use. Also, physician judgment is not a predictor of who is or is not taking medications according to the prescribed schedule. Achieving optimal compliance involves a process of:

- Medication selection
- Choice of initial dose, dose interval, and subsequent adjustments
- Assessment of outcome
- Use of information from the patient and family or other caregiver
- Reexamination of the need for medications
- The attempt to avoid clinically significant drug–disease and drug–drug interactions

There have been many theories about compliance, and many interventions to foster compliance have been studied. There is no simple factor or explanation. Drug compliance requires a patient to perform at varying cognitive levels. The patient's health literacy plays a critical role in communicating with the patient and evaluating responses. Some causes of noncompliance are more common in the elderly or somewhat different compared with factors involved in younger age groups. As previously noted, a higher percentage of the elderly take multiple drugs. Use of three or more drugs daily places elderly patients at risk of poor compliance, as does living alone. The elderly may exhibit unintentional noncompliance due to forgetfulness, confusion, or impaired physical function, especially decreased vision. Hospital admissions for drug-related illness due to unintentional noncompliance are approximately double those seen in the general population. Elderly patients also may exhibit intentional noncompliance because of side effects or financial barriers. Prescription noncompliance also contributes to increased emergency department visits. Some patients use more drug than prescribed in the mistaken belief that this will speed recovery. As many as 10% of elderly people take drugs prescribed for others. More than 20% may take drugs not currently prescribed by a physician.

Techniques for improving medication compliance in the elderly begin with personalized, effective communication between the physician and the patient. Use of charts and written instructions to augment verbal communication can be helpful. Timing of medication administration should be matched to the patient's daily schedule. Mechanical aids and color-coding for packaging and organizing pill counts can be very helpful. Physicians may need to specify that medications should not be dispensed in safety-cap containers.

EXPLICIT CRITERIA IN PRESCRIBING PRACTICE: PROS AND CONS

Prescribing medications is a complex skill. Complications may occur because of interactions between two drugs or between a drug and dietary supplement or because of physiological and functional changes associated with aging or age-related diseases. Nonpharmacological factors also play a critical role in the safety and effectiveness of drug therapy in the elderly.

Physician prescribing skills are developed and evolve in the "real-world" setting beginning with internship and residency training. Subsequently, behaviors are influenced by peers, pharmaceutical company marketing efforts, pharmaceutical benefit managers, and patient demands and expectations.

There is a compelling argument in favor of using explicit criteria in prescribing practice, based on the concept that standardization and improvements in therapeutic practices, with reduction in medication-related ADEs, will increase the quality of care and patient safety, enhance patient outcome, optimize resource utilization, and promote fiscal prudence.

Six scaled domains to measure inappropriate prescribing were identified by Lipton et al,[27,28] including:

- Lack of indication
- Improper schedule
- Inadequate dosage
- Potential drug interactions
- Therapeutic duplication
- Allergy

Application of these criteria found that 22% of older outpatients have serious problems with one or more of these categories.

Some of the biggest players in the health care industry, the Institute of Medicine, the Centers for Medicare and Medicaid Services, the Agency for Healthcare Research and Quality, and the American Association of Health Plans (now America's Health Insurance Plans), to name a few, are among the biggest proponents of explicit criteria and evidence-based prescribing. In *Crossing the Quality Chasm,* discussed in Chapter 1, the Institute of Medicine presented a template for the future, when the traditional values of physician integrity, altruism, knowledge, skill, and dedication to lifelong patient care are seamlessly integrated into an information era of point-of-care, computerized decision support that facilitates appropriate care using the available resources. The updated Beers criteria represent one aspect of that movement, enabling all parties, from providers to insurers, to integrate the recommendations into clinical information systems.

Although it is hard to find dissent for using explicit criteria in prescribing practice, there are some challenges. These criteria, though widely used, have been somewhat controversial because of:

- Their adoption by nursing home regulators
- Their appearance to some as too simplistic
- Concerns about potentially limiting the freedom of physicians to prescribe
- Challenges in translating research into measurable quality improvement
- Widespread concerns that perhaps cost containment is the principal driver of change in the health care world

Individual health care providers and organizations should demand objective evidence that implementation of the updated Beers criteria (or, indeed, other appropriate medication guides) will result in objective, quantifiable improvements in the clinical effectiveness and cost-effectiveness of health care services. However, thoughtful application of the updated 2002 Beers criteria and other tools for identifying potentially inappropriate medication use should enable everyone from individual physicians to health care systems to:

- Plan interventions aimed at decreasing drug-related costs and overall health care costs
- Reduce ADE-related admissions in elderly patients
- Improve care and patient safety
- Integrate the new criteria-based prescribing recommendations into their organic, mechanical, and electronic information support systems

Simple electronic prescription programs can eliminate errors caused by handwriting and transcription errors, assist with dosing, and provide quick access to drug information. More sophisticated programs can be integrated with laboratory test results or complete EHRs, and these programs have the potential to prevent drug–drug interactions, drug–disease interactions, and allergic reactions to medications and to assist with patient-specific dosing. Electronic prescribing programs will be further discussed in the next chapter.

These and other similar criteria, or modifications thereof, have been widely used in epidemiological studies to estimate inappropriate prescribing in elderly patients in skilled nursing facilities, board and care facilities or hospitals, in homebound adults and patients within a Medicare health maintenance organization, and for prescriptions originating in outpatient clinics or from office-based physicians. The application of the Beers criteria and other tools for identifying potentially inappropriate medication use should continue to enable providers to plan interventions to minimize drug-related problems. With the continuous release of new drugs on the market, increased knowledge about older drugs, and removal of older drugs, these criteria must be updated on a regular basis and must take into account the ever-increasing, evidence-based literature in the area of medication use in older adults. Despite the frequent published reference to these criteria over the past decade, inappropriate medication use in elderly patients remains a serious problem.[29]

FOLLOWING UP ON PATIENTS' TEST RESULTS

Failure to review and follow up on outpatient test results in a timely manner is a major patient safety concern. In a study to identify problems in current test result management systems and possible ways to improve these systems, 262 physicians working in 15 internal medicine practices affiliated with two large urban teaching hospitals were surveyed (response rate, 64%).[30] The physicians were queried about systems they used, the amount of time they spent managing test results, delays in reviewing test results, overall satisfaction with their management of test results, and features they would find useful in a new test result management system.

Overall, 83% of respondents reported at least one delay in reviewing test results during the previous two months. Although they spent on average 74 minutes per clinical day managing test results, only 41% of physicians reported being satisfied with how they managed test results. Satisfaction was associated with fewer self-reported delays in reviewing test results. Physicians who actively tracked their test orders to completion were also more likely to be satisfied. The most highly desired features of a test result management system were tools to help physicians generate result letters to patients, prioritize their workflow, and track test orders to completion. In conclusion, delays in test result review are common, and many physicians are not satisfied with how they manage test results. Tools for improving test result management in office practices need to track test orders to completion and increase workflow efficiency.

In a 1996 survey of practicing primary care physicians,[31] 32% reported having a fair, poor, or no test-tracking system. Seventy-two percent of physicians did not notify patients of normal results. Only 55% of physicians always notified their patients of abnormal results. After notifying patients of abnormal results, only 23% had a reliable system to ensure that appropriate follow-up on the abnormal test was completed by the patient. Patients may be expected to be seen soon in the office but often skip or cancel these crucial appointments.

Almost a decade later, another study confirmed that practicing physicians are well aware that follow-up on test results and consultations is often incomplete.[11] Tests that are ordered may not get done. Test results may not be forwarded to the ordering physician. Patients may neither make nor keep appointments with specialists. The referring physician may not receive a report from the consultant. In a 1998 study, only 55% of referring physicians received feedback from the consultant.[32] These missteps can lead to harmful delays in diagnosis or treatment.

TEST-TRACKING SYSTEMS

Keenan, et al, provided some practical suggestions to tackle the problem.[11]

In the absence of an electronic tracking system, one practical approach involves the creation of a test-tracking logbook for individual physicians or the entire practice. Examples of essential components of this manual tracking system, which can be easily moved into an electronic medical record system in the future are every test ordered is entered into the book either at the time of order or at the end of the workday. As test results arrive, they are logged and given to the physician for review. If results are not received within a designated time, the patient is contacted to make certain that the test was done and the ordering physician notified. Patients can be routinely notified of results using letter templates, with a copy placed in the chart for documentation. Abnormal results often will be relayed by phone, and the notification, too, should be documented. Any recommended follow-up on abnormal test results must be logged and then tracked until completion. A staff member should be in charge of maintaining the logbook each day and responsible for following up on incomplete orders. The workflow must be set up so that all matters relating to test ordering, results, and follow-up are managed through the staff person and the logbook. Requests for consultation can be managed in the same way as tests and tracked in either the same system or a separate one.

REMINDER TOOL BAG

Keenan, et al, also suggested the use of manual reminder systems in physician offices to facilitate efficient ways to ensure consistent care in the absence of EHR system support[11]:

- A summary sheet that is kept in the patient's chart and reviewed at each visit is a commonly used reminder system for preventive and disease-specific care. Involving ancillary or nursing staff in the process can improve performance. For example, nurses can often prepare the necessary paperwork ahead of time and review pertinent information with the patient at each visit.

- Disease-specific flow sheets for chronic conditions like diabetes, coronary heart disease, and congestive heart failure are also in wide use and cover preventive care, counseling, and medication recommendations.

- Preventive care should be addressed at each visit, as implementation often involves minimal effort by the physician. Alternatively, some physicians use an annual preventive care visit to address all health maintenance issues at one time. A preventive care brochure for patients can be effective.

- Computers can provide patient-specific information and reminders and clinical guidelines in real time to physicians at the point of care. Standardized order sets that are based upon established guidelines for specific diseases can also be used in computerized order-entry systems, when available.

- Physician practices need to establish reliable systems to ensure that all patients receive necessary follow-up, whether for abnormal findings on a mammogram or for routine preventive care. All "no show" charts and cancellations that are not rescheduled should be reviewed by the physician who can assess whether follow-up is in fact necessary and, if it is, determine the appropriate time frame.

Although these manual processes are important stopgaps in preventing adverse events and errors from inadequate tracking and communicating test results, they are not able to cover all of the complexities of managing critical information in the physician office. Fortunately, tracking and alerting technologies are an integral component in electronic health record systems.

ELECTRONIC HEALTH RECORDS

Technology has benefited many industry sectors (banking, transportation, manufacturing, and defense, to name a few) by providing drastically improved productivity, efficiencies, accuracy, and service levels. Many organizations within these industries, by failing to "keep up" and adopt essential new technologies, either failed or were "gobbled up" by others (ie, Pan American Airways, FirstUnion Bank, MetLife, Travelers Health Insurance). The promises and the threat of nonadoption of IT has yet to be fully realized in health care. There exists an urgent and unmet need to:

- Reduce paper processes
- Increase patient safety
- Implement process improvements for:
  - Patient satisfaction
  - Provider satisfaction
  - Increased efficiency and elimination of waste (ie, ineffective processes)
  - Greater cost controls

Definitions

Several terms are used for the electronic systems that replace paper medical records. *Electronic health record* (EHR) is a generic term for electronic patient care systems. *Computer-based patient record* (CPR) is a lifetime patient record that includes all information from all specialties (eg, dentist, psychiatrist) and requires full interoperability, even potentially internationally.[33] EHR core functions and implementation phases can be summarized as follows[39]:

Core Functions

Health information and data: Patients' diagnoses, allergies, and lab results

Results management: New and past test results by all clinicians involved in treating a patient

Order management: Computerized entry and storage of data on all medications, tests, and other services

Decision support: Electronic alerts and reminders to improve compliance with best practices, ensure regular screenings and other preventive practices, identify possible drug interactions, and facilitate diagnoses and treatments

Patient support: Tools offering patients access to their medical records, interactive education, and the ability to do home monitoring and testing

Administrative processes: Tools including scheduling systems that improve administrative efficiencies and patient service

Reporting: Electronic data storage that uses uniform data standards to enable physician offices and health care organizations to comply with federal, state, and private reporting requirements in a timely manner

Electronic communication and connectivity: Secure and readily accessible communication among clinicians and patients

---

Typical Phases of EHR Implementation

Analysis: Study health care provider's work environment, including work flow, and create report. Develop project plan.

Selection: Use functional requirements to create a request for proposal (RFP). Project the total cost of ownership (TCO) and return on investment (ROI). Select vendors for hardware, software, and network.

Procurement: Negotiate acquisition of hardware, software, and network. Purchase hardware, software, and network.

Installation: Install hardware, software, and network. Fully document configurations and system administration functions. Customize the EHR system as needed (eg, additional forms and templates). Integrate the EHR system with the existing embedded system as needed (eg, billing, scheduling). Perform data conversions (eg, paper to digital, digital from existing system to digital of new system) as needed. Test new environment.

Training: Initially train all staff users. Evaluate, on an ongoing basis, the staff's feature usage and retrain or coach, as needed. Train new staff users.

Maintenance: Arrange for the help desk to handle all issues (eg, user questions, repair, outages, new installations) with dispatch capabilities 24 hours/day, 7 days/week or on a limited basis, as required. Install hardware, software, and network upgrades. Arrange for routine daily maintenance (eg, backups, preventive maintenance). Develop and test disaster recovery plans.

The American Academy of Family Practice Center for Information Technology is a rich source of practical information available to physicians in their efforts to implement an EHR system. Much of the information is reproduced in Appendix L. Other medical specialty societies also offer patient safety information to their members, summarized in Appendix N.

A summary of EHR features and functions can be found in Appendix M.

IMPROVING THE PHYSICIAN PRACTICE

A Healthvision paper,[34] analyzing drug prescribing in ambulatory care practice, raised a question: "Will physician practices, as we know them today, survive or thrive?" It depends on how physician practices address the complex challenges and opportunities of today's health care delivery environment.

The trends in ambulatory care are well established and unmistakable. In order for the physician practice to survive, there must be attention to and management of a rapidly growing list of vexing issues. A few of the daily frustrations and challenges that threaten practice survival are:

- Rising medical malpractice costs
- Declining reimbursement
- Increasingly complex and burdensome administrative and regulatory practice activities
- Rapidly changing benefit structures from health plans and pharmacy benefit managers for formularies, copayments, and preauthorizations

Not only does survival demand finding ways to acknowledge, manage, and minimize the challenges, but also physicians must:

- Seize and adopt opportunities for improved efficiencies and productivity (as well as new and emerging sources of significant practice revenue)
- Acknowledge a persistent and alarming reality that the workflow and business processes of a typical physician practice are, at best, inefficient and inadequate, and at worst, rapidly becoming completely broken and increasingly dangerous

In this highly complex and confusing ambulatory care environment, how can clinicians be expected to simultaneously manage the complexities of clinical care; implement and administer the arcane regulatory requirements of state and local governments; and follow the rapidly changing business rules for formulary compliance, copayment, preauthorization, quantity limitations for drugs, etc? Given at least some understanding of the mind-boggling dilemma that confronts physician practices, what can they possibly do about it? Currently available and projected new information technologies are poised to radically reshape the way both the business and practice of medicine are conducted. Reliable, mobile, and inexpensive new technologies and solutions are remaking physician workflow, while providing anytime-anywhere access to critical patient information.

IS YOUR PRACTICE READY FOR AN ELECTRONIC HEALTH RECORD SYSTEM?

A 2004 publication by Kenneth Adler provided an excellent review of the reasons why electronic health records (EHRs) are now ready for prime time.[35] A number of questions and concerns were answered and there was a clear message for physicians: The time has come.

Why It's Time to Purchase an Electronic Health Record System

Kenneth G. Adler, MD, MMM

Why Now?

Since 1991, with the publication of its report "The Computer-Based Patient Record: An Essential Technology for Health Care," the Institute of Medicine has been urging us to adopt EHRs—originally called computerized patient records (CPRs) or, more recently, electronic medical records (EMRs).[1] Then it was a vision, not a practical mandate. So why do it now? What's changed?

Well, hardware and software. With the speed of current computers, broadband connections and improved scanning technology, information can typically be filed and retrieved electronically faster than it can be manually. Patient note creation speed has improved dramatically with point-and-click technology, more sophisticated templates and integration of dictation with templates. With the addition of functions such as electronic prescribing, allergy checking, drug-interaction checking and remote chart access, EHRs can do things that paper charts just can't. EHRs are now more user-friendly than ever, and with each new software version release, things just keep getting better.

"But I've heard EHRs are really expensive and require a lot of training." While it's true they represent a significant expense, you'll see below that EHRs now offer you substantial opportunities for cost reduction and revenue enhancement. And while it's true that changing to an EHR will require a definite investment of personal time and effort, hopefully you'll conclude by the end of this article that this particular change is worth it.

What Is an EHR Anyway?

An EHR is software that allows you to create, store, organize, edit and retrieve patient records on a computer. But it's more than just the electronic equivalent of paper. Advanced EHRs also allow you to automate many time-consuming, paper-driven office tasks. They allow for electronic prescribing and medication refills, automatic formulary checking, electronic lab, imaging and referral ordering, automated charge capture, automated coding advice, interoffice and intraoffice clinical messaging, multiple note creation options, remote access to the chart, results flow charting, clinical alerts, patient education and disease management.

Creating, handling, filing and copying paper documents, forms and messages invariably involve more steps and time than performing the same functions electronically. Just witness what has happened in banking and the airlines. Paper processes cost more and take longer. Fully implemented EHRs lead toward a "paperless" office, not as a goal but as a byproduct of the benefits they offer.

How EHRs Improve Care

EHRs improve communication, access to data and documentation. This leads to better clinical and service quality.

Clinical quality is improved by having more ready access to all relevant clinical information at the time of the patient encounter or phone call, receipt of clinical alerts at the point of care (e.g., being reminded of a drug interaction or allergy as you're writing a prescription), the ability to easily monitor and analyze patient outcomes, and the ability to easily identify patients who are due for health maintenance or other clinical tests and/or follow-up.

Service quality is improved through direct e-faxing of prescriptions to pharmacies, customized, typed patient education instructions and handouts printed at the point of care and, if desired, even the ability to provide copies of clinical notes to patients and/or consultants at the completion of a patient visit. Your office can be much more responsive to patients on the phone as well. Since the patient chart will be available at the time of the first call, many "we'll pull your chart and call you back later" interactions can be eliminated.

Patient perception of your clinical acumen may benefit as well. One seasoned EHR user I talked to said that he is no smarter now than he was five years ago when he began using an EHR, but his patients sure think so.

Coming improvements in patient service quality include the ability to offer patients secure Internet access to parts of their medical record such as medication lists, problem lists and test results.

How Can I Afford This?

Cost estimates can be hard to pin down. You need to include not just the software vendor's quote, but also the cost of hardware, network upgrades and computer personnel (contracted and/or hired). For a top-of-the-line EHR, plan on an initial investment of $15,000 to $30,000 per physician for software, hardware, implementation and training. But remember, you'll be amortizing that cost over five years or so. Also expect a 15-percent to 18-percent annual software support fee, which covers upgrades and service. In total, expect annual costs of $5,000 to $15,000 over the first five years. That sounds daunting until you look at the savings.

EHRs are expensive, but in talking to numerous users around the country, I learned that if an EHR is implemented well, it will pay for itself through cost reductions and revenue enhancements. It could even make you money or allow you to go home earlier. A friend of mine brags that using an EHR allows him to go home at least 30 minutes earlier than he did in his pre-EHR days, without any reduction in his income. Savings include the following:

- **Reduced transcription costs.** If you currently dictate your notes, you're probably spending $3,600 to $12,000 per year on transcription. Using an EHR typically cuts these costs by 50 percent to 100 percent.
- **Savings in paper-chart-related costs.** Consider how much of your budget for staffing, supplies, copying, printing and storage is devoted to the care and management of charts.
- **Improved staff efficiency.** With an EHR, staff time currently devoted to searching for charts, entering charges manually, etc. can be devoted to value-added activities or eliminated, thereby reducing overtime charges.

Revenue enhancements include increased income through improved coding, improved charge-entry accuracy, and improved provider productivity:

- **Coding.** EHRs improve coding by reducing the common tendency to undercode, because they provide better documentation and typically incorporate an automated coding adviser. This feature alone may pay for the system. In a recent paper, the Central Utah Medical Clinic, a 59-physician predominantly primary care group, documented a substantial overall increase in the appropriate use of 99214 codes for visits that would previously have been coded 99213, approximately one year after implementing an EHR. They went from having 33 percent to having 44 percent of their visits coded 99214. Their reduction in down-coding due to their EHR produced an average billable gain of $26 per patient visit.[2]
- **Charge capture.** Automated charge entry eliminates missed or overlooked charges.
- **Productivity.** With an EHR, provider productivity increases as a result of improved office efficiency. If you eliminate half an hour of paperwork, that's two more patients you could see per day or 30 more minutes you could spend with your family.

But I Don't Want to Change!

It's true: Using an EHR will require some new skills and some changes in your office procedures. You won't pick up everything immediately. But you probably will pick it up quickly. Most experts recommend implementing an EHR incrementally, starting with the functions that change your day-to-day processes the least and moving to the ones that require larger changes (like using note templates) later. Be realistic. You won't go paperless overnight. More likely it will take you a year or two of working with the EHR, and a clear plan, before you'll be able to warehouse or shred all those old cumbersome paper charts and free your chart room for more productive use. Be forewarned: Converting your records from paper to electronic format will require many months of extra time and effort on your part. But the long-term gain will more than justify the short-term pain.

If you're inspired to investigate FHRs, consider talking to anyone in your community who is using one.

1. Institute of Medicine Committee on Improving the Patient Record. The computer-based patient record: an essential technology for health care. Dick RS, Steen EB, eds. Washington, DC: National Academy Press, 1991.

2. Barlow S, Johnson J, Steck J. The economic effect of implementing an EMR in an outpatient clinical setting. *J Healthc Inf Manag.* 2004;18(1):46-51.

There are many reasons for all ambulatory care providers, physician practices in particular, to actively begin (and move to finalize) the process of implementing an EHR system. The task, like any other major improvement initiative, could be viewed as monumental but should not be considered insurmountable. Some of the reasons why physicians have not made the move to EHR systems include:

"It would be too costly and disrupt my practice."

"It would slow me down and force me to spend more time with a computer than with my patients."

"I'm not a 'techie' type who knows how to fiddle with computers and programs."

A 2005 *Medical Economics* survey revealed some useful information[36]:

- The number of primary care physicians who have EHRs (also known as EMRs) is growing fast, but EHR users, at 15%, are still a small minority of all generalists.

- There is no doubt, however, that EHR adoption is growing fast. Of the physicians using an EHR, half have had them for less than two years. Twenty-three percent plan to acquire an EHR within the next 12 months.

- A higher percentage of young physicians are EHR users. Some began using a computerized record on their first day in practice. One physician was quoted as saying, "Since I was going to start a new practice, I thought, 'Why wait to convert later?' I'd rather start it up the way I think it ought to be done."

- To no one's surprise, more physicians in medium-sized and large groups have EHRs. The systems can be very expensive.

Larger practices have deeper pockets and are more likely to have information technology people and administrators who can help the practice implement the system. Yet, despite the "digital divide" between large and small groups, there are signs that small practices are trying to catch up: 60% of soloists with EHRs have bought them within the past two years and 20% of physicians in solo or two-physician practices plan to buy EHRs within the next 12 months.

The Features Physicians Want Most

When asked, physicians who use EHRs are most interested in workflow features, cost, return on investment, and electronic charting. The next most common features are:

- Practice management system interface
- Electronic charge capture
- Electronic prescribing
- Ability to import scans of paper documents
- Messaging systems that allow physicians to exchange patient-related information with their staffs
- Availability of drug reference and formulary data
- Ability to call up lists of patients with specific diagnoses
- Clinical alerts regarding allergies and drug interactions
- Care reminders

Developing an Integrated Electronic Physician Practice

At the beginning of 2004, more than 90% of the physicians in the United States were using paper medical records in their practices.[37] The fact is, EHRs are rapidly becoming a necessity rather than a "nice to have." Current health record systems are capable of integrating both the clinical and business aspects of the practice. Business functionality usually includes:

- Billing and collections
- Scheduling (patient, provider, equipment)
- Productivity
- Revenue analysis

The objective of this "holistic environment" is to:

- Establish a seamless interaction between
  - All offices of the physician practice
  - The systems at affiliated hospitals, clinics, laboratories, and other ancillary services

- Create an up-to-date, accurate, and complete medical record that enables optimum-quality care to be provided regardless of where the patient is treated
- Support the business aspects of the practice to optimize practice efficiencies, effectiveness, and profitability

Electronic Prescribing: An Essential for Prescription Practice Reform

The magnitude of medication adverse events in health care, discussed at length earlier in this chapter, is so enormous that it deserves special attention when planning and implementing an EHR. The effect of electronic prescribing in outpatient settings has not yet been specifically studied, but studies from the inpatient arena show impressive results. Bates and his colleagues[17] found an 88% reduction in serious medication errors and an 81% reduction in all medication errors (excluding missed doses) at Brigham and Women's Hospital in Boston, Mass, after the introduction of a sophisticated computerized order-entry system.

The main problems with electronic prescribing and computerized order-entry systems are the cost and the significant changes in physician workflow. In addition, their effect on errors and cost of care has yet to be fully elucidated in the ambulatory arena. Nonetheless, cost-effectiveness analyses suggest that electronic prescribing can be a good investment for some practices, particularly large ones.[38]

The previously cited Healthvision paper[34] summarized the benefits of an electronic prescribing (e-prescribing) implementation for a 1300-physician, multiple-specialty group, with 300 primary care physicians.

Improving Drug Prescribing in the Ambulatory Environment

Healthvision

From a patient safety perspective, as well as from a cost-savings perspective, improving drug prescribing begins with an understanding of the weaknesses in the current process. . . .

E-prescribing holds the potential to improve many areas of the ambulatory practice. In addition to improving patient safety by reducing upstream adverse drug events (ADEs) and medical errors, e-prescribing reduces costs and can actually help increase practice revenue. These opportunities are a direct result of advanced application logic and workflow improvements, which provide more accurate formulary information and operational efficiencies—which, in turn, result in reduced pharmacy call backs for clarification. Finally, in certain geographic markets, e-prescribing can actually increase practice revenue by using clinical and business logic to align paid incentives between payers and physician groups for the improved use of low-cost generics and more cost-efficient brands.

Improved ambulatory practice productivity and efficiency reduces the cumbersome and frustrating "frictions" involved in the delivery of care to patients. By streamlining the prescribing process, e-prescribing reduces practice overhead and allows resources to refocus on value-producing patient activities. In short, e-prescribing allows physicians and care givers to spend less time on administrative activities and more time working with patients.

. . .

One of the healthcare delivery processes that is in desperate need for improvement is the area of drug prescribing. The current prescribing process is antiquated, inefficient and ripe for reform. It is well known that the rate of drug spending continues to increase at an alarming rate, and prescription errors leading to ADEs are becoming more common.

E-prescribing has established itself as a core healthcare technology to address the inadequacies of the current prescribing process. . . .

. . .

Unavailable patient data can contribute to ADEs when the prescriber does not have ready access to information about the patient's current and previous medication usage, allergy history or lab data. Of course, this data is most important and difficult to find at the point of care.

. . .

Fortunately, e-prescribing holds enormous promise for improving practice efficiencies, particularly in the area of prescription-related messaging.

Within six months of deploying an e-prescribing application at a 15-physician primary care practice in Kokomo, Ind., formulary phone calls dropped from 15 per day to two per day.

Similarly, when Gateway Medical Group in Anaheim, Calif. implemented an intelligent e-prescribing solution, the number of pharmacy call backs due to illegible or non-formulary-compliant prescriptions dropped by more than 90 percent.

. . .

Clearly, then, a thriving physician practice encompasses more than just quality clinical care. A thriving practice employs intelligent e-prescribing solutions to deliver superior clinical care, enable cost-effective business practice and provide vastly improved patient and provider satisfaction through all stages of the process.

. . .

The best e-prescribing solutions include advanced intelligent business and clinical logic to provide effective clinical utility, improved efficiencies and productivity, as well as configurable business logic that aligns payer and provider incentives to maximize the capture of new pay for performance revenue opportunities. . . .

. . .

. . .The analysis focuses on quantifiable return derived from significant improvements in three areas: improved patient safety, lower drug spending and improved efficiencies. . . .

. . .

. . .Other studies [have] shown the value of an e-prescribing solution to be as much as $12,000 per physician per year, based on the total value derived from the solution.

. . .

Although the most difficult to quantify, the first area of value to examine is patient safety. The economic value is derived primarily through the reduction of ADEs. The CITL estimates that electronic prescription writing with drug/drug, drug/allergy and duplicate therapy checking can eliminate more than 2 million ADEs and more than 190,000 hospitalizations. The Academy of Managed Care Pharmacy estimates similar savings, with one of its studies placing the savings at $10,375 per ADE-related hospitalization. . . .

Further evidence of the savings generated by the reduction in ADEs is that many malpractice insurance carriers now offer reductions of between 3 and 7 percent for physicians that use e-prescribing solutions with clinical decision support functions. Although many groups will be able to work with their insurance carriers to realize these savings, the Test Group is self-insured and, therefore, these savings were not used to calculate its ROI.

. . .

. . . the second largest savings after the reduction of ADEs and their associated hospitalization is in reducing medication expenditures.[11] An e-prescribing solution that provides basic business logic tied to formularies and generics has resulted in improvements of up to 12 percent. With intelligent business logic prompting for generic alternatives, Healthvision's e-prescribing solution has resulted in improvements of up to 28 percent.

. . .

. . .There is a potential to generate between three and five times more revenue through programs with other payers.

The final area of demonstrated value from the Healthvision pilot program is in a reduction in time spent managing calls from pharmacies to resolve prescription issues and renewal requests. According to the California HealthCare Foundation report Improving Drug Prescribing Practices in the Outpatient Setting, several studies have been completed by independent, third-party organizations as well as technology vendors that attribute e-prescribing with a reduction in call backs from pharmacies, time saved in the practice and overall improvement in efficiencies. It is estimated that each physician requires between 10 and 13 hours a week for his or her staff to handle call backs from pharmacies.

In the Healthvision pilot, physicians have seen a significant reduction in call backs for prescription issues, such as illegible prescriptions, formulary compliance or drug/drug interaction issues. . . .

. . .

. . . In the Healthvision pilot, the typical physician had between eight and 10 calls per day for renewals. Currently, Healthvision is able to reduce about 30 percent of these calls through its connectivity to pharmacies for electronic renewal messages. The company's connectivity partners estimate that this will be at the 50 percent level by the end of 2004 and in the 75 to 80 percent level by 2005. At the current 30 percent level, the Test Group has an opportunity to reduce approximately 2,033 hours per month, with an annual savings of $558,900. . . .

The potential savings is expected to increase to more than $1 million in the next two years, as additional pharmacies move toward EDI connectivity. . . .

. . . By rolling out Healthvision's intelligent e-prescribing solution, the Test Group positions itself to achieve more than just cost-effective, efficient and higher quality care. It also sets itself to access an ROI that exceeds $4,000 for each of the practice's 300 physicians—a total of more than $1.2 million . . .

Physicians and practice managers should keep these and other studies of ROI in mind when planning to implement e-prescription technology. A prepurchase ROI assessment for the practice should make the budgeting process more accurate and meaningful.

ENDNOTES

1. Weingart SN, Wilson RM, Gibbert RW, et al. Epidemiology of medical error. *BMJ.* 2000;320:774-777.

2. Physician Adoption of Information Technology. 2004 VHA Research Series. Available at: www.vha.com/portal/server.pt/gateway/PTARGS_0_38363_0_0_18/Knowledge%20Directory/VHA.COM/public/research/docs/physician_it.pdf. Accessed February 23, 2006.

3. Audet AM, Doty MM, Peugh J. Information technologies: when will they make it into physicians' black bags? *Medscape General Medicine.* 2004;6(4). Available at: www.medscape.com/viewarticle/493210. Accessed February 23, 2006.

4. Transforming Health Care: The President's Health Information Technology Plan. 2004. President George W. Bush, State of the Union Address, January 2004. Available at www.whitehouse.gov/infocus/technology/economic_policy200404/chap3.html. Accessed October 17, 2006.

5. Kuperman GJ, Teich JM, Tanasijevic MJ, et al. Improving response to critical laboratory results with automation: results of a randomized controlled trial. *J Am Med Inform Assoc.* 1999;6:512-522.

6. Sittig DF, Stead WW. Computer-based physician order entry: the state of the art. *J Am Med Inform Assoc.* 1994;1:108-123.

7. Classen DC, Pestotnik SL, Evans RS, Burke JP. Computerized surveillance of adverse drug events in hospital patients [published erratum appears in *JAMA.* 1992;267:1922]. *JAMA.* 1991;266: 2847-2851.

8. Durieux P. Electronic medical alerts—so simple, so complex. *N Engl J Med.* 2005;352:1034-1036.

9. Bates DW, Leape LL, Cullen DJ, et al. Effect of computerized physician order entry and a team intervention on prevention of serious medication errors. *JAMA.* 1998;280:1311-1316.

10. Bates DW, Miller EB, Cullen DJ, et al. Patient risk factors for adverse drug events in hospitalized patients. *Arch Intern Med.* 1999;159:2553-2560.

11. Keenan CR, Adubofour K, Daftary AV. Reducing medical errors in primary care. *Patient Care.* 2003;37:28-36. Reprinted with permission.

12. Lazarou J, Operand BH, Corey PN. Incidence of adverse drug reactions in hospitalized patients: a meta-analysis of prospective studies. *JAMA.* 1998;279:1200-1205.

13. Gurwitz JH, Field TS, Harrold LR, et al. Incidence and preventability of adverse drug events among older persons in the ambulatory setting. *JAMA.* 2003;289:1107-1116.

14. Gandhi TK, Weingart SN, Borus J, et al. Adverse drug events in ambulatory care. *N Engl J Med.* 2003;348:1556-1564.

15. Gurwitz JH, Field TS, Judge J, et al. The incidence of adverse drug events in two large academic long-term care facilities. *Am J Med.* 2005;3:251-258.

16. Leape LL. Error in medicine. *JAMA.* 1994;272:1852-1857. Reprinted with permission.

17. Bates DW, Teich JM, Lee J, et al. The impact of computerized physician order entry on medication error prevention. *JAMA.* 1999; 6:313-321.

18. Bebout KL. Safely prescribing take-home medications for ambulatory care patients. *P&T News,* University of Iowa Hospitals and Clinics. August 2004. Available at: www.healthcare.uiowa.edu/ pharmacy/PTNews/2004/august.html. Accessed March 23, 2006.

19. Improving the quality of geriatric pharmacology. American Medical Association Council on Scientific Affairs, June 2002. Available at: www.ama-assn.org/ama/pub/category/ print/13592.html. Accessed May 23, 2006. Reprinted with permission.

20. Lazarou J, Pomeranz BH, Corey PN. Incidence of adverse drug reactions in hospitalized patients: a meta-analysis of prospective studies. *JAMA.* 1998;279:1200-1205.

21. Beers MH, Ouslander JG, Rollingher I, Reuben DB, Brooks J, Beck JC. Explicit criteria for determining inappropriate medication use in nursing home residents. UCLA Division of Geriatric Medicine. *Arch Intern Med.* 1991;151:1825-1832.

22. Beers MH. Explicit criteria for determining potentially inappropriate medication use by the elderly: an update. *Arch Intern Med.* 1997;157:1531-1536.

23. Fick DM, Cooper JW, Wade WE. Updating the Beers criteria for potentially inappropriate medication use in older adults. *Arch Intern Med.* 2003;163:2716-2724. Available at: http://archinte.ama -assn.org/cgi/content/full/163/22/2716. Accessed May 22, 2006.

24. Hanlon JT, Schmader KE, Boult C, et al. Use of inappropriate prescription drugs by older people. *J Am Geriatr Soc.* 2002;50:26-34.

25. Graves T, Hanlon JT, Schmader KE, et al. Adverse events after discontinuing medications in elderly outpatients. *Arch Intern Med.* 1997;157:2205-2210.

26. Forster AJ, Murff HJ, Peterson JF, et al. The incidence and severity of adverse events affecting patients after discharge from the hospital. *Ann Intern Med.* 2003;138:161-167.

27. Lipton HL, Bird JA, Bero LA, et al. Assessing the appropriateness of physician prescribing for geriatric outpatients: development and testing of an instrument. *J Pharm Technol.* 1993;9:107-113.

28. Lipton HL, Bero LA, Bird JA, McPhee SJ. The impact of clinical pharmacists' consultations on physicians' geriatric drug prescribing: a randomized controlled trial. *Med Care.* 1992;30:646-658.

29. Zhan C, Sangl J, Bierman AS, et al. Potentially inappropriate medication use in the community dwelling elderly. *JAMA.* 2001;286:2823-2829.

30. Poon EG, Gandhi TK, Sequist TD, et al. "I wish I had seen this test result earlier": dissatisfaction with test result management systems in primary care. *Arch Intern Med.* 2004;164:2223-2228.

31. Boohaker EA, Ward RE, Uman JE, et al. Patient notification and follow-up of abnormal test results: a physician survey. *Arch Intern Med.* 1996;156:327-331.

32. Bourgeut C, Gilchrist V, McCord G. The consultation and referral process: a report from NEON. Northeastern Ohio Network Research Group. *J Fam Pract.* 1998;46:47-53.

33. EHR vs CPR vs EMR. Healthcare Informatics Online. Available at: www.providersedge.com/ehdocs/ehr_articles/EHR_vs_CPR_vs_EMR.pdf. Accessed March 2005.

34. Improving drug prescribing in the ambulatory environment. Healthvision. Available at: www.healthvision.com/solutions/physicians/erx/er_physician.pdf. Accessed March 2005. Reprinted with permission.

35. Adler KA. Why it's time to purchase an electronic health record system. *Fam Pract Manag.* 2004;11(10):43-46. Available at: www.aafp.org/fpm/20041100/43whyi.html. Accessed June 19, 2005. Reprinted with permission.

36. Terry K. Exclusive survey: doctors and EHRs. *Med Econ.* Jan 21, 2005. Available at: www.memag.com/memag/article/articleDetail.jsp?id=143144. Accessed March 2005.

37. Electronic health records overview: an integrated electronic physician practice. Available at: www.providersedge.com/ehr_overview.htm. Accessed March 2005.

38. Institute of Medicine. Key capabilities of an electronic health record system. July 2003. Available at: www.providersedge.com/ehdocs/ehr_articles/Key_Capabilities_of_an_EHR_System.pdf. Accessed May 22, 2006.

chapter 5

Business Models

Do we need to make a business case for patient safety? The short answer is no. Few would argue that patient safety is not a worthwhile goal, and, of course, ensuring that medical errors do not occur is the right thing to do. However, for many reasons, not the least of which is budgeting for the significant expenditures in technology that were previously discussed, efforts should be made to show the financial, as well as clinical, impact of providing safer care. Vance and Wilson[1] suggested that, intuitively, it would seem that improving patient safety should add significant costs to the operation of a health care enterprise. However, whether it be a hospital system or a single physician office, there are limited data demonstrating financial returns. Furthermore, funding sources to support these efforts are limited.

There are three goals of this chapter:

- Recap the financial impact of medical adverse events and errors
- Examine return on investment (ROI) analysis of electronic health record (EHR) systems for ambulatory medical practices
- Review pay-for-performance initiatives (See Appendix D.)

It is hoped that physicians and other ambulatory care providers will find useful information that can be applied to their own practices and organizations.

UNNECESSARY ANTIBIOTICS

Null and colleagues,[2] through a review of medical peer-review journals and government health statistics, discovered some disturbing information (statistics based on annual rates):

- 2.2 million people had in-hospital adverse drug reactions to prescribed medications
- 20 million unnecessary antibiotics were prescribed for viral infections
- Tens of millions of unnecessary antibiotics were prescribed
- 7.5 million unnecessary medical and surgical procedures were performed

■ 8.9 million people were exposed to unnecessary hospitalization
■ Comparative death rates (annual):
  • Iatrogenic (summarized in the following table), 783,936
  • Heart disease, 699,697
  • Cancer, 553,251

The following table summarizes potential annual physical and economic costs of medical errors.

Condition	Deaths	Estimated Cost (in Billions)
Adverse drug reactions	106,000	$12
Medical error	98,000	$2
Decubitus ulcers	115,000	$55
Infection	88,000	$5
Malnutrition	108,800	
Outpatients	199,000	$77
Unnecessary procedures	37,136	$122
Surgery, related	32,000	$9
Potential total	**783,936**	**$482**
Adverse drug reaction/medication error	20,000	$200
Revised total	**999,936**	

Source: Adapted from Null et al.[2]

There also are public relations considerations on both community and personal levels. The news media continues to make the public keenly aware of patient safety and medical error issues. For instance, a widely publicized report by The Commonwealth Fund said one fifth of adults surveyed, or 22.8 million people, reported they or a family member had experienced a medical error of some kind; of these, an estimated 8.1 million households reported experiencing a medical "error that became a serious problem."[3]

MEDICAL COMPLICATIONS

Although medical injuries are recognized as a major hazard in the health care system, little is known about their impact. Excess length of stay, charges, and deaths attributable to medical injuries during hospitalization were assessed in a study that used the Agency for Healthcare Research and Quality (AHRQ) Patient Safety Indicators (PSIs) to identify medical injuries in 7.45 million hospital discharge abstracts from 994 acute-care hospitals across 28 states in 2000 in the AHRQ Healthcare Cost and Utilization Project Nationwide Inpatient Sample database.[4] The findings revealed that:

- Excess length of stay attributable to medical injuries ranged from 0 days for injury to a neonate to 10.89 days for postoperative sepsis.
- Excess charges ranged from $0 for obstetric trauma (without vaginal instrumentation) to $57,727 for postoperative sepsis.
- Excess mortality ranged from 0% for obstetric trauma to 21.96% for postoperative sepsis.
- Postoperative wound dehiscence was the second most serious event, with 9.42 extra days in the hospital, $40,323 in excess charges, and 9.63% attributable mortality.
- Infection due to medical care was associated with 9.58 extra days, $38,656 in excess charges, and 4.31% attributable mortality.

The authors concluded that often-preventable complications contributed to more than 2.4 million extra days in the hospital, 32,000 US hospital deaths, and more than $9 billion in extra costs each year, but that the effect of such injuries was highly variable. The findings greatly underestimated the problem because many other complications occur that are not listed in hospital administrative data. Many of the 18 complications, including medical objects left in the operative site after surgery, were preventable medical errors. Others, like postoperative bleeding, might not always be avoidable. The figures could not capture all complication-related costs. For example, trauma during a normal vaginal delivery without use of forceps or other instruments (51,223 such injuries were studied) resulted in virtually no extra hospitalization costs or deaths but likely led to other complications in mothers or their infants. The study could not answer whether progress had been made since the 1999 Institute of Medicine report.[5]

In an editorial accompanying the article by Zhan et al, Weingart and Iezzoni[6] of Harvard's Beth Israel Deaconess Medical Center state, "Given their staggering magnitude, these estimates are clearly sobering."

Another study designed to examine the effect of safety initiatives on clinical and financial outcomes[7] showed that hospitals with the highest compliance to recommended protocols for coronary artery bypass grafting (CABG) had fewer potentially preventable adverse events (identified by means of AHRQ PSIs), lower risk-adjusted mortality rates, and lower excess variable costs per case. The year-long study, involving 134 hospitals and more than 40,000 patients, examined the effectiveness of care using widely accepted protocols (ie, use of aspirin, β-blockers, and an internal mammary grafting procedure) and their relationship to patient safety and costs. The findings showed variance in compliance with the protocols of as much as 22% between top-and-bottom quintile (ie, 20% increments) hospitals. For example, β-blockers were used 97.9% of the time in the top-quintile hospitals and 75.1% for the bottom quintile. The top quintile also had a 14% difference in risk-adjusted mortality (2.4% vs 2.8%). Variable costs per case for hospitals in the bottom quintile of compliance with indicators were 18% higher (about $2400) than costs incurred by the top performers. The study also found that adverse events led to excess variable costs per case of $15,620 and an additional per-case length of stay of 9.2 days. Four percent of all patients undergoing CABG were found to have one or more potentially preventable adverse events by means of the AHRQ-identified PSIs.

Additional conclusions were made. There was no correlation between hospital volume of CABG procedures and observed patient safety indicators, although hospitals that performed fewer than 200 procedures had much wider variances in performance. There was a correlation between surgeon volume and adverse events, which is consistent with current literature. Study results supported the protocols recommended by AHRQ, the Joint Commission on Accreditation of Healthcare Organizations (JCAHO), National Quality Forum, and others. They demonstrated that quality and effective care is safer and costs less. In addition, AHRQ's PSIs are a meaningful and useful starting point to screen for potential problems that may lead to further investigation and for implementation of corrective measures, when appropriate, to improve patient safety.

The AHRQ PSIs provide information on potential in-hospital complications and adverse events following surgeries, procedures, and childbirth, using readily available inpatient administrative data and based on:

■ A comprehensive literature review
■ Analysis of International Classification of Diseases, Ninth Revision, Clinical Modification codes
■ Review by a clinician panel
■ Implementation of risk adjustment
■ Empirical analyses

The complete contents of the AHRQ PSIs are reproduced in Appendix O.

ELECTRONIC HEALTH RECORD SYSTEMS

Enormous waste and costs are generated from medical errors, many of which are preventable. It is imperative to implement system support and solutions for improved patient safety. One of the most effective ways to do this is for physician practices to adopt electronic health record (EHR) systems. The ROI information that follows must consider the current adverse financial impact of maintaining the status quo.

In a 2004 interview, Dr Mark Leavitt[8] (medical director and ambulatory care director for the Healthcare Information and Management Systems Society) gave several reasons why physicians are slow to adopt EHRs:

- Physicians are so busy that they avoid information technology systems that slow them down.

- EHRs may be economically valuable for hospitals, health maintenance organizations, and health plans, but physicians are reluctant and often unable to capitalize on EHR installation.

- Physicians are not paid for quality, reducing errors, and enhancing safety.

- Physicians are paid for volume: numbers of procedures and office visits, be they of high or low quality. There is no incentive to do the right thing.

- The main benefits of EHRs flow to health plans, patients, and those who study health care (ie, those who want digital data on what is really going on in the physician's office).

How can EHRs be brought into the fragmented physician market, with 60% practicing in groups of six or fewer? Leavitt stressed the importance of understanding the four *Cs*:

- **Costs:** System costs must be more affordable. There has been good progress with driving down hardware costs while ramping up performance, but the cost of software remains a problem.

- **Culture:** In this context, *culture* refers to physician mindset. They are not technophobes; their cars are loaded with high-tech gadgets and they use high-tech equipment in their offices. Another cultural obstacle is that many physicians feel they need to spend most of their time with patients. Physicians never step back and ask how they can make their practices more efficient.

- **Connectivity:** Physicians do not work in a vacuum. They need connectivity for EHRs to work. A successful EHR must import information from other physicians and other care settings and send information back out electronically. Unfortunately, connectivity is not within the physician's control. Despite the price paid for an EHR, without cooperation it will not retrieve test results from a laboratory or send admitting information to the hospital.

- **Community:** Physicians were trained to try to solve problems one at a time, by themselves. In today's complex world they must act in concert. For instance, specialty societies could follow the example of the American Academy of Family Physicians, which is working with their nearly 100,000 members to act with one voice, drive down the price, and enhance standards.

Other considerations in choosing a medication-safety system include[9]:

- **Compliance:** Determine whether the system will address compliance with issues such as the JCAHO National Patient Safety Goals.
- **Compatibility:** Determine whether the system will integrate successfully with existing systems.
- **Prioritizing error-prevention strategies:** Analyze where most errors occur, and then decide where to focus error-prevention resources.
- **Ease of use:** Analyze training requirements and consider disruption of office routines.
- **Implementation costs:** Consider software, hardware, training, licensing, and other ongoing costs
- **Nonimplementation costs:** Consider potential legal liability.

For larger organizations, the considerations include:

- **Acceptance:** Develop a communication and training plan to ensure acceptance of implementing the technology across the organization. Implementation must be concurrent with, or after the development of, a nonblaming, nonpunitive culture that encourages error reporting.
- **Executive buy-in:** Secure buy-in from senior management. Hospital leadership must be 100% in favor of implementation. This support should be promoted and communicated throughout the organization.

INFORMATION TECHNOLOGY: RETURN ON INVESTMENT: HOW LONG AND HOW MUCH?

In the ideal world, all physicians would be using EHRs, records could be easily transferred, and automatic guidelines would prevent errors and promote safety. However, until computerization can also do something for the physician pocketbook, there will be a less than optimal rate of progression toward paperless medical records. It is argued that the ROI is not good enough, but it must be understood that an EHR investment provides both tangible and intangible benefits. Tangible benefits include:

- Fewer costly medication errors
- Increased staff satisfaction
- Positive identification of patients
- Increased communication among caregivers
- Improved safety in the use of high-alert medications

The implementation of an EHR may allow also the elimination of transcription costs. Even a solo physician who dictates, with average costs of about $10,000 to $15,000 a year, can see a payback in three years. The returns can be seen even sooner in larger groups, as described in the next section.

Intangible benefits include public perception of the organization's commitment to safety, word-of-mouth value from former patients, and patient satisfaction.

When planning to implement an EHR system, much more goes into the decision than a straight ROI calculation. It impossible to just "dig in" and find a completely fact-based ROI calculation. An ROI calculation should include intuitive judgments, doing the right thing for the patient: the right patient, the right diagnosis, the right place, the right time, and the right reason.

What is the current state of EHR ROI in small to medium-sized physician offices? A review of the ROI literature for EHRs revealed that because of the lack of current widespread adoption of EHRs in small to medium-sized practices, only specific case studies of EHR implementations currently exist.[10] Accurate estimations of average state or national ROIs that can be generalized to a population of physician offices are not yet available. The reasons are summarized in Table 5-1.

Tables 5-2 and 5-3 provide some insight into how long it is taking to achieve a positive ROI. As to what is working, the analysis of a wide range of case studies found that ROI can be maximized if common barriers and benefits are addressed at the onset of EHR implementation. Key success factors for physician practices that have realized a qualitative and quantitative ROI from EHR implementation include:

- Champion for EHR implementation identified at the onset
- Physicians in the practice committed to EHR implementation at the onset
- Maximized electronic data exchange with laboratories and vendors

T A B L E   5-1

Variations in ROI

Reasons for Variation	Specific Variations
Variations in the determinate variables for ROI for EHRs may explain the wide variations in ROIs realized by smaller physician practices that have implemented EHRs.	■ Physician support of EHR implementation ■ EHR implementation support ■ Office activities and expenditures (eg, office square footage, staffing hours, patient volume, and physician numbers) ■ EHR software and data management ■ EHR component selection, implementation, and use (the broad spectrum of EHR components offer a varied ROI when selected in different combinations)
It is only recently that physicians in smaller practices have begun implementing EHRs and exploring variables that directly impact ROI.	■ Issues with patient privacy ■ Lack of compatibility of EHR systems with private and government insurance reimbursement systems ■ The current absence of national interoperability of EHR applications ■ EHR needs generally not yet compatible with office workflow design

Adapted from Current Return on Investment (ROI) Literature for EHRs in Small to Medium-Sized Physician Offices. Available at: www.providersedge.com/ehdocs/ehr_articles/Current_ROI_Literature _for_EHRs_in_Small_to_Medium-Sized_Physician_Practices.pdf. Accessed February 24, 2006.

■ Established comprehensive EHR support at the onset

■ Identified specific improvement opportunities for the EHR system

■ Assisted in EHR vendor selection and focused the EHR implementation efforts

■ Complete conversion to a paperless system from onset

Establishing an ROI for technology support to reduce medical errors is both a science and an art.[2] Even without the mounting pressure from the JCAHO, the Institute of Medicine (IOM), and purchaser consortiums such as the Leapfrog Group to employ patient-safety information technology, health care is feeling the palpable rising public expectations as more people employ technology in other aspects of their lives outside of health care. More and more patients also are learning about advances in health care technology that may not be available in their communities. As a result, some organizations may soon need to catch up to their competitors to retain their patients.

To explore the ROI for EHR programs, providers should approach them like any other investment, using the concepts,

T A B L E   5-2

EHR ROI per Physician: Five-Year Implementation Period

ROI	Year 1	Year 2	Year 3	Year 4	Year 5
Average	−$21,700	$21,200	$14,600	$47,200	$47,200
Minimum	−$11,900	$8,000	$4,700	$20,100	$20,100
Maximum	−$26,600	$41,300	$31,400	$85,100	$85,100

Adapted from Current Return on Investment (ROI) Literature for EHRs in Small to Medium-Sized Physician Offices. Available at: www.providersedge.com/ehdocs/ehr_articles/Current_ROI_Literature _for_EHRs_in_Small_to_Medium-Sized_Physician_Practices.pdf. Accessed February 24, 2006.

T A B L E   5-3

Five-Year ROI per Physician Based on the Scope of EHR Features

Feature	Light EHR	Medium EHR	Full EHR
Online patient charts	X	X	X
Electronic prescribing		X	X
Laboratory ordering			X
Radiology ordering		X	
Electronic charge capturing		X	
Average ROI	−$18,200*	$44,600*	$86,400*

Adapted from Current Return on Investment (ROI) Literature for EHRs in Small to Medium-Sized Physician Offices. Available at: www.providersedge.com/ehdocs/ehr_articles/Current_ROI_Literature _for_EHRs_in_Small_to_Medium-Sized_Physician_Practices.pdf. Accessed February 24, 2006.
*Assuming a 5% discount rate.

tools, and language of finance in the planning process. Even though the process starts with the volume and cost of medical errors, it is ultimately tied to the organization's mission and future survival. Projected return from an EHR should be based on intangible benefits to the organization as well as an ROI calculation. Some of the costs that go into an ROI calculation on technology implementation for patient safety information are reimbursed, but in the long term, higher-quality care and reduced costs, regardless of whether reimbursed, should result in a more efficient, safer, and profitable provider organization. Higher quality and efficiency can put those organizations in a better future bargaining position with payers compared with other organizations and also can enhance patient loyalty and employee satisfaction. Kinninger[9] cited a comment made by John Byrnes, MD, Spectrum Health's corporate vice president of quality: "I think the 1999 IOM report raised awareness to the point where patient safety became more of a have-to item rather than one of those issues where we have to argue the [return on technology]." The decision to invest in an EHR system should take into account not only implementation costs but also

reduced costs for treating complications resulting from medication errors and potential liability. Investment in EHR systems
can be justified in terms of risk management and legal liability.

However, ROI is not the only barrier. There are deeper issues
related to physician core values to satisfy a hierarchy of personal
and professional needs. Every physician would like provide the
best, most efficient, safe, coordinated care tempered with the
reality that every physician also has constraints (time, money,
energy) that limit the personal time one can give to that cause.
This will likely remain a catch-22 until technology investment
delivers a real ROI to the individual physician and/or the
investment is shared by other stakeholders. Technology can
eliminate medical errors, but not in a vacuum. A medical error
is a culmination of events between technology and human
beings. Technology cannot fix an error based on human judgment. Until the information-delivery process is redesigned,
technology alone cannot eliminate medical errors. Although
there is no government or payer mandate to implement patient-
safety information technology systems, it is likely that such systems eventually will become part of the cost of doing business
in health care.

THE BASICS OF PAYING FOR PERFORMANCE

The third aspect of the business case for patient safety to be covered in this chapter is the evolving movement toward providing
physicians, and hospitals, greater financial incentives for improving the quality and safety of patient care.

The AMA believes that PFP programs, to be effective, fair, and
ethical, must do the following:

- **Ensure quality of care.** Fair and ethical PFP programs are
  committed to improved patient care as their most important
  mission. The programs use evidence-based quality of care
  measures created by physicians across appropriate specialties.
  Variations in an individual patient care regimen are permitted
  based on a physician's sound clinical judgment and should
  not adversely affect PFP program rewards.

- **Foster the relationship between patient and physician.** Fair
  and ethical PFP programs support the patient/physician relationship and overcome obstacles to physicians treating
  patients, regardless of patients' health conditions, ethnicity,
  economic circumstances, demographics, or treatment compliance patterns.

- **Offer voluntary physician participation.** Fair and ethical PFP
  programs offer voluntary physician participation, and do not

undermine the economic viability of nonparticipating physician practices. These programs support participation by physicians in all practice settings by minimizing potential financial and technological barriers including costs of start-up.

■ **Use accurate data and fair reporting.** Fair and ethical PFP programs use accurate data and scientifically valid analytical methods. Physicians are allowed to review, comment, and appeal results prior to the use of the results for programmatic reasons and any type of reporting.

■ **Provide fair and equitable program incentives.** Fair and ethical PFP programs provide new funds for positive incentives to physicians for their participation, progressive quality improvement, or attainment of goals within the program.

Source: American Medical Association. Policy H-450.947, Pay-for-Performance Principles and Guidelines. http://www.ama-assn.org/apps/pf_new/pf_online?f_n=resultLink&doc=policyfiles/HnE/H-450.947.HTM&s_t=H-450.947&catg=AMA/HnE&catg=AMA/BnGnC&catg=AMA/DIR&&nth=1&&st_p=0&nth=1&Accessed June 11, 2007

The JCAHO Web site features a document titled "Principles for the Construct of Pay-for-Performance Programs."[11] Following is JCAHO's take on PFP:

. . . pay-for-performance programs are operating in a complex reimbursement environment that often creates—by omission or commission—barriers to reaching the goal of consistent, high quality care for all patients. For example, payment systems frequently do not recognize the nuances of care delivery, nor do they always pay fairly for important aspects of care, such as activities that support patient education, continuity of care, or integration of services. . . . Alignment of payment policies to support the provision of safe, high quality care is a complex undertaking. Such policies and programs must be credible, must minimize unintended negative consequences, and most importantly, must be transparent and attentive to ethical considerations. It is important to recognize as well that non-financial incentives can also drive positive behavior changes.

Notwithstanding their recent proliferation, pay-for-performance programs are largely untested. It is important that these programs be well-designed, make every effort to encompass all affected stakeholders for whom the incentives must be aligned, and be designed and implemented in a manner that engenders, maintains, and continually promotes trust among all of the participating parties. Just as important, the broad-scale implementation and success of these programs must necessarily rest upon the timely creation and deployment of an electronic health infrastructure that facilitates the collection, transmittal, and analyses of the performance data that will drive these programs. . . .

Alignment of payment program incentives to support the provision of safe, high quality care is a complex undertaking, for it must simultaneously achieve fair reimbursement for necessary services; promote desired behavior change; and avoid unintended consequences. In the end, new payment policies and programs must work to the advantage of the patient and support the provision of patient-centered care.

. . . the following principles are offered to guide the development and refinement of current and future pay-for-performance programs.

Principles

A. The goal of pay-for-performance programs should be to align reimbursement with the practice of high quality, safe health care for all consumers.
    - Payment systems should recognize the cost of providing care in accordance with accepted standards of practice and should guard against any incentives that could undermine the provision of safe, high quality care.
    - Reward programs should encourage qualified clinical staff to accept patients where complexity, risk, or severity of illness may be considerations.
    - Performance incentives should be aligned with professional responsibility and control.

B. Programs should include a mix of financial and non-financial incentives (such as differential intensity of oversight; reduction of administrative and regulatory burdens; public acknowledgment of performance) that are designed to achieve program goals.
    - The type and magnitude of incentives should be tailored to the desired behavior changes. Rewards should be great enough to drive desired behaviors and support consistently high quality care.
    - A sliding scale of rewards should be established to allow for recognition of gradations in quality of care, including service delivery.
    - The reward structure should take into account the unique characteristics of a provider organization's mission.

C. When selecting the areas of clinical focus, programs should strongly consider consistency with national and regional efforts in order to leverage change and reduce conflicting or competing measurement. It is also important to attend to clinical areas that show significant promise for achieving improvements because they represent areas where unwarranted differences in performance have been documented.

D. Programs should be designed to ensure that metrics upon which incentive payments are based are credible, valid and reliable.
    - Quality-related program goals should be transparent, explicit and measurable.
    - Metrics should be evidence-based or, in the absence of strong science, be based on expert consensus.
    - Metrics should also be standardized, be risk-adjusted where appropriate, and have broad acceptance in the provider and professional communities.
    - Credible and affordable mechanisms to audit data and verify performance must be developed and implemented.
    - The measurement set should be constructed to fulfill program objectives with the minimum amount of measurement burden needed.

E. Programs must be designed to acknowledge the united approach necessary to effect significant change, and the reality that the provision of safe, high quality care is a shared responsibility between provider organizations and health care professionals.

- Incentive payments should recognize systemic drivers of quality in units broader than individual provider organizations and practitioner groups and encourage improvement at these aggregate levels.
- Incentive programs should support team approaches to the provision of health care, as well as integration of services, overall management of disease, and continuity of care.
- Incentive programs should encourage strong alignment between practitioner and provider organization goals, while also recognizing and rewarding the respective contributions of each to overall performance.

F. The measurement and reward framework should be strategically designed to permit and facilitate broad-scale behavior change and achievement of performance goals within targeted time periods. To accomplish this, providers and practitioners should receive timely feedback about their performance and be provided the opportunity for dialogue when appropriate. Rewards should follow closely upon the achievement of performance.

G. Programs should reward accreditation, or have an equivalent mechanism that recognizes health care organizations' continuous attention to all clinical and support systems and processes that relate to patient safety and health care quality.

H. Incentive programs should support an interconnected health care system and the implementation of "interoperable" standards for collecting, transmitting and reporting information.

I. Programs should incorporate periodic, objective assessment into their structure. The evaluations should include the system of payment and incentives built into the program design, in order to evaluate its effects on achieving improvements in quality, including any unintended consequences. The program and, where appropriate, its performance thresholds should be re-adjusted as necessary.

J. Provisions should be made to invest in sub-threshold performers who are committed to improvement and are willing to work themselves or with assistance to develop and carry out improvement plans. Such investments should be made after considering both the potential for realistic gains in improvement relative to the amount of resources necessary to achieve that promise, and what is a reasonable timeframe for achieving program performance goals.

ENDNOTES

1. Vance JE, Wilson N. Outlining the business case for patient safety. In: Youngberg BJ, Hatlie M, eds. *The Patient Safety Handbook.* Sudbury, Mass: Jones & Bartlett Publishers; 2004:436-474.

2. Null G, Dean C, Feldman M, Rasio D, Smith D. Death by medicine. Available at: www.mercola.com/2003/nov/26/death_by _medicine.htm. Accessed February 24, 2006.

3. Davis K, Schoenbaum SC, Collins KS, Tenney K, Hughes DL, Audet AJ. *Room for Improvement: Patients Report on the Quality of Their Health Care.* New York, NY: Commonwealth Fund; April 2002:7.

4. Zhan C, Miller MR. Excess length of stay, charges, and mortality attributable to medical injuries during hospitalization. *JAMA.* 2003;290:1868-1874.

5. Kohn LT, Corrigan JM, Donaldson MS, eds. *To Err Is Human: Building a Safer Health System.* Washington, DC: Institute of Medicine; 1999.

6. Weingart SN, Iezzoni LI. Looking for medical injuries where the light is bright. *JAMA.* 2003;290:1817.

7. Premier study indicates compliance with CABG protocols improves outcomes, reduces cost. Presented at: Sixth Annual National Patient Safety Foundation Congress. Available at: www.premierinc.com/all/safety/publications/05-04_full _txt.htm#Premier. Accessed February 24, 2006.

8. Reece RL. The four Cs of physician EMR adoption. *HealthLeaders News.* May 19, 2004. Available at: www.healthleadersmedia.com/ view_feature.cfm?content_id=54770. Accessed February 24, 2006.

9. Kinninger T. Establishing ROI for technology to reduce medication errors is both a science and an art—the business case for medica-tion safety—return on investment. Healthcare Financial Management, February 2003. Available at: www.findarticles.com/ cf_dls/m3257/2_57/97786236/print.jhtml. Accessed February 24, 2006.

10. Current Return on Investment (ROI) Literature for EHRs in Small to Medium-Sized Physician Offices. Available at: www.providersedge .com/ehdocs/ehr_articles/Current_ROI_Literature_for_EHRs_in _Small_to_Medium-Sized_Physician_Practices.pdf. Accessed February 24, 2006.

11. Principles for the construct of pay-for-performance programs. Available at: www.jcaho.org/about+us/public+policy+initiatives/ pay_for_performance.htm. Accessed February 24, 2005. Reprinted with permission.

chapter 6

Case Studies

The following case studies provide excellent insight into innovative patient safety initiatives in several large provider groups in the state of Washington.

CASE STUDY I: THE EVERETT CLINIC[1]

The Everett Clinic, based in Everett, Washington, has 1200 employees, including more than 210 physicians and other providers. The stated "core values" of The Everett Clinic include "doing what is right for each patient." Influenced by *To Err is Human* and subsequent discussions about patient safety throughout the country, in 2001 the clinic's leadership decided that, based on those core values, the clinic needed to take specific steps to address safety issues. The clinic strives to be a highly reliable organization; its leaders recognized that other such organizations were now talking about safety separately from quality.

Richard J. Rafoth, MD, gastroenterologist and associate medical director for quality, is leading the effort to change the culture of The Everett Clinic to emphasize safety. Taking a page from the Federal Aviation Administration/airline model, employees, including physicians, are encouraged to report problems for the purpose of making care safer, without fear of penalty or backlash. "It's everybody's responsibility to report," said Dr Rafoth. The clinic has developed a simple intranet-based reporting system that takes an employee no more than 30 seconds to access and type in a three to four-line report about what he or she has observed. "We needed an easy way to report," said Dr Rafoth. He tracks, analyzes and follows up on these messages, makes changes, and reports back to the employee if requested to do so.

The clinic set up meetings with groups of employees, from small groups of 1-2 people to larger groups of 15-20, to let them know that reporting is regarded as a positive step because it can lead to safer care. The clinic stressed how important it was for all employees to tell what they know when things are not going right. It delivered the same messages in articles in its employee newsletter. The clinic board of directors revised a clinic policy to make it explicit that unless an employee is under the influence of controlled substances or engaged in illegal activity, the reports cannot be used against them. It publicized the policy revision and persuaded the human resource department that the policy is a wise one. "It removes the fear factor," said Dr Rafoth. "But there's a certain level of paranoia in all organizations and also the attitude that 'you want us to rat on our fellow employees.'" Building a track record month by month is helping change attitudes.

The reports come under the clinic's state-qualified quality improvement program—legislation to create the program was supported by the WSMA—and are not discoverable. Dr Rafoth has received reports on late radiology reports, lab values sent to the wrong place, the improper filling out of data sheets, and interpreters not showing up for scheduled appointments. He recently received a report from a float nurse who wrote that the sharps container on the back of a door was a potential hazard (a person almost got stuck). The clinic moved the container. More than 90% of the concerns raised are systems issues, he noted. "They're about the way we do our work." He and a quality improvement employee read the reports and decide which department should address them. If it is a "medications" issue, it goes to one of the clinical pharmacists. The pharmacists have the authority to work with physicians to improve processes.

In the second quarter of 2003, Dr Rafoth received seven reports. In the first quarter of 2004, he received 131. His goal is to have 600-700 reports per quarter. He is beginning to analyze the reports for clusters or patterns of problems. Over the next three to five years, he expects the clinic's malpractice exposure to decrease. "If I'm successful, it has to," he said. "It really is about changing the culture. You say the same message over and over and then you walk the talk."

CASE STUDY II: VIRGINIA MASON MEDICAL CENTER[1]

The Virginia Mason Clinic has 5000 staff members and more than 365 physicians.

Some three years ago Virginia Mason Medical Center (VMMC) embraced the management philosophy of "lean thinking," pioneered and applied by Toyota in its production system. Michael G. Glenn, MD, chief of surgery at VMMC and a member of the Washington State Patient Safety Coalition, explained that lean thinking is fundamentally about eliminating waste and improving quality. "We think that when we eliminate waste we make patient care safer," he said.

In one operational aspect of lean thinking, the medical center runs frequent week-long "rapid process improvement workshops," attended by physicians, other staff, and in some cases, patients who offer their perspective. One of the goals in every workshop is the reduction or elimination of defects. Workshop participants focus on developing "standard work," ie, a detailed description of the safest, most efficient, and most reproducible way to perform a given task. During the week of the workshop, the group attempts to simultaneously carry out improvements. Groups often shorten or simplify complex processes that result in a simpler and safer system of care delivery. To ensure that employees engage in such "change" work, the medical center has promised that employees will not "improve" themselves out of a job. When processes are simplified, "it becomes more obvious when problems or mistakes do occur, and they are easier to correct in real time, before they become 'defects,'" said Dr Glenn. He and others involved in the workshops are working to extend improvements made via the workshops to all medical center departments. Ultimately, every aspect of the hospital and clinic's processes will be evaluated through the prism of lean thinking.

The medical center leadership believes that care must be safe 100% of the time. That does not mean that mistakes do not happen. It does mean "you don't send something along the [production] line until it's fixed," said Dr Glenn. "That's how lean thinking at Toyota is applied. We're trying to adapt that philosophy to health care. Every provider needs to be an 'inspector,' as well "as a deliverer of care."

The medical center also uses "patient safety alerts" (PSAs) to encourage employees to improve care. If an employee notices something unsafe or a process that has not gone well, he or she can initiate a PSA by notifying the Office of Patient Safety (formerly the Office of Risk Management), either by filling out a form on-line or by telling their supervisor or manager. The organization's traditional quality improvement (QI) program has essentially been rolled into the PSA program. As an example, said Dr Glenn, if patients experience an increased rate of complications from their IVs, "we would immediately try to figure out the root cause and make the necessary changes. The person who called this to our attention would not be hassled. Instead, we would celebrate that individual and thank him or her for making patient care safer. Basically, the idea is to create a culture of safety and get away from a culture of blame. We want everybody to be empowered to speak up."

It's too early to see an impact on malpractice claims, he said. "Our primary goal is to make health care safer. If we have a safer environment, we'll have fewer incidents; fewer claims will be a welcome side effect."

CASE STUDY III: WENATCHEE VALLEY MEDICAL CENTER[1]

The Wenatchee Valley Medical Center, Wenatchee Washington has 1170 employees and 170 physicians in seven clinics throughout North Central Washington. The Wenatchee Valley Medical Center soon will begin using an electronic prescription-writing system developed by the Everett Clinic, and now in use there. The two clinics have collaborated on a number of projects over the past decade. With the prescription-writing system, physicians will be able to electronically prescribe and send the order to the pharmacy while automatically updating the patient's computerized medical record.

The patient safety benefits are numerous: the system generates legible prescriptions; it permits the prescriber to prescribe only feasible options (ie, the prescriber cannot prescribe for 250 milligrams if the drug comes only in a 200-milligram form); it prevents prescribing drugs to which the patient is allergic; and with planned future enhancements it will prevent prescribing incompatible drugs. It can also be programmed to check the patient's insurer's formulary to make sure the drug is covered.

William Gotthold, MD, medical informatics officer with the clinic, said, "This system is designed to reduce the incredible effort that goes into avoiding a mistake by letting the computer help." He expects the system to decrease the clinic's exposure to errors. "If you look at just the process, you can see that the software catches 'X' number of allergy problems or drugs that interact with each other. If we don't harm patients, we won't be sued." The prescribing system should be in full use throughout the medical center by the end of 2005. At the medical center's 20-bed hospital, nursing supervisors review all charts daily to check whether drugs are delivered appropriately and whether labs are done on time. Pharmacists also review the charts, making sure they contain all relevant information so that caregivers can make the proper assessments. Rob Pollard, pharmacy director of the medical center, said that medication errors continue to decline.

The medical center medication error work group analyzes errors reported by nurses and others and then makes system adjustments. That has helped push the error rate down, too, he said, as has modifying the hospital's formulary. For example, where there are sound-alike and look-alike drugs, one may be removed from the formulary. Tylenol #3 was taken off the formulary because of its low efficacy, high incidence of patient allergies, and high incidence of gastrointestinal upset. If a physician writes a prescription for Tylenol #3, Vicodin is now the therapeutic substitution.

The medical center has expanded its computerized medical record system so that when patients are hospitalized at Central Washington Hospital, the large community hospital in Wenatchee, physicians can access both their hospital and medical center records. Dr Richard Tucker, medical director of quality and education, said, "One of our underlying theses is that errors occur when the physician does not have all the available data at the time of taking care of patients." Other physicians in the community can also participate in the system via an organization called Community Choice. Dr Tucker said that emergency department physicians "have a tremendous opinion" of the system because they now have immediate access to records on many of their ED patients.

The medical center's top management supports patient safety initiatives. "Lack of patient safety is an indicator of inefficient systems," said Dr Tucker. "Making care safer eliminates waste and drives risk down. It is better for patients, and there is every financial reason in the world to do this."

CASE STUDY IV: UNIVERSITY OF WASHINGTON MEDICAL CENTER[1]

The University of Washington, Seattle Washington, has 3500 employees and 700 physicians. Like many other hospitals and medical centers, the 1999 report *To Err is Human* by the Institute of Medicine prompted the University of Washington Medical Center in Seattle to focus more closely on patient safety, including modifying the health system's entire operating plan to explicitly stress safety and quality. "Those issues are now the strategic glue around operations," said Julie B. Duncan, RN, director of quality improvement.

The health system is actively promoting a culture of safety and attempting (within the constraints of the current tort system environment) to move away from a culture of "blame and shame," she said. "It's at least a three- to five-year undertaking." Beginning July 20, 2004, on every desktop in every clinical area of the medical center—inpatient and outpatient—will be a Web-based electronic adverse event reporting system. With a click of an icon, anyone employed at the medical center can write up a near miss, a near harm or a harm event. The system will allow real-time notification of the event to those who need to know-managers, pharmacy, risk mangers, quality managers and as appropriate, clinical chiefs. Those reporting can do so anonymously if they prefer; other centers have found that only about 10% choose to remain anonymous, partly because people want to find out what has been done to address their concerns. "Overall, we're promoting the concept of reporting as a way to make improvement; it's a blame-free non-punitive tool," said Duncan.

Physicians and others can still call the risk manager if an unto-ward event occurs, said Duncan. "They can do whatever is most comfortable for them. We wouldn't mandate that they change that. Convenience equals compliance. But others may be more comfortable with computers." However physicians report, they are immune from discovery under the state quality assurance and peer review statute. "We would fall on our sword and die for that statute. Being without it would be the worst possible thing," she said. Even with it, some physicians are still reluctant to report for fear of being sued, she said.

Nonetheless, other academic centers that have implemented the same reporting system are finding it useful. The product was developed by the University Health System Consortium, an organization of some 100 academic medical centers, and is current-ly in use by 21 medical academic centers. Said Duncan, "In some cases, there has been a 300% increase volume of reporting. And there's been more process improvement around patient safety. It's wonderful; it's a concept whose time is come. But it wouldn't work if you had a blame culture."

The medical center, following recommendations by the Insti-tute of Medicine, has redefined its performance expectations so that senior executives, department chairpersons, service chiefs and managers are accountable for safety and quality.

- Safety is a "distinct and clear line item," said Duncan. "Performance is measured against it."
- They are now receiving regular reports, called "dashboards" on how they are doing, so they can see where they are against benchmarks and identify areas of improvement.

Employee surveys include questions about safety, as do patient surveys.

- Every patient is offered a brochure detailing the role the patient plays in assuring his or her safe care.
- For instance, the brochure states that it is permissible to ask health care workers if they have washed their hands, and it encourages patients to ask about their plan of care.

Duncan is also developing a curriculum on patient safety.

- It will eventually be presented to the entire staff and faculty.
- The JCAHO seven national Patient Safety Goals will be covered.
- Other content, such as the importance of team concepts and effective communication will also be covered.

Beginning July 1, 2004, for the first time the UW has an associate director for quality, a physician.

■ He is to be part of a new systemwide "center of clinical excellence" where individuals with expertise in quality improvement work together with analysts with expertise in collecting and analyzing the system's clinical data.

■ The data will include:
  • Patient safety indicators
  • Clinical outcomes
  • Adverse events
  • Service data
  • Patient satisfaction data.

■ The center's experts will be available to work beside and consult with individual physicians, services and departments.

■ Duncan and the new associate medical director for quality will co-lead the center.

CASE STUDY V: LAKESHORE CLINIC[1]

The Lakeshore Clinic, with locations in Bothell, Totem Lake and Kirkland, Washington has 153 employees, and 25 providers in family practice and internal medicine. Creating a culture of safety and decreasing the stigma associated with reporting errors are essential to Lakeshore Clinic's efforts to make care safer for patients. Tess Morton-Trask, RN, director of operations and quality improvement, says that the clinic's seven-physician governing board has been paying steadily closer attention over the past three years to system changes that will improve patient safety and quality.

■ The governing board oversees and supplies resources to the quality improvement committee and the safety committee. Both committees are represented by a number of areas within the clinic-critical for organizational change, according to Trask.

■ The board also reviews the clinic's data and progress toward the goals established by these committees.

■ The board supports physician peer review:
  • A process of reviewing feedback and data about each provider
  • If a problem area is identified, a plan is developed and followed until the problem is resolved.

The closer scrutiny has been driven in part by escalating malpractice premiums and a desire to minimize their malpractice exposure.

- "Patient safety is really a test of how our entire organization and community function," she said. "It is truly the end product of putting the patient's needs in the middle of our mission statement, and more importantly, in our actions."

- Despite good risk experience, the rising cost of the clinic's malpractice premiums means that safety efforts and other needed improvements do not get as much attention as Trask would like.

  - "We're structurally thin," she said.
  - "We need the community to understand that we need better compensation for organizational structure.
  - We're juggling priorities."

The clinic has had an incident reporting system for several years, which any employee can use to report an error, a near miss or something more serious.

- More recently, the clinic has broadened its description of what constitutes an incident to now include any event that is considered inconsistent with routine operations and expectations, no matter how small.

- A physician is assigned to every incident involving a patient.

  - Said Trask, "Patients aren't sicker today.
  - But we have realized that the results of seemingly minor actions or mishaps have fairly significant impact."

Like the other institutions presented in this report, the clinic's policy is to look at errors primarily as system problems, rather than finding an individual to blame. The reason is pragmatic. "If you have a medical assistant who comes forward to say he or she has made an error, and you fire them, no one is going to report anything for a very long time," said Trask. "You have to be very careful and cautious and not overreact to an error." Instead, the clinic performs root cause analysis—"we ask why, and why and why" to figure out what has gone awry. More often than not, the underlying cause is correctible with better orientation, more education or more supervision, for example.

Patients routinely receive a follow-up to their complaints and requests, so that they know the clinic is listening to them. About half the time, the problems have arisen because of miscommunications or misunderstanding, she said. "Once we talk with patients and explain, they're happier." Consumer demand has played a role in helping the clinic do a better job in delivering care safely. "It's a good thing," said Trask. "When patients come, they should get their medications injected by someone skilled; they should get the right medications at the right time; and they should receive lab results that are accurate and timely."

Within the next year, the clinic will implement an electronic medical record that will help improve care in a variety of ways, including generating recall lists to assure that patients receive appropriate follow up. Said Trask, "We'll also be able to automate our medical records audits to review for quality outcomes. Having access to this data will allow us to negotiate better health plan contracts which will support our organizational infrastructure."

The clinic is also beginning to use CHILD Profile, a statewide repository of immunizations, sponsored by the Washington State Department of Health. Providers with proper clearance can access patient immunization information in a shared, secure database, including immunization histories, recommendations of immunizations needed, recall lists and mailing labels for patients who have missed immunizations, vaccine usage reports, data for practice-specific immunization assessment reports and tracking of children eligible for state-supplied vaccine. If a child changes health care providers, the new provider may access the CHILD Profile immunization registry to review the child's record. Trask said that although CHILD Profile is a good idea for patient care, the clinic still had to work to find the staff and time to in put the data into the computer. "We use it because it is another way to automate our recall. It's a really hard sell to do things that don't result in that kind of win–win," she said.

The clinic's goal is to embed quality and safety into its entire structure. "It takes two to three years to get there," she said. "We're almost there. The medical community used to think of patient safety in just the hospital. But the more care is provided in outpatient settings, the more need there is for safety in the outpatient setting."

LESSONS TO LEARN

In conclusion, these case studies portray the intense commitment to improve patient safety, using tools and concepts that work for the particular organization. Even though the cases represented large organizations, there are lessons to be learned and concepts that can be applied across the spectrum of ambulatory care, including in the solo practice.

ENDNOTE

1. Colley J, Heineccius L. Patient Safety and Error Reduction Initiatives in the State of Washington and Recommendations for Action. Report. Washington State Medical-Education and Research Foundation. July 2004. Reprinted with permission.

chapter 7

The Future of Patient Safety

The health care patient safety movement has created many exciting and innovative approaches to the enhancement of more efficient, cost-effective, and, most importantly, safer patient care. Several of these initiatives are outlined in this chapter.

THE PATIENT SAFETY AND QUALITY IMPROVEMENT ACT OF 2005

The Patient Safety and Quality Improvement Act (Public Law 109-41) was signed into law in July, 2005. The law was enacted in response to growing concern about patient safety in the US and the Institute of Medicine's 1999 report, *To Err is Human: Building a Safer Health System.* The goal of the Act is to improve patient safety by encouraging voluntary and confidential reporting of events that adversely affect patients.

Here is a summary of the Act provided by the Agency for Healthcare Research and Quality (AHRQ) on its Web site (http://www.ahrq.gov/qual/psoact.htm):

The Patient Safety and Quality Improvement Act calls for Patient Safety Organizations (PSOs) to collect, aggregate, and analyze confidential information reported by health care providers. Currently, patient safety improvement efforts are hampered by the fear of discovery of peer deliberations, resulting in under-reporting of events and an inability to gather sufficient patient safety event data for analysis. By analyzing patient safety event information, PSOs will be able to identify patterns of failures and propose measures to eliminate patient safety risks and hazards.

Many providers fear that patient safety event reports could be used against them in medical malpractice cases or in disciplinary proceedings. The Act addresses these fears by providing Federal legal privilege and confidentiality protections to information that is assembled and reported by providers to a PSO or developed by a PSO ("patient safety work product") for the conduct of patient safety activities. The Act also significantly limits the use of this information in criminal, civil, and administrative proceedings. The Act includes provisions for monetary penalties for violations of confidentiality or privilege protections.

Additionally, the Act specifies the role of PSOs and defines "patient safety work product" and "patient safety evaluation systems," which focus on how patient safety event information is collected, developed, analyzed, and maintained. In addition, the Act has specific requirements for PSOs, such as:

- PSOs are required to work with more than one provider.
- Eligible organizations include public or private entities, profit or not-for-profit entities, provider entities, such as hospital chains, and other entities that establish special components.
- Ineligible organizations include insurance companies or their affiliates.

Finally, the Act calls for the establishment of a Network of Patient Safety Databases (NPSD) to provide an interactive, evidence-based management resource for providers, PSOs, and other entities. It will be used to analyze national and regional statistics, including trends and patterns of patient safety events. The NPSD will employ common formats (definitions, data elements, and so on) and will promote interoperability among reporting systems. The Department of Health and Human Services will provide technical assistance to PSOs.[1]

EVIDENCE-BASED MEDICINE

The Agency for Healthcare Research and Quality (AHRQ), in cooperation with the American Medical Association and the American Association of Health Plans (now America's Health Insurance Plans), created the National Guideline Clearinghouse (NGC),[2] a public resource for evidence-based clinical practice guidelines. The NGC mission is to provide physicians, nurses, other health professionals, health care providers, health plans, integrated delivery systems, purchasers, and others an accessible mechanism for obtaining objective, detailed information on clinical practice guidelines and to further their dissemination, implementation, and use.

Key components of NGC include the following:

- Structured abstracts (summaries) about the guideline and its development
- Links to full-text guidelines, where available, and/or ordering information for print copies
- Palm-based personal digital assistant (PDA) downloads of the complete NGC summary for all guidelines represented in the database
- A guideline comparison utility that gives users the ability to generate side-by-side comparisons for any combination of two or more guidelines
- Unique guideline comparisons, called *guideline syntheses* and prepared by NGC staff, that compare guidelines covering similar topics and highlighting areas of similarity and difference. NGC guideline syntheses often provide a comparison of guidelines developed in different countries, providing

insight into commonalities and differences in international health practices.

- An electronic forum—NGC-L—for exchanging information on clinical practice guidelines, their development, implementation, and use.

- An annotated bibliography database where users can search for citations for publications and resources about guidelines, including guideline development and methodology, structure, evaluation, and implementation

Other user-friendly features include the following:

- **What's New** enables users to see what guidelines have been added each week and includes an index of all guidelines in NGC.

- **NGC Update Service** is a weekly electronic mailing of new and updated guidelines posted to the NGC Web site (www.guideline.gov/whatsnew/subscription.aspx).

- **Detailed Search** enables users to create very specific search queries based on the various attributes found in the NGC classification scheme.

- **NGC Browse** permits users to scan for guidelines available on the NGC site by disease or condition, treatment or intervention, or developing organization.

- **PDA/Palm List** provides users with information regarding the availability of full-text guidelines and/or companion documents available through the guideline developer that can be downloaded for the handheld computer (PDA, Palm, etc).

- **AHRQ Evidence Reports/Technical Assessments List** provides users with links to the summaries and full-text reports for evidence reports and technology assessments produced under the AHRQ Evidence-Based Practice Center Program.

- **Glossary** provides definitions of terms used in the standardized abstracts (summaries).

- Sister sites include www.qualitytools.ahrq.gov/.

- The 2004 NHQR including state resources and National Healthcare Disparities Report are now available on AHRQ's QualityTools Web site.

MODELS OF CARE

Recommendations for a new model of practice were described by Spann.[3] The task force that created the concept presented financial models that would reward family physicians for reshaping their practices and offered recommendations for how those goals could be realized. The model was:

> . . . based on the concept of a relationship-centered *personal medical home,* which
> serves as the focal point through which all individuals—regardless of age, gender,
> race, ethnicity, or socioeconomic status participate in health care. In this new medical
> home, patients receive a basket of acute, chronic, and preventive medical care serv-
> ices that are accessible, accountable, comprehensive, integrated, patient-centered,
> safe, scientifically valid, and satisfying to both patients and their physicians. This New
> Model will include technologies that enhance diagnosis and treatment for a large por-
> tion of problems that patients bring to their family physicians. Business plans and
> reimbursement models will be developed to enable the reengineered practices of fam-
> ily physicians to thrive as personal medical homes, and resources will be developed to
> help patients make informed decisions about choosing a personal medical home. A
> financially self-sustaining national resource will be implemented to provide practices
> with ongoing support in the transition to the New Model of family medicine.
>
> The major characteristics of the New Model of family medicine include:

- Personal medical home
- Patient-centered care
- Team approach to care
- Elimination of barriers to access
- Advanced information systems, including a standardized electronic health
  record (EHR)
- Redesigned, more functional offices
- Whole-person orientation
- Care provided in a community context
- Focus on quality and safety
- Enhanced practice finance
- Defined basket of services

Family physicians would need to retool their medical practices
and provide:

- Open-access scheduling
- Online appointment
- EHRs
- Group visits
- E-mail consultations
- Chronic disease management
- Web-based information
- Use of clinical practice software and outcomes analyses

The task force analysis estimated that national health care
expenditures could be reduced by a minimum of 5%, or $67 bil-
lion, in 2004 if all patients were to adopt a primary care physician
as their primary source of care. Payments to family physicians for

preventive, chronic, and acute care services under the current fee-for-service system could increase annual compensation by 26% (from $167,457 to $210,288). Family physicians who elected to manage chronic diseases and provide medical advice via e-mail and who demonstrated clinical skills that merited an overall performance bonus could realize a compensation increase of as much as 66% (up to $277,800).

Significant obstacles remain, especially the "transition costs" incurred from purchasing EHRs and other electronic communication systems, recruiting and training new personnel, and lost productivity. Costs could range from $23,443 to $90,650 per physician, depending on the productivity loss associated with implementing an EHR.

However, a physician practice that adopted all features of the new model could be expected to add nearly $49,000 in compensation and recoup transition costs in less than one year under the best-case scenario or more than two years under the worst case.

CHRONIC DISEASE MANAGEMENT

Kennan, et al, point out that a multitude of data support the importance of preventive care measures. Likewise, there are proven interventions that can reduce morbidity and mortality for many common diseases. Nonetheless, implementation is unsatisfactory, as exemplified in data from Medicare beneficiaries from 2000 to 2001 showing low rates of mammography (77%); pneumonia and influenza vaccination (64% and 71%, respectively); β-blocker and aspirin therapy after myocardial infarction (78% and 84%, respectively); angiotensin-converting enzyme inhibitor in congestive heart failure (66%); and eye examinations in patients with diabetes (74%).[4] Systematic reminders and computer-based decision support systems have been shown to improve preventive and disease-specific care.[5,6]

Every primary care physician can evaluate his or her practice and identify where errors either are occurring or may be likely to occur. When primary care physicians are proactive and improve the systems of care that they use in their practices, they will dramatically improve the safety of their patients and improve the quality of care that they provide.

PUBLIC REPORTING

HealthGrades, Inc, a health care ratings, information, and advisory services company, publishes a consumer-oriented directory of hospitals, nursing homes, and physicians. According to HealthGrade's Web site,[7] online physician profiles on its site are accessed by the following groups:

Patients.   Patients access our Web site for quality information to make better informed health care choices.

Major Search Engines.   Individuals using major search engines (Google, Yahoo, etc) to locate [physician profiling] information are directed to HealthGrades.

Health Plan Members.   Health plan members can use incorporated HealthGrades' quality information within their online benefits portal as a valuable tool to find the best health care providers.

Employees.   Many employees receive our provider information as an employee benefit. They rely on HealthGrades when looking for the highest quality of care within their health plan networks.

Media.   The media often cites HealthGrades on consumer-driven health care and related trends, which drives visitors to our site. Our studies and press releases help educate the public on health care quality.

Insurance Underwriters.   Insurance underwriters obtain valuable data from us to evaluate business risk and quality of providers.

Another HealthGrades feature, obtained through the acquisition of the CompareYourCare online patient-education and physician care-rating tool from the Foundation for Accountability, allows patients to log on to the Web site and complete questionnaires based on their experiences with their physicians in four disease states—heart disease, asthma, diabetes, and depression—or in the category of "staying healthy."[8]

Results from the questionnaire are compared instantly with national and regional quality guidelines, and patients are given a grade that measures how closely their physicians adhere to optimal care. Patients, too, are rated on the basis of their level of compliance with basic care plans. Unlike other HealthGrades metrics, these rankings will not be publicly displayed. Patients are able to print out a report showing the grades, areas where the care was good, and suggested areas of improvement.

Also, for the third year in a row, HealthGrades is issuing the results of its Study of Distinguished Hospitals for Clinical Excellence.[9]

- Unlike the annual HealthGrades Hospital Quality in America Study, which focuses on individual procedures at the nation's nearly 5000 hospitals and is issued in the fall, this study examines overall quality at each of the nation's hospitals.

- The 229 hospitals that fall into the top 5% in the nation in terms of mortality and complication rates across 28 common procedures and diagnoses are identified in the study as HealthGrades Distinguished Hospitals for Clinical Excellence™.

- Each year, HealthGrades researchers examine millions

of patient records submitted by hospitals to the Centers for Medicare and Medicaid Services (CMS) and the US Department of Health and Human Services (HHS).

■ Patient records cover three federal fiscal years: 2001, 2002, and 2003.

The following are key findings from the current study:

■ Of the 28 medical procedures and diagnoses that Health-Grades used to evaluate the nation's hospitals for this study, four are analyzed in greater detail in the study.

■ The findings showed significantly lower complication and mortality rates when comparing hospitals in the top 5% in the nation to the rest for:
  • Coronary bypass surgery
  • Treatment of heart attack (comparing only those hospitals with angioplasty and stent treatments available)
  • Treatment of stroke
  • Treatment of community-acquired pneumonia

In those four categories, Medicare patients treated at the 229 HealthGrades Distinguished Hospitals for Clinical Excellence had, on average, the following improved chances of survival when compared to patients treated at the rest of hospitals nationwide:

■ 15.30% for coronary bypass surgery

■ 12.62% for heart attack (angioplasty or stent available)

■ 15.40% for stroke

■ 19.55% for community-acquired pneumonia

Extrapolating these data to the entire patient population nationally, HealthGrades found that:

■ Approximately 52,949 lives could have been saved if all patients treated at other hospitals for these four categories during 2001, 2002, and 2003 had instead gone to a Distinguished Hospital.

■ Hospitals in the top 5% in terms of clinical excellence treated:
  • Substantially more patients per hospital—for some diagnoses in some regions, more than twice the average hospital level
  • Sicker patients with higher expected mortality rates

Another source of hospital quality data is provided by the National Healthcare Quality Report (NHQR),[10] an Agency for Healthcare Research and Quality (AHRQ)-led effort on behalf of HHS. This is the second annual NHQR. The purpose of the report is to track the state of health care quality for the nation on an annual basis. The 2004 report extends the baseline established in the 2003 report for a set of health care quality measures across four dimensions of quality:

■ Effectiveness

■ Safety

■ Timeliness

■ Patient centeredness

The report also spans nine clinical condition areas or care settings within the effectiveness component:

■ Cancer

■ Diabetes

■ End-stage renal disease

■ Heart disease

■ HIV/AIDS

■ Maternal and child health

■ Mental health

■ Respiratory diseases

■ Nursing home and home health care

Using data from the 2004 NHQR,[10] resources have been developed for State Resources for Selected Measures Report.[11] This report, mandated by Congress and published annually by AHRQ, is based on a detailed analysis of measures designed to help track health care quality across the nation. It includes state-level statistics for approximately 100 of these measures. The state data are presented in three different formats:

■ **State rankings on 14 selected measures.** These rankings show how well each state is performing on 14 selected measures of health care quality that are featured in the 2004 NHQR. These data show where states are doing well and where they may need to improve.

■ **State summary tables.** These tables provide a complete listing of the entire set of about 100 quality measures for each state. Each individual state's table shows the all-states average and that state's estimate for each measure. (The state summary tables do not provide rankings on all of the measures because data on all measures were not available for all states.)

■ **State snapshots.** These snapshots give more detail on specific measures. Each state snapshot shows two areas in which the health care system of a particular state is doing well in providing high-quality health care and two in which it might be able to improve.

An example 2004 NHQR: State Ranking on Selected Measures is reproduced in Appendix Q.

COMPARING HOSPITALS

That appears to be the case, not only from the previously cited sources but also from probably the largest health care provider database in the world, HHS. HHS has provided a tool[12]—called Hospital Compare (see Appendix R)—to the public that will provide anyone with information on how well the hospitals in their area are caring for adult patients with certain medical conditions. This information will help compare the quality of care hospitals provide. Hospital Compare was created through the efforts of the CMS and organizations that represent hospitals, physicians, employers, accrediting organizations, other federal agencies, and the public.

HSS recommends that patients talk to their physicians about this information when making hospital care decisions. This is likely to represent just the beginning of public reporting of hospital and physician quality and patient safety data based on the provider's own billing data.

ENDNOTES

1. The Patient Safety and Quality Improvement Act of 2005. Overview, June 2006. Agency for Healthcare Research and Quality, Rockville, MD. http://www.ahrq.gov/qual/psoact.htm

2. National Guideline Clearinghouse. Available at: www.guideline .gov/. Accessed February 24, 2005.

3. Spann SJ, for the members of Task Force 6 and the Executive Editorial Team. Report on financing the new model of family medicine. *Ann Fam Med.* 2004;2:S1-S21. Available at: www.annfammed .org/cgi/content/full/2/suppl_3/s1. Accessed April 2005.

4. Jencks SF, Huff ED, Cuerdon T. Change in the quality of care delivered to medicare beneficiaries, 1998-1999 to 2000-2001. *JAMA.* 2003;289:305-312.

5. Hunt, DL, Haynes B, Hanna SE, et al. Effects of computer-based clinical decision support systems on physician performance and patient outcomes: a systematic review. *JAMA.* 1998;280:1339-1346.

6. Balas EA, Wiengarten S, Garb CT, et al. Improving preventive care by prompting physicians. *Arch Intern Med.* 2000;160:301-308.

7. HealthGrades program overview. Available at: www. healthgrades .com/physician/index.cfm?fuseaction=mod&modtype =PUT&SubType=NonAuth&modact=put_news. Accessed February 24, 2006.

8. Compare Your Care survey selection page. Available at: www .compareyourcare.org/?id=5017. Accessed February 24, 2006.

9. Study naming hospitals in top 5% for clinical quality released by HealthGrades (press release). Available at: www.healthgrades.com/ media/DMS/pdf/DHPCEPress2005.pdf. Accessed February 24, 2006.

10. Welcome to the Web-enabled 2004 National Healthcare Quality Report (NHQR). Available at: www.qualitytools.ahrq.gov/ qualityreport/browse/browse.aspx. Accessed February 24, 2006.

11. State resources for selected measures from the 2004 National Healthcare Quality Report. Available at: www.qualitytools.ahrq .gov/qualityreport/state/. Accessed February 24, 2006.

12. Hospital Compare. Available at: www.hospitalcompare.hhs.gov/. Accessed February 24, 2006.

Rules for Satisfying Patient Needs

Accessible	Easy and convenient patient access to the system; face-to-face visits not the sole interaction
Flexible	Standardize to efficiently meet patient needs; customized for unique needs
Informed patient decision making	Give patients all information to make decisions; clinician or patients share in decisions
Free access to information and knowledge	Patient access to medical records and clinical information 24 hours per day
Evidence based	Based on best scientific information available; physician or provider preferences should not lead to random variations in care; same standard of care wherever care is given
Safe	"First do no harm"; all providers should engage in risk reduction and patient safety
Transparent	Providers share all information needed for informed decision, including their own performance
Anticipates needs	Standardize care based on scientific evidence and their outcomes; customize when needed

Adapted from Institute of Medicine. Formulating New Rules to Redesign and Improve Care. Chapter 3 in *Crossing the Quality Chasm: A New Health System for the 21st Century.* Washington, DC: National Academy Press; 2001:61-62. Reprinted with permission.

Decrease waste	Organizations focus on decreasing waste of time and resources; resources needed for best long-term outcome vs short-term cost
Collaboration	Open collaboration and communication between clinicians to ensure best patient outcomes

The Patient Safety and Quality Improvement Act of 2005

The Patient Safety and Quality Improvement Act of 2005 (Public Law 109-41), signed into law on July 29, 2005, was enacted in response to growing concern about patient safety in the United States and the Institute of Medicine's 1999 report, *To Err is Human: Building a Safer Health System.* The goal of the Act is to improve patient safety by encouraging voluntary and confidential reporting of events that adversely affect patients.

The Patient Safety and Quality Improvement Act signifies the Federal Government's commitment to fostering a culture of patient safety. It creates Patient Safety Organizations (PSOs) to collect, aggregate, and analyze confidential information reported by health care providers. Currently, patient safety improvement efforts are hampered by the fear of discovery of peer deliberations, resulting in under-reporting of events and an inability to aggregate sufficient patient safety event data for analysis. By analyzing patient safety event information, PSOs will be able to identify patterns of failures and propose measures to eliminate patient safety risks and hazards.

Many providers fear that patient safety event reports could be used against them in medical malpractice cases or in disciplinary proceedings. The Act addresses these fears by providing Federal legal privilege and confidentiality protections to information that is assembled and reported by providers to a PSO or developed by a PSO ("patient safety work product") for the conduct of patient safety activities. The Act also significantly limits the use of this information in criminal, civil, and administrative proceedings. The Act includes provisions for monetary penalties for violations of confidentiality or privilege protections.

Additionally, the Act specifies the role of PSOs and defines "patient safety work product" and "patient safety evaluation systems," which focus on how patient safety event information is collected, developed, analyzed, and maintained. In addition, the Act has specific requirements for PSOs, such as:

- PSOs are required to work with more than one provider.
- Eligible organizations include public or private entities, profit or not-for-profit entities, provider entities, such as hospital chains, and other entities that establish special components.
- Ineligible organizations include insurance companies or their affiliates.

Finally, the Act calls for the establishment of a Network of Patient Safety Databases (NPSD) to provide an interactive, evidence-based management resource for providers, PSOs, and other entities. It will be used to analyze national and regional statistics, including trends and patterns of patient safety events. The NPSD will employ common formats (definitions, data elements, and so on) and will promote interoperability among reporting systems. The Department of Health and Human Services will provide technical assistance to PSOs.

Source: The Patient Safety and Quality Improvement Act of 2005. *Overview, June 2006. Agency for Healthcare Research and Quality, Rockville, MD. http://www.ahrq.gov/qual/psoact.htm. Accessed April 17, 2007.*

Potentially Problematic Drug List for Office-Based Surgery

Drugs*	Potential Problem(s)
Platinol (cisplatin) and **Paraplatin** (carboplatin)	Similarity in names can lead to confusion between these two products. Doses appropriate for carboplatin usually exceed the maximum safe dose of cisplatin. Severe toxicity and death has been associated with accidental cisplatin overdoses. Install maximum dose warnings in computer systems. A boxed warning notes that cisplatin doses greater than 100 mg/m² once every 3 to 4 weeks are rarely used and that the package insert should be consulted for further information. Use safe handling recommendations and safety stickers for cisplatin as provided by manufacturer. Do not store these two agents next to each other. Use generic names when prescribing and not chemical names or abbreviations.
Concentrated liquid morphine products: **Roxanol,** MSIR vs conventional liquid morphine concentrations, morphine oral liquid	Concentrated forms of oral morphine solution (20 mg/mL) have often been confused with the standard concentration (listed as 10 mg/5 mL or 20 mg/5 mL), leading to serious errors. Accidental selection of the wrong concentration and prescribing or labeling the product by volume, not milligrams, contributes to these errors, some of which have been fatal. For example, "10 mg" has been confused with "10 mL." If concentrated product is used, this represents a 20-fold overdose. Dispense concentrated oral morphine solutions only when ordered for a specific patient (not as unit stock). Segregate the concentrated solution from the other concentrations wherever it is stored. Purchase and dispense concentrated solutions in dropper bottles (available from at least two manufacturers) to help prevent dose measurement errors

*Brand name drugs are provided in boldface.

Drugs*	Potential Problem(s)
	and differentiate the concentrated product from the conventional products. Verify that patients and caregivers understand how to measure the proper dose for self-administration at home. For inpatients, dispense concentrated solutions in unit-doses.
Adrenalin (epinephrine) and ephedrine	The names of these two medications look very similar, and their clinical uses make storage near each other likely, especially in obstetrical areas. Both products are available in similar packaging (1 mL amber ampuls and vials). See general recommendations in Appendix E.
Sublimaze (fentanyl) and **Sufenta** (sufentanil)	The products are not interchangeable. Confusion has resulted in episodes of respiratory arrest due to potency differences between these drugs. Some errors occurred when using sufentanil during drug shortages of fentanyl. Do not stock sufentanil in patient care units outside OR/PACU settings. Do not store these agents near one another if both products are available (eg, pharmacy, anesthesia supplies).
Dilaudid (hydromorphone) injection and **Astramorph, Duramorph, Infumorph** (morphine) injection	Some health care providers have mistakenly believed that hydromorphone is the generic equivalent of morphine. However, these products are not interchangeable. Fatal errors have occurred when hydromorphone was confused with morphine. Based on equianalgesic dose conversion, this may represent significant overdose, leading to serious adverse events. Storage of the two medications in close proximity to one stock specific strengths for each product that are dissimilar. For example, stock units with hydromorphone 1 mg unit dose cartridges, and morphine in 2 mg unit dose cartridges. Ensure that health care providers are aware that these two products are not interchangeable with one another and in similar concentrations may contribute to such errors. Confusion has resulted in episodes of respiratory arrest due to potency differences between these drugs.
Insulin products: **Lantus** (insulin glargine) and **Lente** (insulin zinc suspension); **Humulin** (human insulin products) and **Humalog** (insulin lispro); **Novolin** (human insulin products) and **Novolog** (human insulin aspart); **Novolin** 70/30 (70% isophane	Similar names, strengths and concentration ratios of some products (eg, 70/30) have contributed to medication errors. Mix-ups have also occurred between the 100 unit/mL and 500 units/mL insulin concentrations. Limit the use of insulin analog 70/30 mixtures to just a single product. Limit the variety of insulin products stored in patient care units and remove patient-specific insulin vials from stock upon discharge. For drug selection screens, emphasize the word *mixture* or *mix* along with the name of the insulin product mixtures. Consider

*Brand name drugs are provided in boldface.

Drugs*	Potential Problem(s)
insulin and 30% insulin injection); and **Novolog Mix 70/30** (70% insulin aspart protamine suspension and 30% insulin (aspart)	auxiliary labels for newer products to differentiate them from the established products. Also apply bold labels on atypical insulin concentrations.
Lipid-based daunorubicin and doxorubicin products **Doxil** (doxorubicin liposomal); **Daunoxome** (daunorubicin citrate liposomal) vs conventional forms of daunorubicin and doxorubicin; **Cerubidine** (daunorubicin, conventional) **Adriamycin, Rubex** (doxorubicin, conventional)	Many drugs now come in liposomal formulations indicated for special patient populations. Confusion may occur between the liposomal and the conventional formulation because of name similarity. The products are not interchangeable. Lipid-based formulation dosing guidelines differ significantly from conventional dosing. For example, a standard dose of doxorubicin liposomal is 20 mg/m^2 given at 21-day intervals, compared to doses of 50 to 75 mg/m^2 every 21 days for conventional drug. Staff involved in handling these products should be aware of the differences between conventional and lipid-based formulations of these drugs. Encourage staff to refer to the lipid-based products by their brand names and not just their generic names. Stop and verify that the correct drug is being used if staff, patients, or family members notice a change in the solution's appearance from previous infusions. Lipid-based products may be seen as cloudy rather than a clear solution. Storage of lipid-based products in patient care areas and automated dispensing cabinets is highly discouraged. Include specific method of administration for these products. Doses of liposomal daunorubicin are typically 40 mg/m^2 repeated every two weeks, while doses of conventional daunorubicin vary greatly and may be administered more frequently. Accidental administration of the liposomal form instead of the conventional form has resulted in severe side effects and death.
Lipid-based amphotericin products: **Ambisome** (amphotericin B liposomal); **Abelcet** (amphotericin B lipid complex); **Ampnotec** (amphotericin B cholesteryl sulfate complex for injection) vs conventional forms of amphotericin; **Amphocin, Fungizone Intravenous** (amphotericin B desoxycholate)	Many drugs now come in liposomal formulation indicated for special patient populations. Confusion may occur between the liposomal and the conventional formulations because of name similarity. The products are not interchangeable. Lipid-based formulation dosing guidelines differ significantly from conventional dosing. Conventional amphotercin B desoxycholate doses should not exceed 1.5 mg/kg/day. Doses of the lipid-based products are higher, but vary from product to product. If conventional amphotericin B is given at a dose appropriate for a lipid-based product, a severe adverse event is likely. Confusion between these products has resulted in episodes of respiratory arrest and other dangerous, sometimes fatal outcomes due to

*Brand name drugs are provided in boldface.

Drugs*	Potential Problem(s)
	potency differences between these drugs. Staff involved in handling these products should be aware of the differences between conventional and lipid-based formulations of these drugs. Encourage staff to refer to the lipid-based products by their brand names and not just their generic names. Stop and verify that the correct drug is being used if staff, patients, or family members notice a change in the solution's appearance from previous infusions. Lipid-based products may be seen as cloudy rather than a clear solution. Storage of lipid-based products in patient care areas and automated dispensing cabinets is highly discouraged. To reduce potential for confusion, consider limiting lipid-based amphotericin B products to one specific brand.
Taxol (paclitaxel) and **Taxotere** (docetaxel)	Confusion between these two drugs can result in serious adverse outcomes since they have different dosing recommendations and use in various types of cancer. Install maximum dose warnings in computer systems to alert staff to name mix-ups during order entry. Do not store these agents near one another.
Velban (vinblastine) and **Oncovin** (vincristine)	Fatal errors have occurred, often due to name similarity, when patients were erroneously given vincristine intravenously, but at the higher vinblastine dose. A typical vincristine dose is usually capped at around 1.4 mg/m^2 weekly. The vinblastine dose is variable but, for most adults, the weekly dosage range is 5.5 to 7.4 mg/m^2. Install maximum dose warnings in computer systems to alert staff to name mix-ups during order entry. Do not store these agents near one another. Staff involved in handling these products should be aware of the differences. Use brand names or brand and generic names when prescribing and do not use abbreviations for these drug names.

Source: Adapted from Institute of Medicine. Formulating New Rules to Redesign and Improve Care. Chapter 3 in *Crossing the Quality Chasm: A New Health System for the 21st Century.* Washington, DC: National Academy Press; 2001:61-62. Reprinted with permission.

*Brand name drugs are provided in boldface.

These safety strategies are not inclusive of all possible strategies to reduce name-related errors. See also Appendix E.

A list of potentially problematic drug names can be accessed at www.jcaho.org/accredited +organizations/patient+safety/lasa.pdf.

Potentially Problematic Drug List for Ambulatory Care

Drugs*	Potential Problem(s)
Amaryl (glimepiride) and **Reminyl** (galantamine hydrobromide)	Handwritten orders for Amaryl (used for type II diabetes) and Reminyl (used for Alzheimer's disease) can look similar. Patients receiving Amaryl in error would not be provided with blood glucose monitoring which could lead to a serious error. See general recommendations in Appendix E.
Avandia (rosiglitazone) and **Coumadin** (warfarin)	Poorly handwritten orders for Avandia (used for type II diabetes) have been misread as Coumadin (used to prevent blood clot formation), leading to potentially serious adverse events. Mix-ups originally occurred due to unfamiliarity with Avandia (ie, staff read the order as the more familiar Coumadin). However, mix-ups between these two products continue to occur. Neither medication is safe without appropriate monitoring that is specific to the drug. See general recommendations in Appendix E.
Celebrex (celecoxib) and **Celexa** (citalopram hydrobromide) and **Cerebyx** (fosphenytoin)	Patients affected by a mix-up between these three drugs may experience a decline in mental status, lack of pain or seizure control, or other serious adverse events. See general recommendations in Appendix E.
Catapres (clonidine) and **Klonopin** (clonazepam)	The generic name for clonidine can easily be confused as the trade or generic name for clonazepam. See general recommendations in Appendix E.
Concentrated liquid morphine products, **Roxanol,** MSIR vs conventional liquid morphine concentrations, morphine oral liquid	Concentrated forms of oral morphine solution (20 mg/mL) have often been confused with the standard concentration (listed as 10 mg/ 5 mL or 20 mg/5 mL), leading to serious errors. Accidental selection of the wrong concentration and prescribing or labeling the product by volume, not milligrams, contributes to these errors, some of which have been fatal. For

*Brand name drugs are provided in boldface.

Drugs*	Potential Problem(s)
	example, "10 mg" has been confused with "10 mL." If concentrated product is used, this represents a 20-fold overdose. Dispense concentrated oral morphine solutions only when ordered for a specific patient (not as unit stock). Segregate the concentrated solution from the other concentrations wherever it is stored. Purchase and dispense concentrated solutions in dropper bottles (available from at least two manufacturers) to help prevent dose measurement errors and differentiate the concentrated product from the conventional products. Verify that patients and caregivers understand how to measure the proper dose for self-administration at home. For inpatients, dispense concentrated solutions in unit-doses.
Dilaudid (hydromorphone) injections and **Astramorph, Duramorph, Infumorph** (morphine) injections	Some health care providers have mistakenly believed that hydromorphone is the generic equivalent of morphine. However, these products are not interchangeable. Fatal errors have occurred when hydromorphone was confused with morphine. Based on equianalgesic dose conversion, this may represent significant overdose, leading to serious adverse events. Storage of the two medications in close proximity to one another and in similar concentrations may contribute to such errors. Confusion has resulted in episodes of respiratory arrest due to potency differences between these drugs. Stock specific strengths for each product that are dissimilar. For example, stock units with hydromorphone 1 mg unit dose cartridges, and morphine in 2 mg unit dose cartridges. Ensure that health care providers are aware that these two products are not interchangeable.
Insulin products: **Lantus** (insulin glargine) and **Lente** (insulin zinc suspension); **Humulin** (human insulin products) and **Humalog** (insulin lispro); **Novolin** (human insulin products) and **Novolog** (human insulin aspart); **Novolin** 70/30 (70% isophane insulin and 30% insulin injection) and **Novolog Mix** 70/30 (70% insulin aspart protamine suspension and 30% insulin (aspart)	Similar names, strengths and concentration ratios of some products (eg, 70/30) have contributed to medication errors. Mix-ups have also occurred between the 100 unit/mL and 500 units/mL insulin concentrations. Limit the use of insulin analog 70/30 mixtures to just a single product. Limit the variety of insulin products stored in patient care units, and remove patient-specific insulin vials from stock upon discharge. For drug selection screens, emphasize the word *mixture* or *mix* along with the name of the insulin product mixtures. Consider auxiliary labels for newer products to differentiate them from the established products. Also apply bold labels on atypical insulin concentrations.

*Brand name drugs are provided in boldface.

Drugs*	Potential Problem(s)
Serzone (nefazodone) and **Seroquel** (quietapine)	Beyond name similarity, these medications are both available in 100 mg and 200 mg strengths; both have similar instructions and dosage ranges; and both are used in similar clinical settings. Sedation or dizziness has occurred when Seroquel was dispensed instead of Serzone. Decompensation of mental status has occurred when Serzone was given instead of Seroquel. Further, there are many potentially dangerous drug interactions with Serzone. For example, there are reports of serious, sometimes fatal, reactions when patients receiving monoamine oxidase inhibitors are given drugs with pharmacologic properties similar to nefazodone. See general recommendations in Appendix E.
Zyprexa (olanzapine) and **Zyrtec** (cetirizine)	Name similarity has resulted in frequent mix-ups between Zyrtec, an antihistamine, and Zyprexa, an antipsychotic. Patients who receive Zyprexa in error have reported dizziness, sometimes leading to a related injury from a fall. Patients on Zyprexa for a mental illness have relapsed when given Zyrtec in error. See general recommendations in Appendix E.

Source: Adapted from Institute of Medicine. Formulating New Rules to Redesign and Improve Care. Chapter 3 in *Crossing the Quality Chasm: A New Health System for the 21st Century.* Washington, DC: National Academy Press; 2001:61-62. Reprinted with permission.

*Brand name drugs are provided in boldface.

These safety strategies are not inclusive of all possible strategies to reduce name-related errors. See also Appendix E.

A list of potentially problematic drug names can be accessed at www.jcaho.org/accredited +organizations/patient+safety/lasa.pdf.

Supplemental List of Potentially Problematic Drugs

Acetohexamide	acetazolamide
Advicor	Advair
Avinza	Evista
Bretyllium	Brevibloc
chlorpropamide	chlorpromazine
Diabeta	Zebeta
Diflucan	Diprivan
folic acid	leucovorin calcium ("folinic acid")
heparin	Hespan
idarubicin	doxorubicin daunorubicin
lamivudine	lamotrigine
Leukeran	leucovorin calcium
opium tincture	paregoric (camphorated opium tincture)
Prilosec	Prozac
Primacor	Primaxin
Retrovir	Ritonavir
tizanidine	tiagabine
Wellbutin SR	Wellbutrin XL
Zantac	Xanax
Zantac	Zyrtec

Adapted from Institute of Medicine. Formulating New Rules to Redesign and Improve Care. Chapter 3 in *Crossing the Quality Chasm: A New Health System for the 21st Century.* Washington, DC: National Academy Press; 2001:61-62. Reprinted with permission.

A list of potentially problematic drug names can be accessed at www/jcaho.org/accredited+organizations/patient+safety/lasa.pdf.

Recommendations for Preventing Drug Name Mix-Ups

- Maintain awareness of look-alike and sound-alike drug names published by various safety agencies.
- Clearly specify the dosage form, drug strength, and complete directions on prescriptions. These variables may help staff differentiate products.
- With name pairs known to be problematic, reduce the potential for confusion by writing prescriptions using both the brand and generic name.
- Include the purpose of medication on prescriptions. In most cases drugs that sound or look similar are used for different purposes.
- Alert patients to the potential for mix-ups, especially with known problematic drug names. Advise ambulatory care patients to insist on pharmacy counseling when picking up prescriptions, and to verify that the medication and directions match what the prescriber has told them.
- Encourage inpatients to question nurses about medications that are unfamiliar or look or sound different than expected.
- Give verbal or telephone orders only when truly necessary, and never for chemotherapeutics. Include the drug's intended purpose to ensure clarity. Encourage staff to read back all orders, spell the product name, and state its indication.
- Maintain awareness of look-alike and sound-alike drug names as published by various safety agencies. Regularly provide information to professional staff.
- Whenever possible, determine the purpose of the medication before dispensing or drug administration. Most products with look or sound-alike names are used for different purposes.

Adapted from Institute of Medicine. Formulating New Rules to Redesign and Improve Care. Chapter 3 in *Crossing the Quality Chasm: A New Health System for the 21st Century*. Washington, DC: National Academy Press; 2001:61-62. Reprinted with permission.

- Accept verbal or telephone orders only when truly necessary, and never for chemotherapy. Encourage staff to read back all orders, spell the product name, and state its indication.
- Consider the possibility of name confusion when adding a new product to the formulary. Review information previously published by safety agencies.
- Computerize prescribing. Use preprinted orders or prescriptions as appropriate. If possible, print out current medications daily from the pharmacy computer system and have physicians review for accuracy.
- When possible, list brand and generic names on medication administration records and automated dispensing cabinet computer screens. Such redundancy could help someone identify an error.
- Change the appearance and of look-alike product names on computer screens, pharmacy and nursing unit shelf labels and bins (including automated dispensing cabinets), pharmacy product labels, and medication administration records by highlighting, through bold face, color, and/or tall man letters, the parts of the names that are different (eg, hydrOXYzine, hydrALAzine).
- Install and utilize computerized alerts to remind providers about potential problems during prescription processing.
- Configure computer selection screens and automated dispensing cabinet screens to prevent the two confused drugs from appearing consecutively.
- Affix "name alert" stickers to areas where look or sound-alike products are stored (available from pharmacy label manufacturers).
- Store products with look- or sound-alike names in different locations in pharmacies, patient care units, and in other settings, including patient homes. When applicable, use a shelf sticker to help locate the product that has been moved.
- Continue to employ independent double checks in the dispensing process (one person interprets and enters the prescription into the computer and another reviews the printed label against the original prescription and the product prior to dispensing).
- Encourage reporting of errors and potentially hazardous conditions with look- and sound-alike product names and use the information to establish priorities for error reduction. Also maintain awareness of problematic product names and error prevention recommendations provided by ISMP (www.ismp.org), FDA (www.fda.gov), and USP (www.usp.org).

REFERENCES

ISMP. What's in a name? ways to prevent dispensing errors linked to name confusion. *ISMP Medication Safety Alert!* 2002;7(12).

JCAHO. *Sentinel Event Alert.* May 2001; Issue 19.

A list of potentially problematic drug names can be accessed at www.jcaho.org/accredited+organizations/patient+safety/lasa.pdf.

Worksheets

ELECTRONIC HEALTH COST–BENEFIT WORKSHEET

The following worksheet can be used to estimate the net annual financial benefit that can be potentially derived from an Electronic Health Record system (EHR). Benefits can be calculated either by individual physician or for an entire practice. An interactive Excel file can be downloaded from www.aafp.org /fpm/20041100/43whyi.html. The file combines this worksheet and the "Increased annual E/M revenue worksheet" in the next section of this appendix.

Expense Type	Total 5-Year Cost	Annualized Cost (Total ÷ 5)
Software license(s)		
Software implementation		
Hardware (obtain hardware specifications from the software vendor)		
Network upgrade		
Personnel		
Annual software support		
Total annual cost	$	

Savings Type	Estimated Annual Savings
Transcription	
Printing supplies	
Chart supplies	
Increased E/M revenue (from bottom row in "Increased Annual E/M Revenue Worksheet")	
Total annual savings	$
Minus total annual cost (from above)	−
Equals net annual benefit (or cost, if negative)	=

This does not take into account savings from reduction in staff hours or include an estimate of increased revenue from better charge capture. Nor does it attempt to quantify any possible decrease in physician productivity during EHR implementation or increase in physician productivity after the EHR is fully operational. It also does not quantify any increased office productivity you may gain from eliminating on-site (and/or off-site) chart storage and regaining that space for patient care (ie, exam rooms). Finally, this tool assumes that you are making up-front payments for expenses. Alternatively, you could apply leases to many of these expenses. This will improve your cash flow but cost you somewhat more in the long run.

INCREASED ANNUAL EVALUATION AND MANAGEMENT REVENUE WORKSHEET

This worksheet can be used to estimate the net increase in evaluation and management (E/M) revenue that can be potentially derived from an electronic health record system (EHR) either per physician or for a whole practice. The assumptions in the worksheet are conservative:

- Only one out of 10 visits currently coded 99213 (10%) should be coded 99214 and that the EHR makes that adjustment.
- There are no coding changes on new patient visits, 99211, 99212, 99214, or preventive care visits.
- All 99213 and 99214 visits are paid at Medicare rates.

Current Medicare payment for 99214 in your area (eg, $73.72):	A	$
Current Medicare payment for 99213 in your area (eg, $47.08):	B	$
Additional income per 99214 visit (A - B):	C	$
Current annual number of visits coded 99213:	D	
Additional visits coded 99214 with improved coding (0.1 × D):	E	
Estimated increase in revenue from improved coding (C × E):		$

Source: Kenneth G. Adler. Why it's time to purchase an electronic health record system. *Fam Pract Manage.* November-December 2004. Available at www.aafp.org/fpm/20041100/43whyi.html. Accessed June 19, 2005. Reprinted with permission.

Patient Safety Tips: Tracking Cytology and Laboratory Test Results

Appropriate and timely follow-up on cytology and other outpatient tests is of paramount importance in avoiding medical errors. Every physician's office should have mechanisms in place to ensure that results are obtained for each test ordered. When planning a cytology/laboratory tracking mechanism, consider the following questions:

1. Is a log kept of all cytology samples submitted to different labs? By whom?

2. Is there a mechanism for tracking delayed reports or those that were never received?

3. As a secondary safety net, are all patients instructed to contact the office regarding Pap results within a specific time period?

4. Who is responsible for receiving the cytology reports?

5. Does the physician see and initial all reports before they are filed in the patient's chart?

6. Is the cytology report attached to the chart at the time it is triaged by the physician (rather than put in a stack of "loose" reports)?

7. Are all reports triaged by the physician, or only abnormal reports?

8. If the physician reviews only the abnormal reports, who determines what constitutes an abnormal report? Are there written guidelines for the office staff?

Source: Bruder KL. Patient safety tips: tracking cytology and lab test results. *ACOG Today.* September 2001. Available at www.acog.org/departments/dept_notice.cfm?recno=28&bulletin=1968. Accessed November 17, 2005. Reprinted with permission.

9. What are the level of education and qualifications of non-physician office staff who participate in the triage process? RN? LPN? colposcopy nurse? medical assistant? clerk?

10. Does the office have a "no-show" policy and mechanism in place?

11. At the end of the workday does the physician personally review the medical record of all patients who "no-show?"

12. Who is responsible for the recall of patients with abnormal cytology? Is a log kept to ensure that the patient was seen and the abnormal results addressed?

13. Is there a policy for the recall of patients who are not accessible by telephone?

14. Does the laboratory have a policy for notifying the clinician about abnormal results?

15. Is there a system for the physician to discuss results directly with the pathologist if needed?

Patient Safety Principles for Office-Based Surgery Utilizing Moderate Sedation/Analgesia, Deep Sedation/Analgesia, or General Anesthesia

The following statement was approved by the ACS Board of Regents at its October 2003 meeting.

Over the past few years, there has been a noticeable increase in the number of invasive procedures being performed in the office setting. Recognizing that many states still haven't issued patient safety guidelines in this area, the American College of Surgeons (ACS) sponsored a resolution, which was passed at the American Medical Association's (AMA's) December 2002 Interim Meeting of its House of Delegates. In brief, the resolution called on the AMA to work with the ACS in "convening a work group of interested specialty societies and state medical associations to identify specific requirements for optimal office-based procedures and utilize those requirements to develop guidelines and model state legislation for use by state regulatory authorities to assure quality of office-based procedures."

On February 5, 2003, the ACS convened a meeting of interested surgical specialty societies to discuss the surgical community's perspective on this issue. In addition, the College invited representatives from the American Society of Anesthesiologists (ASA) to provide information and guidance regarding ASA's anesthesia guidelines. As a result of this meeting, a majority of

Source: Bulletin of the American College of Surgeons, Vol. 89, No. 4, April 2004. Available at www.facs.org/fellows_info/statements/st-46.html. Accessed November 17, 2005. Reprinted with permission.

the surgical community reached consensus on a set of 10 core principles that states should examine when moving to regulate office-based procedures.

Having observed the College's catalytic efforts in this area, the AMA quickly followed suit with a March 17, 2003, meeting of interested parties including: surgical and medical specialty societies; state medical associations; the National Committee on Quality Assurance; and the major accrediting organizations for ambulatory and office-based surgery (Joint Commission on Accreditation of Healthcare Organizations [JCAHO], Accreditation Association for Ambulatory Health Care, Inc., American Association for Accreditation of Ambulatory Surgical Facilities, Inc., and the American Osteopathic Association [AOA]). The March meeting, which was held in consultation with the ACS, used the 10 principles from the College's meeting as the foundation for discussion and debate.

The AMA meeting was co-chaired by LaMar S. McGinnis, Jr., MD, FACS, of the ACS and Clair Callan, MD, of the AMA. The discussion focused on a walk-through of the College's principle document with the work group debating the merits of each principle. After a few minor changes, the members of the work group unanimously approved the revised set of 10 principles.

The following principles were based on a document that was unanimously agreed to by the following groups during a March 17, 2003, ACS/AMA coordinated consensus meeting on office-based surgery:

Accreditation Association for Ambulatory Health Care, American Academy of Cosmetic Surgery, American Academy of Dermatology, American Academy of Facial Plastic and Reconstructive Surgery, American Academy of Ophthalmology, American Academy of Orthopaedic Surgeons, American Academy of Otolaryngology-Head and Neck Surgery, American Academy of Pediatrics, American Association for Accreditation of Ambulatory Surgery Facilities, American College of Obstetricians and Gynecologists, American College of Surgeons, American Medical Association, American Osteopathic Association, American Society for Dermatologic Surgery, American Society for Reproductive Medicine, American Society of Anesthesiologists, American Society of Cataract and Refractive Surgery, American Society of General Surgeons, American Society of Plastic Surgeons, American Urological Association, Federation of State Medical Boards, Indiana State Medical Society, Institute for Medical Quality-California Medical Association, Joint Commission on Accreditation of Healthcare Organizations, Kansas Medical

Society, Massachusetts Medical Society, Medical Association of the State of Alabama, Medical Society of the State of New York, Missouri State Medical Association, National Committee for Quality Assurance, Pennsylvania Medical Society, and Society of Interventional Radiology.

- **Core Principle #1**—Guidelines or regulations should be developed by states for office-based surgery according to levels of anesthesia defined by the American Society of Anesthesiologists' (ASA's) "Continuum of Depth of Sedation" statement dated October 13, 1999, excluding local anesthesia or minimal sedation.[1]

- **Core Principle #2**—Physicians should select patients by criteria including the ASA patient selection Physical Status Classification System[2] and so document.

- **Core Principle #3**—Physicians who perform office-based surgery should have their facilities accredited by the JCAHO, AAAHC, AAAASF, AOA, or by a state-recognized entity such as the Institute for Medical Quality, or be state licensed and/or Medicare-certified.

- **Core Principle #4**—Physicians performing office-based surgery must have admitting privileges at a nearby hospital, a transfer agreement with another physician who has admitting privileges at a nearby hospital, or maintain an emergency transfer agreement with a nearby hospital.

- **Core Principle #5**—States should follow the guidelines outlined by the Federation of State Medical Boards (FSMB) regarding informed consent.[3]

- **Core Principle #6**—States should consider legally privileged adverse incident reporting requirements as recommended by the FSMB[3] and accompanied by periodic peer review and a program of Continuous Quality Improvement.

- **Core Principle #7**—Physicians performing office-based surgery must obtain and maintain board certification from one of the boards recognized by the American Board of Medical Specialties, AOA, or a board with equivalent standards approved by the state medical board within five years of completing an approved residency training program. The procedure must be one that is generally recognized by that certifying board as falling within the scope of training and practice of the physician providing the care.

- **Core Principle #8**—Physicians performing office-based surgery may show competency by maintaining core privileges at an accredited or licensed hospital or ambulatory surgical center, for the procedures they perform in the office setting.

Alternatively, the governing body of the office facility is responsible for a peer review process for privileging physicians based on nationally recognized credentialing standards.

- **Core Principle #9**—At least one physician, who is credentialed or currently recognized as having successfully completed a course in advanced resuscitative techniques (Advanced Trauma Life Support®, Advanced Cardiac Life Support, or Pediatric Advanced Life Support), must be present or immediately available with age- and size-appropriate resuscitative equipment until the patient has met the criteria for discharge from the facility. In addition, other medical personnel with direct patient contact should at a minimum be trained in basic life support.

- **Core Principle #10**—Physicians administering or supervising moderate sedation/analgesia, deep sedation/analgesia, or general anesthesia should have appropriate education and training.

REFERENCES

1. American Society of Anesthesiologists: Continuum of Depth of Sedation. American Society of Anesthesiologists Web site. Internet (http://www.asahq.org/publicationsAndServices/standards/20.htm).

2. American Society of Anesthesiologists: ASA Physical Status Classification System. American Society of Anesthesiologists Web site. Internet (http://www.asahq.org/clinical/physical status.htm).

3. Report of the FSMB Special Committee on Outpatient [Office-Based] Surgery, adopted April 2002. American Society of Anesthesiologists Web site. Internet (http://www.fsmb.org/policydocumentsandwhite papers/outpatient_surgery_cmt_rpt.htm).

Universal Protocol For Preventing Wrong Site, Wrong Procedure, Wrong Person Surgery

Wrong site, wrong procedure, wrong person surgery can be prevented. This universal protocol is intended to achieve that goal. It is based on the consensus of experts from the relevant clinical specialties and professional disciplines and is endorsed by more than 40 professional medical associations and organizations.

In developing this protocol, consensus was reached on the following principles:

- Wrong site, wrong procedure, wrong person surgery can and must be prevented.
- A robust approach—using multiple, complementary strategies—is necessary to achieve the goal of eliminating wrong site, wrong procedure, wrong person surgery.
- Active involvement and effective communication among all members of the surgical team is important for success.
- To the extent possible, the patient (or legally designated representative) should be involved in the process.
- Consistent implementation of a standardized approach using a universal, consensus-based protocol will be most effective.
- The protocol should be flexible enough to allow for implementation with appropriate adaptation when required to meet specific patient needs.
- A requirement for site marking should focus on cases involving right/left distinction, multiple structures (fingers, toes), or levels (spine).

Source: Joint Commission on Accrediation of Healthcare Organizations. 2006. Available at www.jcaho.org/accredited+organizations/ patient+safcty/universal+protocol/universal_protocol.pdf. Accessed November 17, 2005. Reprinted with permission.

- The universal protocol should be applicable or adaptable to all operative and other invasive procedures that expose patients to harm, including procedures done in settings other than the operating room.

In concert with these principles, the following steps, taken together, comprise the Universal Protocol for eliminating wrong site, wrong procedure, wrong person surgery:

- Pre-operative verification process
  - Purpose: To ensure that all of the relevant documents and studies are available prior to the start of the procedure and that they have been reviewed and are consistent with each other and with the patient's expectations and with the team's understanding of the intended patient, procedure, site and, as applicable, any implants. Missing information or discrepancies must be addressed before starting the procedure.
  - Process: An ongoing process of information gathering and verification, beginning with the determination to do the procedure, continuing through all settings and interventions involved in the preoperative preparation of the patient, up to and including the "time out" just before the start of the procedure.
- Marking the operative site
  - Purpose: To identify unambiguously the intended site of incision or insertion.
  - Process: For procedures involving right/left distinction, multiple structures (such as fingers and toes), or multiple levels (as in spinal procedures), the intended site must be marked such that the mark will be visible after the patient has been prepped and draped.
- "Time out" immediately before starting the procedure
  - Purpose: To conduct a final verification of the correct patient, procedure, site and, as applicable, implants.
  - Process: Active communication among all members of the surgical/procedure team, consistently initiated by a designated member of the team, conducted in a "fail-safe" mode, i.e., the procedure is not started until any questions or concerns are resolved.

Medication Dosages for the Elderly

Drug	Recommended Initial Dose[a]	Effective Lower Dose
Acebutolol hydrochloride	400	200
Amitriptyline hydrochloride	50–75	10–25
Amiodipine besylate	5	2.5
Atenolol	50	25
Atorvastatin calcium	10	2.5 and 5
Bisoprolol fumarate	5	2.5[b]
Bupropion hydrochloride	100 BID	50 BID
Celecoxib	100 BID	50 BID
Cerivastatin sodium	0.4	0.2 or 0.3
Chlorthalidone	15	12.5
Cimetidine hydrochloride	800 HS	400 HS
Estrogens, conjugated[c]	0.625	0.3
Diclofenac sodium	50 BID-QID	25 TID
Doxepin hydrochloride	75	10, 25, or 50
Ethacrynic acid	50	25
Famotidine	20 BID or 40 QD or BID	10 BID or 20 QD
Felodipine	5	2.5
Fexofenadine hydrochloride	60 BID	20 TID or 40 BID
Fluoxetine hydrochloride	20	2.5, 5, or 10
Flurazepam hydrochloride	30 QHS	15 QHS
Furosemide	80	40
Hydrochlorothiazide	25	12.5
Ibuprofen	400 TID-QID	200 TID
Imipramine hydrochloride	75	10–25
Lisinopril	10	5
Losartan potassium	50	25

a Dose values are given as milligrams per day unless otherwise indicated. BID, 2 times daily; HS, at bedtime; QID, 4 times daily; TID, 3 times daily; QD, daily; QHS, every night; and XL, extended release.

b Product labeling states the "usual" initial dose is 5mg/d, but notes that 2.5 mg/d may be sufficient for "some patients." The sixth report of the Joint National Committee on Prevention, Detection, Evaluation, and Treatment of High Blood Pressure recommends 2.5 mg/d initially for all patients.

c For vasomotor symptoms

Drug	Recommended Initial Dose[a]	Effective Lower Dose
Lovastatin	20	10
Metoprolol tartrate	50–100	50
Misoprostol	200 μg	50 or 100 μg QID
Nefazodone hydrochloride	100 BID	50 QD or BID
Nizatidine	150 BID or 300 HS	25 BID or 100 HS
Nortriptyline hydrochloride	50–75	10 or 25
Omeprazole	20	10
Ondansetron hydrochloride	8 BID	1–4 TID
Penbutolol sulfate	20	10
Pravastatin sodium	10–20	5-10
Propranolol hydrochloride	80	40
Ramipril	2.5	1.25
Ranitidine hydrochloride	150 BID or 300 HS	100 BID
Sertraline hydrochloride	50	25 once daily
Simvastatin	10–20	2.5, 5, or 10
Spironolactone	50–100	25
Torsemide	10	5
Trazodone hydrochloride	150	25–100
Triamterene	100 BID	25–100 QD
Venlafaxine hydrochloride	75	37.5 or 50 (in divided doses)
Verapamil hydrochloride	120–180	90
Zolpidem tartrate	10 mg vs 5 mg	7.5 HS

Source: Cohen JS. Dose discrepancies between the Physicians' Desk Reference and the medical literature, and their possible role in the high incidence of dose-related adverse drug events. *Arch Intern Med.* 2001;161:957-964. Available at http://archinte.ama-assn.org/cgi/reprint/161/7/957 .pdf. Accessed November 17, 2005. Reprinted with permission. Copyright ©2001, American Medical Association. All rights reserved.

a Dose values are given as milligrams per day unless otherwise indicated. BID, 2 times daily; HS, at bedtime; QID, 4 times daily; TID, 3 times daily; QD, daily; QHS, every night; and XL, extended release.

Selecting and Implementing an Electronic Health Record

Making the transition to an automated, digital office requires nothing less than a transformation of your office. The resources in this section are provided to help you understand the issues and processes involved and to give you the tools to make the transformation a success.

PREPARING YOUR OFFICE

Preparation is the first step in the transition to an EHR. The following resources map out the tasks involved in getting your team assembled and getting your practice ready. It is critical to determine the level of interest and support for an EHR initiative among your colleagues and staff. If you can identify and empower champions, you enhance the likelihood of success. You must also uncover potential resistance. Address individuals' concerns directly and invite them to be involved in the process.

FEAR OF THE UNKNOWN

Change makes people feel uneasy. Such is human nature. You will enhance your chance of success (and minimize trauma to your staff) by tackling this fear head on. Start by making certain your staff and colleagues understand why this change, although

American Academy of Family Practice. Available at www.centerforhit .org/. Accessed March 17, 2005. Reproduced with permission from the EHR Readiness Assessment. Copyright © American Academy of Family Physicians. All rights reserved.

171

difficult, is essential. Do not forget to keep those who are not directly involved in the process updated about its progress. One easy way to do this is to schedule regular meetings to review major decisions and milestones. It is also a good idea to share anticipated timelines with the whole office so they can track the project as it unfolds.

SET EXPECTATIONS

The amount of work required during the transition (and even after) can be substantial. Do not let this come as a surprise to anyone. Make sure your colleagues and staff know what is expected of them. For example, explain that a temporary drop in productivity during the implementation phase is expected and acceptable.

EXPLAIN BENEFITS

Communicate the expected benefits of the EHR implementation—not only the benefits to patients and the practice as a whole, but also to individual staff. For example, highlight benefits such as ready access to charts, fewer chart pulls, improved intra-office communication, and more efficient handling of medication refills.

CHANGE MANAGEMENT AND QUALITY IMPROVEMENT PROCESSES

Implementing an EHR causes many changes in a practice. Use it as an opportunity to improve your practice's efficiency, quality, and safety. Look critically at how things are to be done in the practice. If you have a process for quality improvement (QI), build on it to form a framework to manage the EHR initiative. Your QI activities can serve as a model for how to manage the change introduced by an EHR.

Resources

Change Management Learning Center—This tutorial series offered by the Change Management Learning Center is designed to provide consultants, managers, and practitioners with insight into the field and practice of change management.

Managing Change: An Overview—This article from the *Journal of the American Medical Informatics Association* gives an overview of change management, with special attention to information technology implementation.

Change Management: A Critical Factor in EMR Implementation—A brief article from For the Record magazine about how change management can affect the implementation of an EHR.

AAFP Quality Initiative—The AAFP Quality Initiative is the Academy's effort to establish the discipline of family medicine as the premier medical discipline for quality health care.

ESTABLISH THE EHR TEAM

With any large project, a project team needs to be assembled. There are different roles that need to be filled, but one person may fill more than one role.

Project Manager: This person will manage and oversee all aspects of the EHR project including project administration and resource management.

Clinical Leader: This person will oversee the clinical impact of the project and make decisions about how clinical processes are redesigned.

Business Leader: This person is responsible for overseeing the financial and legal concerns during the project.

Technical Leader: This person is responsible for overseeing the technical aspects of the project. He or she also serves as the technical advisor to the project.

In a small practice, a physician may play all of the roles or they may be split between two physicians. In a medium-sized practice, the champion physician is usually the project manager and the technical leader. Another physician may take the role of clinical leader, and the business manager may take the role of business leader for the project. In a larger practice, the project manager and technical leader may come from outside of the practice.

No matter how these roles are filled, they must be filled. You may want to consider a consultant to fill the role of technical leader and/or project manager. Many EHR vendors can provide consultative services. If a consultant is used, a person in the practice serving in one of the other roles must provide oversight of the consultant.

Resources

Project Management Framework Overview—This handbook sets out a concise, high-level framework for project management. It was developed for the federal government. Although it is geared for larger organizations, it offers great content on people, strategies, and processes in project management.

How to Get More from Your IT Consultant's Time—This article from DM Direct Newsletter outlines strategies to get the most from a consultant.

PERFORM A NEEDS ASSESSMENT

Performing a needs assessment will make it easy to identify products that are suitable for your practice. The size and complexity of your practice will determine the level of detail required in determining your needs. Some factors to consider include:

- Workflow Constraints
- Features/Functionality
- Support/Training
- Hardware
- Consultative Services
- Compatibility
- Connectivity
- Small or Solo Practice

In a small practice, it may be enough to mentally run through these issues. Ask yourself questions such as: How do patients move through my practice? What data do staff and I need? Who collects that data and how does it flow to those that need it? How are my staff and I going to be able to take the time to perform training? What help do I need to get an EHR into my practice?

Medium-sized Practice

In a medium-sized practice, you may need to write down the issues in each area and, as a group, work through what your needs are. It is especially important in medium-sized practices to look for "easy wins" that allow your practice to quickly see the benefits of an EHR. For example, could messaging or e-prescribing be implemented first and improve the efficiency of the practice? If so, they may smooth the way for the rest of the EHR implementation.

Large Practice

In a large practice, there is more of a need for a formal process to define the practice's needs. This may include flow diagrams of patients, data, and staff. It may also include mapping of clinical and business processes.

Resources

Needs Assessment 101—An overview of the steps in a needs assessment and the purpose and goals of those steps.

Needs Assessment—This article from the AAO-HNS Bulletin discusses of the basic facets of a needs assessment.

EXPLORE FINANCING MODELS

Before you begin to consider how to finance your EHR, you need to understand what costs will be incurred and what benefits may be realized. Once you have that information, you can explore different financing options.

Costs

The costs of an EHR implementation include initial expenses as well as ongoing outlays for maintenance.

Costs can be broken down into one of two categories: initial or implementation; and maintenance or recurring. These represent your up-front costs and your annual budgeting costs, respectively. Each category can be subdivided into software, hardware, and services.

Hardware will vary based on the EHR you choose. For example, application service provider (ASP) EHRs will typically have lower hardware requirements than a traditional client-server based EHR. Of course, the size of the practice affects the hardware requirements.

Software costs include the EHR itself but also contain add-on or support applications that are needed (such as interfaces to a practice management or lab system). Support applications may also include faxing, scanning, or word processing applications.

Services include support, training, and any consultants.

Benefits

Benefits of an EHR can include not only productivity and financial improvements but also improved quality of care and enhanced job satisfaction.

Benefits of an EHR can be categorized as follows:

Productivity and Financial Improvement
Fewer chart pulls
Reduced transcription cost
Improved efficiency of handling telephone messages and medication refills

Increased formulary compliance and accurate prescription leading to fewer pharmacy call backs

Improved billing

Improved coding of visits

Additional potential benefits may include: population management and proactive reminders to patients to be seen; improved reimbursement for payers due to using an EHR; and future participation in pay-for-performance programs.

Quality of Care Improvement

Easier preventive care leading to increased preventive care services

Easier chronic disease management

Point-of-care decision support

Integration of evidence-based clinical guidelines

Rapid and remote access to patient information

Job Satisfaction Improvement

Fewer repetitive, tedious tasks

Access to patient information while on-call or at the hospital

Less "chart chasing"

Easier compliance with regulations

Improved intra-office communication

Demonstrable high-quality care

Customer Satisfaction Improvement

Quick access to their records

Improved continuity of care (fewer visits without the chart)

Reduced turn-around time for telephone messages and medication refills

Improved delivery of patient education materials

A more efficient office leads to improved patient access to physicians

Resources—Tools and articles to help assess costs, benefits, and financing options

Return on Investment Calculator for EHRs—This interactive form from www.emrupdate.com can help you understand the potential cost of an EHR.

Running the Numbers: Making Sure Your Spending Pays Off—This article from *American Medical News* describes four steps to ensure that you are spending wisely.

Financing High Tech: You Can Afford It After All—This article in American Medical News decribes financing an EHR from a specialist point of view.

A Beginner's Guide to Financing an EHR—This article from EHR vendor PMSI describes financing an EHR. (PDF file: 8 pages/516 KB)

Cost–Benefit Analysis of an EHR in Primary Care—This article from the *American Journal of Medicine* explores a cost-benefit analysis of a primary care EHR. The authors conclude: "Implementation of an electronic medical record system in primary care can result in a positive financial return on investment to the health care organization." (PDF file: 7 pages/116 KB)

Economic Impact of Implementing an EHR in an Outpatient Setting—This study documents the evaluation of the economic impact of implementing an EHR in a large, multi-specialty, multi-site ambulatory practice. (PDF file: 6 pages/547 KB)

STUDY WORKFLOW PROBLEMS

Identify actual (and perceived) sources of inefficiency, delay, duplication of effort, or wasted time that you hope an EHR can help alleviate. It is a useful exercise to calculate what these workflow issues may be costing you in time and money. Some examples include:

- Time spent on the phone regarding medication changes or prescription refills
- Delays due to trouble finding paper medical records
- Delays in locating laboratory or other clinical results performed outside the practice
- High costs associated with transcription of medical notes and other documents via a transcription service

As you examine workflow problems, it is important to be realistic about what computers and software can really do. No software program can do everything or even perform routine tasks that it has not been designed to do. For example, reports that include lab results cannot be generated unless the lab results have been entered into the database. Similarly, alerts and reminders won't be generated unless someone has programmed them into the system.

It is also important to look critically at how features or functions of EHRs can save time or improve efficiency. Some that at first blush promise to be efficiency gainers in reality turn out to increase administrative costs. For example, e-prescribing software that prints to a printer and then must be faxed to the pharmacy could be more work—not less—for your practice. E-prescribing is truly efficiency gaining only when the prescription can be sent electronically to its place of fulfillment, the PBM or the pharmacy. This scenario cuts down on paperwork and filing, especially when done within the context of a full EHR.

It is critical to identify the features and functions that are of actual importance and likely to benefit your medical practice. The right features make it more likely that the right things will be done consistently, and that quality results will be routine instead of haphazard.

Resources

The Practice Redesign Guide—A compendium of redesign information from the AAFP that provides ideas and tools to make the practice of tomorrow a reality today.

Strategies for Better Patient Flow and Cycle Time—This article from *Family Practice Management* can help you identify problem areas in patient flow and strategies to address issues. Although published in 2002, the issues and strategies hold true.

IHI.org Patient Cycle Tool—This tool from the Institute for Healthcare Improvement helps you look at the total time patients are spending in the office, with the goal of minimizing wait times and maximizing time spent with the physician.

High Performance Physician Institute—The High Performance Physician Institute exposes physicians to solutions developed by colleagues which address pressing issues such as accurate coding, regulatory compliance, payment for work done, detailed documentation, streamlining workflow, and prompt payment with fewer rejected claims.

DEVELOP A CONTENGENCY PLAN FOR DOWNTIME AND DATA LOSS

It might seem early to consider what could go wrong with an EHR, but now is the time to start contingency planning. At this stage it is important to know the potential impact of different architectures and technologies on a contingency plan. In evaluating vendors, consider what capacity they have to help you do this planning. This type of planning is required under the HIPAA security rule. Circumstances to consider:

- Scheduled downtime
- Short-term system outage
- Long-term system outage
- End of life
- Back-up and data loss

Scheduled Downtime

The issue here is understanding the amount of downtime the vendor expects for maintenance, upgrades, etc. Once you have a short list of a couple of EHRs, insist that each vendor schedule downtime that has the least impact on the practice (ie, nights or weekends).

Short-term System Outage

This may be from either scheduled or unscheduled downtime. The issue here is what process and/or resources need to be in place to keep the practice functioning during the downtime. In a short-term outage (< 1 day), workarounds can be put in place, such as stop scheduling non-acute visits until the next day or entering visit information on paper forms and entering it into the EHR when the system is back. It is important is for people to know what to do during the downtime and how to handle emergencies.

Long-term System Outage

Not only are there the same issues as short-term outage, but they are compounded by the length of downtime. Many of the stopgap measures successful in a short-term outage are not sufficient for a long-term outage (> 1 day). This is where the contingency planning can really pay off. Issues such as (1) alternative patient scheduling options, (2) alternative data access, (3) and alternative data entry should be part of the contingency plan.

End of Life

The ultimate in system outages is end of life of the EHR. This may come due to collapse of the vendor and product or need to switch vendors or EHRs. The issue here is data migration. The contingency plan should lay out the responsibilities of the vendor to provide access to the data in a usable form.

Back-up and Data Loss

Part of the contingency plan contains procedures to prevent data loss. The backing-up of data from an EHR is more complicated than copying the data to a disk. The type of EHR purchased will govern the amount of resources needed to maintain adequate back-ups of the data. For example, application service provider (ASP) based system require the vendor to maintain the back-ups. With the ASP model you must confirm that the EHR vendor has the resources and procedures needed to adequately back up the data. (To learn more about back-up methods, check out the NIST guide listed below under "Resources.") In contrast, with a client-server based EHR the server resides in your office and you are solely responsible for backing-up the data.

Resources

NIST Contingency Planning Guide for Information Technology Systems—This contingency planning guide by the National Institute of Standards and Technology (NIST) is a useful reference and contains detailed descriptions of the planning process and each component of such a plan.

Automated Information Systems Security Program Handbook—This Department of Health and Human Services (DHHS) handbook is a complete source for planning security for computer systems in the health care environment. Chapter VI deals with contingency planning.

SELECTING AN ELECTRONIC HEALTH RECORD

Once the office has prepared for an EHR, the next step is selecting the right EHR. These resources map out the tasks involve in selecting an EHR. For each task, resources are available to help you complete the task.

To determine if this is the right place for you to start and to tailor the content for your practice, take the Readiness Assessment (AAFP Members Only).

Once the office has prepared for an EHR, the next step is selecting the right EHR. These resources map out the tasks involved in selecting an EHR. Click each task to learn more and find related resources.

FIND A PERSON LIKE YOU

Your peers may be your best resource during the EHR selection process. They can give you insight into how they prepared for, selected, and ultimately used their EHR. You can adopt what they did right and learn from any missteps. These peers can also give you unbiased or "rightly" biased opinions and experiences with specific vendors and products.

The only caveat is to make sure you find peers who really are like you. You are looking for physicians who have a similarly sized practice. The issues of small practices and large practices are very different. Also make sure they had a similar experience or understanding of information technology when they started. (Of course, they are going to have more experience now that they have implemented an EHR.)

Resources

Find a Doctor Like Me in a Practice Like Mine (AAFP Members Only)—This interactive tool allows you to search for physicians who currently use EHR systems. You may search by product, state, and practice size. All physicians in this tool have agreed to be contacted for advice and feedback for those seeking to implement EHRs

EHR Lectures and Workshops—AAFP and state chapter events on EHRs and health IT

AAFP Electronic Medical Record Discussion List (AAFP Members Only)—Hundreds of family physicians who have an EHR or are looking for one participate in this list. This link will take you to the AAFP Web site; you will need your member ID to log-in (unless you are already logged in). Click the subscribe button beneath "Electronic Medical Record." You will receive an introductory e-mail at the account you have on file with AAFP. The discussion list is moderated by CHiT staff.

DEVELOP AN EHR EVALUATION MATRIX

Now that you have performed the needs assessment and explored the financial options, you can construct an evaluation matrix. The matrix is a simple grid. Across the top are the criteria you want in your EHR and down the side are the EHRs you're considering. You can enter the information about how each EHR meets your criteria and easily compare products. You can also send the empty matrix to each vendor you are considering and ask them complete it.

When EHR certification standards become a reality in the not-too-distant future, it will be easier to evaluate products based on their functionality. Then the evaluation matrix becomes easier and criteria such as vendor stability, compatibility, and interoperability will move to the forefront of the evaluation process.

Resources

California HealthCare Foundation EMR Evaluation Tool—An example of an evaluation matrix, this tool consists of an Excel spreadsheet (compressed as a zip file) and a PDF with instructions.

FPM Vendor Survey—Although the survey data is from 2001, you can use the approach and the matrix to create your own evaluation matrix.

Integrimed Article on EHR Evaluation—This article by Integrimed from 2001 demonstrates another approach to an EHR evaluation matrix. What is important here is to expose you to another set of criteria to consider in your matrix. (PDF file: 4 pages/49 KB)

A Critical Pathway for Electronic Medical Record Selection—This article outlines the selection process used in the COMPETE study—a comprehensive evaluation of EHR implementation in family practices in Canada. They used an evaluation matrix as part of their process.

EHR DEMONSTRATIONS

Several options are available to see an EHR demonstrated. Each method has its pros and cons, and you may choose to use more than one in your evaluation process.

Non-interactive Video

This requires the fewest resources from the practice, but it is also offers the least benefit. This type of video can give you clues into the complexity of the user-interface and a glimpse into the functionality. Keep in mind that the video was produced by the vendor to showcase the best of the product and what the vendor thinks is important. This type of demonstration is useful when your EHR list of contenders is long.

Interactive Trial Demo

This requires more time compared with non-interactive video. Your goal during the demonstration should be to gauge the ease of use. The questions you want answered are: Is the product intuitive? Is it easy and quick to perform repetitive tasks (eg, writing a prescription)? Is it easy to find specific patient information?

Vendor Directed Demo

This will require more time than an interactive trial demo and you will need to schedule it with the vendor. Your goal during the demonstration should be to understand the true functionality available in the system. (If you have not already had an interactive demo, you will need to answer those questions as well.) Come prepared with your list of criteria from your evaluation matrix. You want to see how the functions you require are accomplished. Also bring any issues you uncovered during the interactive trial demo. Besides the functionality, you want to see the workflow. The easiest way to accomplish this is to bring some clinical scenarios that mirror what you see in practice (eg, acute visit for URI; chronic disease care for new and follow-up patients; routine visits such as annual or well child exam). Study how these mock patients flow through the system and how the data is entered and viewed by front desk, nurse, physician, billing, etc.

Live Site Demo

This requires the most resources from the practice, but offers the largest reward in terms of getting data about an EHR. Because of the time, travel, and money involved in this type of demonstration, many physicians limit these to their final few contenders. To set up a live site demo, you first need to find peers like yourself that are using the EHR in their practice. Besides these resources, you can ask the vendor to give you a list of family physicians using their EHR in your region. By asking a vendor for a list, however, you accept the likelihood that these users are happy with their EHR—since it is in the vendor's best interest. You can mitigate this by doing two things: (1) Ask for a list of 10-20 users and (2) Briefly interview the users by telephone before scheduling a site visit. Asking for such a large list and interviewing users can help you find some who may have had a problem with the EHR. You want to ask questions about how they deal with negatives of the system and how well they can explain the functions of the system. This demonstration should build on the previous demonstrations. If you have the resources, doing more than one site visit for a particular EHR is beneficial.

MEASURING SUCCESS

It is useful to consider how you are going to tell whether you were successful in your transition to an EHR. Is it that you use the EHR? Is it that you increased revenue? Is it higher job satisfaction? Or is it some combination of these?

You should make time to think about what you consider a successful transition and how you might demonstrate that it was or was not a success. If you are feeling more ambitious, you can develop a detailed framework with pre- and post-measures to determine whether your EHR implementation succeeded.

Resources

Measuring the Success of Electronic Medical Record Implementation Using Electronic and Survey Data—The COMPETE group developed survey tools to measure medical office processes, including administrative and physician tasks, pre- and post-EMR implementation. They included variables that were expected to improve with EMR implementation, as well as those that were not expected to improve as control measures.

Finding the Value in Healthcare Information Technologies—This Center for Information Technology Leadership article reviews the literature on demonstrating value with health IT. The results of the literature are disappointing, but look at "Sidebar: The Three Dimensions of Value for Healthcare IT" on page 5.

Evaluating Benefits and Return on Investment (ROI) for Clinical Information Systems—Informatics-review.com has put together this list of articles about EHR benefits and return on investment. Currently the resources on this page are slightly aged.

COMPARING EHR SYSTEMS (ARTICLES & REPORTS)

A number of resources exist to help you determine how to go about purchasing EHR software. Below are links to information provided by various companies that work with physicians and others to evaluate needs and choose the best software to meet them. You will also find links to software ratings reports for EHRs.

You may also visit the Center for Health Information Technology's EHR Product Reviews (AAFP members only) where you will find a continually updated list of reviews of EHRs used by family physicians.

Articles

CTS—Articles by CTS, an independent software consulting company. Topics include "20 Insights to Smart Software Buying," "Secrets of Choosing Medical Software," "Medical Software—Time to Change?," "Network Selection Mysteries, Solved," and "Who's in Charge—You or the Reseller?" Free registration is required to view the articles.

Ratings Reports

AC Group—Each year ACG publishes a mid-year report rating the most common EHR systems. AC Group, Inc. (ACG) is an information technology advisory and research service for the health care industry. They provide independent, advisory, and consultative services designed to assist with business strategies, market and customer strategies, competitive analysis, and product profiling. Their mid-year report is available for purchase.

KLAS Reports—The KLAS database reports vendor performance data from 4500+ health care facilities, 300 HIT vendors, and 500 different products. The database is continually updated with reports from health care professionals across the United States, Canada, and selected countries around the world. (Subscription required.)

IMPLEMENTING AN ELECTRONIC HEALTH RECORD

Once you have selected your EHR, you will need to focus on planning and executing a successful implementation. These resources map out the tasks involved in implementing an EHR. For each task, resources are available to help you complete the task.

To determine if this is the right place for you to start and to tailor the content for your practice, take the Readiness Assessment.

Once you have selected you EHR, your focus should shift to planning and executing a successful implementation. These resources map out the tasks involved.

MAINTAINING AND UPGRADING INFORMATION TECHNOLOGY

Once information technology has been implemented in the office, the focus becomes maintaining that infrastructure. These resources can help you maintain and upgrade that technology.

Electronic Health Record Features and Functions

- Support for improved, safer patient care
- Pharmaceutical support, prevent
  - Dosage errors
  - Handwriting misrecognition
  - Medication conflict with allergies
  - Medication conflict with other medications
  - Medication conflict with medical conditions
  - Confirmation for proposed prescriptions: available in the pharmacy, in insurance plan's formulary, affordable
  - Electronic communication with the pharmacy; shorter patient wait time
- Clinical guidelines
- Reminders for current evidence based clinical guidelines
  - Prompts during documentation of a patient visit facilitate awareness of pertinent evidence based evaluation and treatment modalities
  - Notification of new medications, dosages, complications, etc
- Patient support
  - Printed instructions in the appropriate language
  - Patient online participation in chronic illness care, including apprised of current medical status, (eg, HgbA1c)
  - Communication with patients via the Internet
  - View medical history online
  - View laboratory or radiology, etc, results online
  - Schedule appointments online
  - Effective, unique patient education

Adapted from EMR Consultant. http://emrconsultant.com/whyemr.php. Accessed September 30, 2005.

- Language appropriate pamphlets
- Online tutorials
- Continuing medical education
- Reduce risk and malpractice exposure
  - Misdiagnosis
  - Treating outside of current clinical guidelines
  - Lost test results, charts
  - Improper/inadequate documentation
  - In the event of a drug recall (eg, Vioxx,) EHR will allow automatic immediate contact of patients currently taking a recalled medication
- Online connection to with laboratory and radiology facilities
  - Automatic lab and radiology results downloads to patient charts
  - Automatic alerts for abnormal laboratory and test results, permitting prompt response and appropriate action
  - Electronic entry into patient record of other ancillary service reports, such as endoscopies, EKG, ultrasound, etc
  - Minimize or eliminate duplication of documentation of other reports, such as cardiac catheterization, etc
- Support images and full video to be part of the medical documentation
- Direct connectivity with pharmacies
- More effective communication with other physicians through EHR interconnectivity features
- Reduce office overhead costs
  - Improved workflow
  - Eliminate transcription costs
  - Complete documentation in a shorter period of time (once accustomed to using an EHR)
  - Eliminate costs for paper charts
  - Cost of paper itself
  - Cost for employees pulling and filing charts
  - Cost and liabilities of looking for and transfer of lost charts
  - Cost of storage of paper charts
  - Cost of destruction of paper charts
  - Earlier prescription notification
  - Save time telephoning patients with their lab/radiology reports (view online)
  - Allow patients to fill out their past history online, or in a kiosk in the waiting room, minimizing staff expense in obtaining this information

- Allow patients to make and modify their appointment schedules online, thereby minimizing staff expense for scheduling
- Minimize the number of telephone lines required in the office because much of the office or patient interaction will occur via the Internet

■ Enhance reimbursement for physician services
  - Coding compliance for accurate billing
  - Prompts for appropriate documentation to support medical necessity
  - Prompts for medical decision making
  - Documentation templates for history, physical, and medical decision making
  - Prevent performing medical services without billing
  - Avoid lost superbills
  - Avoid failure to code for ancillary services performed
  - Assist with enhanced revenue from "pay-for-performance" associated with higher quality care (eg, DOQ-IT)
  - Support billing for e-mail consultations with patients
  - Support participation in clinical trials, if desired

■ Assist with electronic billing
  - Medical records are already in an electronic and thereby easy to transmit format
  - Billing is already correlated with the medical records and in a format appropriate for electronic billing

■ Enhance reputation in the medical community
  - Documented fewer complications and treatment errors
  - Provide more comprehensive documentation to referral sources
  - Provide consultation/referral reports in a more timely fashion

■ Generate more free time

■ Assist with HIPAA compliance

■ Maintain patient record confidentiality

■ Automatically maintain multiple levels of security, access, etc, records

■ Minimize the exposure due to charts inadvertently left in accessible areas

AMA National Medical Specialty Societies

The following list is adapted from the AMA Web site (www.ama-assn.org/ama/pub/category/7634.html) and features societies that strongly advocate for patient safety.

Aerospace Medical Association (www.asma.org/)

American Academy of Allergy Asthma & Immunology (www.aaaai.org/)

American Academy of Child & Adolescent Psychiatry (www.aacap.org/)

American Academy of Cosmetic Surgery (www.cosmeticsurgery.org/)

American Academy of Dermatology (www.aad.org)

American Academy of Facial Plastic and Reconstructive Surgery (www.facial-plastic-surgery.org/)

American Academy of Family Physicians (www.aafp.org)

On its Web site, AAFP states its mission, goals, and objectives as the following:

Mission[1]

The American Academy of Family Physicians' Developmental Center for Research and Evaluation in Patient Safety-Primary Care (AAFP DCERPS-PC) will improve the safety and quality of medical care in family practice and other primary care office settings through research, evaluation, education, and dissemination.

Goals

1. Patient-focused goal: Patients of family physicians will receive safe care that minimizes risk of injury from the medical system. Patients will perceive that they receive safe medical care.

2. Physician-focused goal: Family physicians will practice a high standard of patient safety.

3. Family practice-focused goal: Family physicians' offices will be safe environments for patient care.

4. AAFP-focused goal: The AAFP DCERPS-PC will be nationally recognized as a center of excellence in patient safety research, evaluation, education, and dissemination.

5. External-focused goal: The AAFP DCERPS-PC will share its findings with other primary care and patient safety organizations.

Objectives

1. Patient-focused objectives:

   a. Decrease adverse outcomes related to medical errors in family physicians' offices.

   b. Educate patients in their roles in improving the safety of primary care practice

2. Physician-focused objectives:

   a. Improve family physicians' knowledge of strategies to improve patient safety.

   b. Assist family physicians in initiating and adopting strategies to improve patient safety in their offices.

   c. Family physicians will know about the activities of the Center and use its resources.

3. Family practice-focused objectives:

   a. Establish and maintain a useful and confidential reporting system to monitor patient safety events in family practice.

   b. Understand threats to patient safety in family physician office settings and to monitor changes.

   c. Develop and test strategies for patient safety improvement in office settings.

The **AAFP Center for Information Technology** (www.centerforhit.org/) is also a robust source of information.

American Academy of Hospice & Palliative Medicine (www.aahpm.org/)
American Academy of Insurance Medicine (www.aaimedicine.org/)
American Academy of Neurology (www.aan.com/)
American Academy of Ophthalmology (www.aao.org/)
American Academy of Orthopaedic Surgeons (www.aaos.org/)
American Academy of Otolaryngic Allergy (www.aaoaf.org/)
American Academy of Otolaryngology—Head and Neck Surgery (www.entnet.org/)
American Academy of Pain Medicine (www.painmed.org/)
American Academy of Pediatrics (www.aap.org/)
American Academy of Pharmaceutical Physicians (www.aapp.org/)

American Academy of Physical Medicine & Rehabilitation
(www.aapmr.org/)

American Academy of Psychiatry & the Law
(www.aapl.org/)

American Academy of Sleep Medicine (www.aasmnet.org/)

American Association for Hand Surgery
(www.handsurgery.org/)

American Association for Thoracic Surgery (www.aats.org/)

American Association of Clinical Endocrinologists
(www.aace.com/)

American Association of Clinical Urologists
(www.aacuweb.org/)

**American Association of Neuromuscular and
Electrodiagnostic Medicine** (www.aaem.net/)

American Association of Gynecologic Laparoscopists
(www.aagl.com/aagl.asp)

American Association of Hip and Knee Surgeons
(www.aahks.org/)

American Association of Neurological Surgeons
(www.aans.org/)

American Association of Plastic Surgeons
(www.aaps1921.org/)

American Association of Public Health Physicians
(www.aaphp.org/)

American Clinical Neurophysiology Society
(www.acns.org/)

American College of Allergy, Asthma, & Immunology
(http://allergy.mcg.edu/home.html)

American College of Cardiology (www.acc.org/)

American College of Chest Physicians (www.chestnet.org/)

American College of Emergency Physicians (www.acep.org/)

American College of Gastroenterology
(www.acg.gi.org/acghome.html)

American College of Medical Genetics (www.acmg.net/)

American College of Medical Quality (www.acmq.org/)

American College of Nuclear Medicine
(www.acnucmed.com/)

American College of Nuclear Physicians
(www.acnponline.org/)

American College of Obstetricians and Gynecologists (www.acog.com/)

Patient safety related articles are available on the ACOG Web site:

- Patient Safety: A New Imperative
- Patient Safety Series: Improving Patient Safety in the Surgical Environment
- Patient Safety Tips: How to Safely Introduce New Technology in Practice
- Patient Safety Series: Safe Medication Prescribing
- Patient Safety Tips: How to Avoid Medication Errors
- Patient Safety Tips: Disclosure of Adverse Outcomes
- Patient Safety Tips: Sentinel Events
- Patient Safety Tips: Tracking Cytology and Lab Test Results

American College of Occupational and Environmental Medicine (www.acoem.org/)

American College of Physician Executives (www.acpe.org/)

American College of Physicians (www.acponline.org/)

The major patient safety activities of the ACP include advocacy efforts for a nonpunitive, systems approach on patient safety, cooperative efforts on patient safety with other organizations, and a wide array of medical education activities aimed at improving clinical performance and minimizing health care errors.

ACP has initiated a robust continuing medical education program titled "Patient Safety: The Other Side of the Quality Equation" (for details, see www.acponline.org/ptsafety/).

American College of Preventive Medicine (www.acpm.org/)

American College of Radiation Oncology (www.acro.org/)

American College of Radiology (www.acr.org/)

American College of Rheumatology (www.rheumatology.org/)

American College of Surgeons (www.facs.org/)

The ACS publishes a 200-page manual titled *Surgical Patient Safety: Essential Information for Surgeons in Today's Environment* that provides guidance and leadership in evolving areas of patient safety.

American Gastroenterological Association (www.gastro.org/)

American Geriatrics Society (www.americangeriatrics.org/)

American Institute of Ultrasound in Medicine (www.aium.org/)

American Medical Directors Association (www.amda.com/)

American Medical Group Association (www.amga.org/)

Along with the National Committee for Quality Assurance (NCQA) and Pharmacia, AMGA is a part of the Safety Collaborative for the Outpatient Environment (SCOPE). The primary goals of SCOPE are to (1) promote patient safety improvement innovations in the ambulatory setting through grants to support improvement initiatives and (2) establish a collaborative of physician-led organizations to standardize patient safety definitions and evaluation criteria, share information on best practices, and recognize outstanding performance.

American Orthopaedic Association (www.aoassn.org/)
American Orthopaedic Foot and Ankle Society (www.aofas.org/)
American Pediatric Surgical Association (www.eapsa.org/)

American Psychiatric Association (www.psych.org/)

The APA site provides a resource page that links to numerous articles and informative sites regarding the following topics:

- Starting points for the psychiatrist
- Office-based issues
- Adverse medication events
- Suicide assessment and interventions
- Information for patients and families
- Inpatient issues
- Seclusion and restraint
- Use of computers
- Psychiatric residence
- Other resources

American Roentgen Ray Society (www.arrs.org/)
American Society for Aesthetic Plastic Surgery (http://surgery.org/)
American Society for Clinical Pathology (www.ascp.org/)
American Society for Dermatologic Surgery (www.asds-net.org/)
American Society for Gastrointestinal Endoscopy (www.asge.org/)
American Society for Reproductive Medicine (www.asrm.org/)
American Society for Surgery of the Hand (www.hand-surg.org/)
American Society for Therapeutic Radiology and Oncology (www.astro.org/)
American Society of Abdominal Surgeons (www.gis.net/~absurg)
American Society of Addiction Medicine (www.asam.org/)

American Society of Anesthesiologists (www.asahq.org/)

The Anesthesia Patient Safety Foundation (www.apsf.org/) has been a leader in the patient safety initiative for more than two decades.

The mission of the Anesthesia Patient Safety Foundation is to ensure that no patient shall be harmed by anesthesia. The purposes of APSF are to foster investigations that will provide a better understanding of preventable anesthetic injuries; encourage programs that will reduce the number of anesthetic injuries; and promote national and international communication of information and ideas about the causes and prevention of anesthetic morbidity and mortality.

American Society of Bariatric Physicians (www.asbp.org/)
American Society of Cataract and Refractive Surgery (www.ascrs.org/)
American Society of Clinical Oncology (www.asco.org/)
American Society of Colon and Rectal Surgeons (www.fascrs.org/ascrs-who.html)
American Society of Cytopathology (www.cytopathology.org/)
American Society of General Surgeons (www.theasgs.org/)
American Society of Hematology (www.hematology.org/)
American Society of Maxillofacial Surgeons (www.maxface.org/left.html)
American Society of Neuroimaging (www.asnweb.org/)
American Society of Neuroradiology (www.asnr.org/)
American Society of Ophthalmic Plastic and Reconstructive Surgery (www.asoprs.org/)

American Society of Plastic Surgeons (www.plasticsurgery.org/)

Patient Advisory Recommendations[2]

Hypothermia. Hypothermia (low body temperature) can develop because of a cold operating room as well as anesthesia's negative effect on the body's ability to regulate temperature. To prevent the condition, temperatures in the office operating room must be adequately monitored and adjustable. The surgery suite should be equipped with warming blankets and intravenous fluid warmers to keep the patient warm. Without these measures, procedures performed should be less than two hours and limited to no more than 20% of the body surface area.

Blood loss. Significant blood loss can lead to an unstable condition during and after the procedure for the patient. Procedures on an average-size adult patient where 500 cc (about a pint) or greater anticipated blood loss is expected should be performed only in facilities where adequate blood products are readily available.

Liposuction with multiple procedures concurrently. The benefits of combining cosmetic procedures, particularly liposuction, must be weighed against the possibility of complications. The removal of fat and liquid should be limited to 5000 cc or less.

Large-volume liposuction, in combination with certain other procedures (such as tummy tucks) where serious complications can arise, should be avoided.

Procedure duration. Most plastic surgery procedures including facelifts, nose reshapings, breast reductions, liposuction, and tummy tucks typically take longer than an hour to complete. Lengthy procedures should be scheduled early in the day, if possible to be completed by 3 p.m. to allow adequate time for patient recovery and discharge. Ideally, the duration of the procedure(s) should be completed within six hours.

Blood clots. The development of blood clots (deep vein thrombosis leading to pulmonary embolus) remains a small but significant risk for surgical patients. As part of the patient history and physical exam, attention should be paid to factors that predispose the patient to thrombosis or embolism, including the use of contraceptives and hormone replacement; family history with attention to past episodes of thrombosis or embolism; genetic disposition to clotting disorders, swelling or other signs of poor circulation in the legs. Next, the patient should be assigned a risk status of low, moderate, or high and necessary measures should be established for each status.

Postoperative recovery problems. Unplanned hospital admission following office-based plastic surgery results primarily from dizziness, pain, and nausea or vomiting. Control of nausea or vomiting, dizziness, and pain is essential to timely postoperative recovery and discharge. Pain management should be based on body mass index and the procedure performed. Additionally, the patient should be sent home with sufficient pain medication and adequate instructions for its use.

Provider qualifications. Regardless of the location of the surgical facility, the physician should have hospital privileges for the procedure being performed and be qualified for examination by or be board-certified in a surgical specialty recognized by The American Board of Medical Specialties, such as The American Board of Plastic Surgery (ABPS).

Surgical facility standards. Plastic surgery performed under anesthesia, other than minor local anesthesia and/or minimal oral tranquilization, should be performed in a facility that meets at least one of the following criteria:

- Accredited by a national or state-recognized accrediting agency/organization such as
  - American Association for Accreditation of Ambulatory Surgery Facilities (AAAAЗГ)
  - Accreditation Association for Ambulatory Health Care (AAAHC)
  - Joint Commission on Accreditation of Healthcare Organizations (JCAHO)
- Certified to participate in the Medicare program under Title XVIII
- Licensed by the state in which the facility operates

All ASPS members who perform plastic surgery in offices where patients are under anesthesia were required to have their offices accredited by July 1, 2002 to promote patient safety in the office-based setting. By choosing an ASPS member plastic surgeon certified by the ABPS, patients are assured that the physician has graduated from an accredited medical school and completed at least five years of additional residency, usually three years of general surgery and two years of plastic surgery.

ASPS, founded in 1931, is the largest plastic surgery organization in the world and the foremost authority on cosmetic and reconstructive plastic surgery. ASPS represents physicians certified by The American Board of Plastic Surgery (ABPS) or The Royal College of Physicians and Surgeons of Canada.

Plastic surgery is serious, and just as with any operation, surgical procedures carry risks. The American Society of Plastic Surgeons (ASPS), the foremost authority on cosmetic and reconstructive plastic surgery, has always led the specialty in safety initiatives and continues to make patient safety the society's number one priority.

"With the increasing popularity of plastic surgery, combined with the reality show Extreme Makeover, it could be easy for the general public to overlook the serious nature of elective cosmetic surgical procedures," said Rod Rohrich, MD, president of the American Society of Plastic Surgeons. "But what the public needs to know is that at the highest level of care, every surgery has risks as well as benefits."

The ASPS has implemented the following initiatives to promote patient safety:

The ASPS created its Patient Safety Task Force in 2000, which developed advisories for members on surgery in the office-based setting. Advisories on general patient safety issues and patient selection were published in *Plastic and Reconstructive Surgery*, the ASPS peer-reviewed medical journal in 2002. Advisories on liposuction as well as pain management and post-operative nausea will be published in 2004 and 2005.

As of July, 2002, all ASPS members who perform plastic surgery under anesthesia, other than minor local anesthesia, are required to perform the procedures in accredited facilities.

The ASPS has a national database "Tracking Operations and Outcomes for Plastic Surgeons" (TOPS), that collects procedure and outcome data that will provide information to demonstrate the quality of care provided by board-certified plastic surgeons.

The ASPS approved a patient safety continuing medical education (CME) requirement for all members.

The ASPS will work with accrediting agencies for office-based surgical facilities to develop a definition of reportable adverse incidents as well as minimum quality assurance standards for office-based surgical facilities.

The ASPS developed the "Statement of Principle on Informed Consent," which details the information that should be discussed and understood by the patient, including: details of the surgery, benefits, possible consequences and side effects of the operation, potential risks and adverse outcomes as well as their probability and severity; alternatives to the procedure being considered and their benefits, risks and consequences; and the anticipated outcome. The ASPS recognizes the physician–patient relationship is one of shared decision-making.

The ASPS fully supports the Patient Safety and Quality Improvement Act, H.R. 663, which would enable surgeons and other health care providers to learn why medical errors and adverse events occur so that the necessary changes can be made. HR 663 was passed by the House of Representatives last year. The Senate is expected to take up similar legislation in early 2004.

Finally, the ASPS offers the following suggestions to anyone interested in having cosmetic plastic surgery.

Check Board Certification: Determine if your physician is certified by a board approved by The American Board of Medical Specialties (ABMS). Members of the ASPS are certified by The American Board of Plastic Surgery, the only board recognized by ABMS that certifies physicians in plastic surgery of the face and all areas of the body. This ensures that the plastic surgeon has graduated from an accredited medical school and completed at least five years of surgical residency, usually three years of general surgery and two years of plastic surgery.

Ensure Safe Facilities: Everyone who chooses cosmetic plastic surgery has the right to a safe procedure. Injectables should be administered in a setting with appropriate medical personnel and necessary equipment to observe patients and manage potential complications, as well as provide for the disposal of medical waste as required by Occupational Safety and Health Administration regulations. ASPS requires all members who perform surgery under anesthesia to do so in an accredited, licensed or Medicare-approved facility.

Require a Medical Evaluation: When considering a cosmetic plastic surgery procedure, consult with a physician for an evaluation, as well as a full medical history, to determine what is most appropriate.

Be Informed: Speak with friends and family about the procedure as well as with a physician. When a treatment decision is made co-operatively between the physician and patient, the physician should explain the risks, benefits, alternatives, and reasoning for the proposed treatment, after which an informed consent document should be signed by the patient.

Look For Specialty Group Affiliation: Membership in the ASPS ensures that not only is the plastic surgeon certified by the American Board of Plastic Surgery, but that the plastic surgeon regularly attends continuing medical education courses and adheres to a strict code of ethics. For referrals to ABPS-certified plastic surgeons call the ASPS at (888) 4-PLASTIC (888-475-2784) or visit www.plasticsurgery.org.

Ask Questions:

1.   Are you certified by The American Board of Plastic Surgery?
2.   What is the best procedure for me?
3.   Where and how will you perform my procedure?
4.   What are the risks involved with my procedure?
5.   Will my procedure need to be repeated?
6.   How much downtime should I expect?
7.   Do you have hospital privileges to perform cosmetic surgery?
8.   How much will my procedure cost?
9.   Are financing options available?
10. How are complications handled?

To aid people considering plastic surgery ASPS has developed an informational brochure, "Making the Right Choice", which offers information on managing expectations and questions to ask before plastic surgery.[3]

American Society of Retina Specialists
(www.vitreoussociety.org/)

American Thoracic Society (www.thoracic.org/)

American Urological Association (www.auanet.org/)

Association of Military Surgeons of the United States
(www.amsus.org/)

Association of University Radiologists (www.aur.org/)

College of American Pathologists (www.cap.org/)

Congress of Neurological Surgeons
(www.neurosurgery.org/cns)

Contact Lens Association of Ophthalmologists
(www.clao.org/)

Infectious Diseases Society of America (www.idsociety.org/)

International College of Surgeons United States Section
(www.ficsonline.org/)

International Spine Intervention Society
(www.spinalinjection.com/ISIS/)

National Association of Medical Examiners
(www.thename.org/)

National Medical Association (www.nmanet.org/)

North American Spine Society (www.spine.org/)

Radiological Society of North America (www.rsna.org/)

Renal Physicians Association (www.renalmd.org/)

Society for Investigative Dermatology (www.sidnet.org/)

Society for Vascular Surgery (www.vascularweb.org/)

Society of American Gastrointestinal Endoscopic Surgeons
(www.sages.org/)

Society of Critical Care Medicine (www.sccm.org/)

Society of Interventional Radiology (www.sirweb.org/)

Society of Laparoendoscopic Surgeons (www.sls.org)

Society of Medical Consultants to the Armed Forces
(www.smcaf.org/)

Society of Nuclear Medicine (www.snm.org)

Society of Radiologists in Ultrasound (www.sru.org/)

Society of Thoracic Surgeons (www.sts.org/)

The Endocrine Society (www.endo-society.org/)

The Triological Society (www.triological.org/)

United States & Canadian Academy of Pathology
(www.uscap.org/)

ENDNOTES

1. www.aafp.org/x16058.xml

2. Iverson RE. Patient safety in office-based surgery facilities: i. procedures in the office-based surgery setting. *Plast Reconstr Surg.* Vol. 110,
   No. 5. October 2002. pp. 1337-1342. Available at: www.plastic
   surgery.org/medical_professionals/Policy_Statements/loader.cfm
   ?url=/commonspot/security/getfile.cfm&PageID=12318. Accessed
   November 18, 2005.

3. Popularity of Plastic Surgery Does Not Diminish Risks: American
   Society of Plastic Surgeons Leads the Specialty with Safety Initiatives.
   Patient Safety Press Release. March 2, 2004. Available at: www.plastic
   surgery.org/news_room/press_releases/Popularity-Of-Plastic
   -Surgery-Does-Not-Diminish-Risks.cfm. Accessed April 2005.

AHRQ Patient Safety Indicators

The *Patient Safety Indicators (PSIs)* are a new tool to help health system leaders identify potential adverse events occurring during hospitalization. The *PSIs* form the third of a three-part set of new AHRQ Quality Indicators developed by Stanford University and the University of California under a contract with the Agency for Healthcare Research and Quality (AHRQ).

The AHRQ Quality Indicators (QIs) measure health care quality by using readily available hospital inpatient administrative data. *Patient Safety Indicators* are a set of indicators providing information on potential in hospital complications and adverse events following surgeries, procedures, and childbirth. The PSIs were developed after a comprehensive literature review, analysis of ICD-9-CM codes, review by a clinician panel, implementation of risk adjustment, and empirical analyses.

THE PATIENT SAFETY INDICATORS (PSIs)

The Patient Safety Indicators provide a perspective on patient safety events using hospital administrative data.

Hospital-Level Patient Safety Indicators

- Accidental puncture and laceration
- Birth trauma—injury to neonate
- Complications of anesthesia
- Death in low mortality DRGs
- Decubitus ulcer
- Failure to rescue
- Foreign body left in during procedure
- Iatrogenic pneumothorax

Reprinted from www.qualityindicators.ahrq.gov/data/hcup/psi.htm. Available at www.premierinc.com/safety/publications/05-04-downloads/02-ahrq-patient-safety-indicators.doc. Accessed April 2005.

- Obstetric trauma—cesarean delivery
- Obstetric trauma—vaginal delivery with instrument
- Obstetric trauma—vaginal delivery without instrument
- Postoperative hemorrhage or hematoma
- Postoperative hip fracture
- Postoperative physiologic and metabolic derangements
- Postoperative pulmonary embolism or deep vein thrombosis
- Postoperative respiratory failure
- Postoperative sepsis
- Postoperative wound dehiscence in abdominopelvic surgical patients
- Selected infections due to medical care
- Transfusion reaction

Area-Level Patient Safety Indicators

- Accidental puncture and laceration
- Foreign body left in during procedure
- Iatrogenic pneumothorax
- Postoperative wound dehiscence in abdominopelvic surgical patients
- Selected infections due to medical care
- Transfusion reaction

Pay-for-Performance Evaluation Tool

INSTRUCTIONS: In the **Health Plan** row, enter the names of the health plans with pay-for-performance programs that you are evaluating. Beginning in the subsequent rows, enter a "1" for each statement that is true; otherwise leave blank.

HEALTH PLAN	Quality Health Plan	Budget Health Plan	Middle Road Health Plan	Other	Other	Other	Other	Other
A health plan rep can explain the compensation formula and how it was derived.	1	1	1					
The program offers a "bonus" rather than a "withhold."	1							
Family physicians were involved in the program's design (e.g. selecting the measures).	1							
The performance measures are nationally recognized (by Medicare, the NCQA, etc.).	1	1	1					
The program offers non-financial assistance, such as guidelines, flowsheets and patient ed materials.	1		1					

HEALTH PLAN	Quality Health Plan	Budget Health Plan	Middle Road Health Plan	Other	Other	Other	Other	Other
The plan uses encounter data, not claims data	1							
If encounter data is used, the health plan provides technical assistance for data collection.	1							
The potential incentive is 5 to 10 percent of income from the plan.	1		1					
TOTAL POINTS	8	2	4	0	0	0	0	0
EVALUATION	Go for It	Forget It	Possible	Forget It	Forget It	Forget It	Forget It	Forget It

KEY
0-2 points = Forget It
3-4 points = Possible
>4 points = Go for It

2004 National Healthcare Quality Report: State Ranking on Selected* Measures—Illinois

The following ranking shows how well this State is performing on 14 selected measures of health care quality that are featured in the 2004 National Healthcare Quality Report. This report, mandated by Congress and published annually by AHRQ, is based on a detailed analysis of measures designed to help track health care quality across the Nation. It includes State-level statistics for around 100 of these measures.

Measure**	National Average***	State Score	State Rank
Cancer			
Percent of adults 50 and older ever receiving flexible sigmoidoscopy or colonoscopy	48.9	45.3	41
Percent of adults 50 and older with fecal occult blood test in last 2 years	31.5	24.7	47
Colorectal cancer deaths per 100,000 population per year	19.8	22.5	46
Heart Disease			
Percent of adults who had their blood cholesterol checked in last 5 years	73.5	70.8	36
Percent of Medicare heart attack patients with beta blocker prescribed when leaving the hospital	83.3	78.1	38
Percent of Medicare heart failure patients with ACE inhibitor prescribed when leaving the hospital	67.2	64.2	34

* These 14 measures were selected because they correspond to quality measures featured in the 2004 National Healthcare Quality Report and have data reported for all 50 States and the District of Columbia.

** Further details on measure specifications are available in the NHQR Measure Specifications Appendix: http://www.qualitytools.ahrq.gov/qualityreport/browse/browse.aspx?id=5011.

*** These national averages are consistently calculated across all measures and differ slightly from those in the National Healthcare Quality Report. For more information, see Methods page.

(continued)

Measure**	National Average***	State Score	State Rank
Maternal and Child Health			
Percent of women receiving prenatal care in first 3 months of pregnancy	83.6	84.0	24
Respiratory Diseases			
Percent of adults 65 and older receiving flu vaccine in the last year	69.2	59.0	48
Percent of Medicare patients hospitalized for pneumonia who got a blood culture before antibiotics	81.8	83.3	18
Percent of Medicare patients hospitalized for pneumonia who got antibiotics within 4 hours	64.5	69.4	9
Percent of Medicare patients hospitalized for pneumonia who got the right antibiotics	68.8	66.3	38
Nursing Home and Home Health Care			
Percent of long-stay nursing home residents who have moderate-to-severe pain	6.0	6.2	17
Percent of home health patients who get better at walking or moving around	35.0	34.6	26
Percent of home health patients who had to be hospitalized	27.5	27.7	25

** Further details on measure specifications are available in the NHQR Measure Specifications Appendix: http://www.qualitytools.ahrq.gov/qualityreport/browse/browse.aspx?id=5011.

*** These national averages are consistently calculated across all measures and differ slightly from those in the National Healthcare Quality Report. For more information, see Methods page.

_____

Source: Quality Tools. April 5, 2005. Available at www.qualitytools.ahrq.gov/ qualityreport/state/srt.aspx?state=IL. Accessed November 16, 2005.

US Department of Health and Human Services Quality Reports

United States Department of
Health & Human Services
Leading America to Better Health, Safety and Well-Being

[   ] Search

Hospital Compare - *A quality tool for adults, including people with Medicare*

✉ **E-mail This Page**

| Search | About | Data Details | Resources |

This tool provides you with information on how well the hospitals in your area care for all their adult patients with certain **medical** conditions. This information will help you compare the quality of care hospitals provide. Hospital Compare was created through the efforts of the Centers for Medicare and Medicaid Services (CMS) and organizations that represent hospitals, doctors, employers, accrediting organizations, other Federal agencies and the public.

Talk to your doctor about this information to help you, your family and your friends make your best hospital care decisions.

This website has:	How would you like to search for a Hospital?	
• **Hospital Information**	**By Geography**	I want to search for all hospitals within a:
Get the address, telephone number and other important information for all Medicare-certified hospitals in the United States.		**State**
		County
• **Quality Measures**		**City**
Learn about treatments that are known to get the best results for most adult patients with heart attack, heart failure, pneumonia, and surgery. See how often hospitals provided recommended treatments for these medical conditions.		**ZIP Code**
	By Name	I want to search for a hospital by entering all/some of its name:
• **Hospital Checklist**		**Hospital Name**
Be prepared. **Click here** to see some important questions to consider before you or your loved one goes to the hospital.		
• **Your Rights When You Are in the Hospital**		
Know your rights. **Click here** to learn more.		

• The information on the website has been provided primarily by hospitals participating in a national project called the **Hospital Quality Alliance (HQA): Improving Care Through Information** (HQA). Participating hospitals agree to submit and report additional quality information for public reporting.

Page Last Updated: September 1, 2005

Top of page

HHS Home | Questions? | Contact HHS | Site Map | Accessibility | Privacy Policy | Freedom of Information Act | Disclaimers

The White House | FirstGov

U.S. Department of Health & Human Services · 200 Independence Avenue, S.W. · Washington, D.C. 20201

220

Source: Available at: www.hospitalcompare.hhs.gov/hospital/ home2.asp. Accessed February 28, 2006.

Time For a Practice Management Check-up?

The AMA offers a range of products to help your office run smooth and effectively

Maximizing Billing and Collections in the Medical Practice

Prevent undue financial losses in today's medical practice. Given the shrinking physician reimbursement environment, practices today need the tools and information necessary to maximize their billing and collections efforts; this book provides that and more. *Maximizing Billing and Collections in the Medical Practice* integrates the patient encounter with the billing and collections function to increase the likelihood of collecting every dollar the physician is entitled to receive.

Softbound with CD-ROM, 8-1/2"x11", 208 pages
Order #: OP318607CCW
ISBN: I-57947-867-0
Price: $75.95   AMA member price: $56.95

A Physician's Guide to Survival and Success in the Medical Practice

This invaluable reference guide details the day-to-day operations of a medical practice offering tools and techniques for managing personnel, finance and operations, marketing and promotion and risk. Up-to-date coverage of EHRs and other technologies are also included. A user friendly, three-ring binder format offers many forms, evaluation and assessment tools and other aids in the included CD-ROM.

Three-ring binder with CD-ROM, 430 pages
Order #: OP401607CCW
ISBN: 978-I-57947-780-6
Price: $135.00   AMA member price: $105.00

Other valuable practice management titles offered by the American Medical Association:
- Starting a Medical Practice
- Assessing the Value of the Medical Practice
- Managing the Medical Practice
- Buying, Selling and Owning a Medical Practice
- Financial Management of the Medical Practice
- Personnel Management in the Medical Practice

For more information on our practice success series or to review additional products and services visit *www.amabookstore.com* or call (800) 621-8335.

The Newest Coding and Documentation Resources
from "The Source" of CPT® – the AMA

Principles of CPT®Coding, Fifth Edition

Updated and revised by the AMA, this resource provides the most in-depth review of the entire CPT® codebook available. Broad enough to educate the beginning coder, while serving as a useful tool for those with more experience, *Principles* explains the use of the codes and guidelines in a practical, easy-to-read style that addresses everyday coding challenges. Instructions on how to code from an operative report and coding tips with hints on codes assignment, bundling, and payer policies are included to increase coding understanding. This new edition contains: additional end-of-chapter exercises, expanded and revised chapter sections for the Surgery, Radiology, Pathology and Laboratory and Medicine.

Available October 2007
Spiralbound, 8-1/2"x11", 580 pages
ISBN: 978-1-57947-967-1   Order #: OP501007CCW
Price: $69.95   AMA member price: $49.95

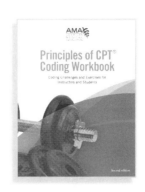

Principles of CPT® Coding Workbook, Second Edition
(formerly CPT® Coding Workbook)

Revised and expanded, the second edition of *Principles of CPT® Coding Workbook* provides in-depth instruction on key coding concepts by CPT code section. Extensive coding scenarios and operative procedure exercises are given at the end of each chapter to test knowledge. New chapters on Category II codes and the appendixes in the CPT codebook are included as well as new illustrations, decision tree flow charts for selected specialties and expanded chapters on E/M, Medicine, Surgery, Anesthesiology and Radiology. Developed as a companion to the bestseller *Principles of CPT® Coding* to provide more coding instruction and exercises, this source can also be used as a stand-alone teaching tool.

Softbound, 8-1/2"x11", 300 pages
ISBN: 978-1-57947-883-4   Order #: OP570407CCW
Price: $59.95   AMA member price: $44.95

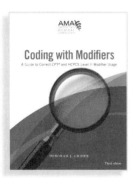

Coding with Modifiers: A Guide to Correct CPT® and HCPCS Level II Modifier Usage, Third Edition

The new third edition of *Coding with Modifiers* explains revisions made to modifiers in CPT® 2008, along with new tools to aid in modifier instruction. This edition contains updated CMS, third party payer, and AMA modifier guidelines to assist in coding accurately and avoiding payment delays. Coding tips and decision tree flow charts help clear up confusion surround modifier usage. A new test-taking tool is provided on CD-ROM, giving users a stimulated test taking environment. New clinical examples and additional test-your-knowledge questions are also included.

Available December 2007
Softbound, 8-1/2"x11", 500 pages
ISBN: 978-1-57947-889-6   Order #: OP322007CCW
Price: $92.95   AMA member price: $69.95

Stedman's CPT® Dictionary

End the guesswork of code assignment by truly understanding CPT® code descriptions. In conjunction with the best-selling *Stedman's Medical Dictionary*, the AMA's CPT experts have developed a reference aimed at reducing this frustration – *Stedman's CPT Dictionary*. This new reference contains definitions of medical terms found within the CPT codebook descriptions. Each entry includes a CPT Stedman's medical definition as it relates to code descriptions. Definitions are organized by CPT section, giving the user the context to further understand the meaning behind these descriptions. Illustrations from *Stedman's Medical Dictionary* and abbreviation and medical terminology appendixes are also included to further understanding

Available December 2007
Softbound, 8"x10", 950 pages
ISBN: 978-1-57947-882-7   Order #: OP300607CCW
Price: $124.95   AMA member price: $94.95

AMERICAN MEDICAL ASSOCIATION

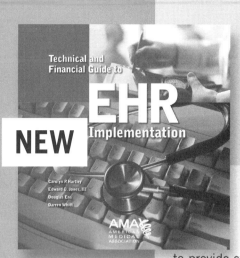

IN A TOWN WITH 50% UNEMPLOYMENT, THE AMA IS HELPING DR. BENJAMIN ACHIEVE 100% MEDICAL COVERAGE.

There are 2,500 people in Bayou LaBatre, Ala. More than half are unemployed. Two-thirds live below the poverty line. If it weren't for the efforts of Dr. Regina Benjamin, they would have no health care at all. She runs the Bayou La Batre Rural Healthcare Clinic where patients are never turned away because they can't pay. Instead, she fights the health care bureaucracy for them.

This is just one of the many reasons Dr. Benjamin is part of the AMA. Not only does being an AMA member provide her with a platform to speak out, it makes her voice even stronger.

By actively working together with her physician colleagues, Dr. Benjamin isn't just helping her patients, she's also helping to change the future for 45 million uninsured Americans who are in need of a good doctor just like her. And just like you.

Regina Benjamin, MD
Family physician
AMA member since 1980

AMA
AMERICAN
MEDICAL
ASSOCIATION

Join Dr. Benjamin and the AMA in our battle for the uninsured.

Be a member of the AMA. Contact your state or local medical society.

Together we are stronger.

www.ama-assn.org